HOW TO DO CONSENT (WITHOUT SOUNDING LIKE A ROBOT)

HOW TO DO CONSENT

(WITHOUT SOUNDING LIKE A ROBOT)

Learning Boundaries, Navigating Discomfort, and Getting to Know What You Really Want

MIA SCHACHTER

North Atlantic Books
Huichin, unceded Ohlone land
Berkeley, California

North Atlantic Books
An educational nonprofit organization
Huichin, unceded Ohlone land
2526 Martin Luther King Jr Way
Berkeley, CA 94704 USA
www.northatlanticbooks.com

Cover design by Jasmine Hromjak
Book design by Happenstance Type-O-Rama

Acquisitions and production editor: Gillian Hamel
Copyeditor: Erin Weigand • Proofreader: Melanie Demmer
Indexer: Ken DellaPenta

North Atlantic Books's publications are distributed to the US trade and internationally by Penguin Random House Publisher Services. For further information, visit our website at www.northatlanticbooks.com.

The authorized representative in the EU for product safety and compliance is Eucomply OÜ, Pärnu mnt 139b-14, 11317 Tallinn, Estonia, hello@eucompliancepartner.com, +33757690241.

PLEASE NOTE: The instructions and advice printed in this book are intended for the use of adults over the legal age of consent in the US, and are not in any way intended as a substitute for medical, mental, or emotional counseling with a licensed healthcare provider.

Library of Congress Cataloging-in-Publication Data

Names: Schachter, Mia, 1989– author
Title: How to do consent (without sounding like a robot) : learning boundaries, navigating discomfort, and getting to know what you really want / Mia Schachter.
Description: Berkeley, California : North Atlantic Books, [2026] | Includes index. | Summary: "Learning boundaries, navigating discomfort, and getting to know what you really want"— Provided by publisher.
Identifiers: LCCN 2026001641 (print) | LCCN 2026001642 (ebook) | ISBN 9798889843665 paperback | ISBN 9798889843672 epub
Subjects: LCSH: Sexual consent | Boundaries (Psychology) | Sex
Classification: LCC HQ32 .S3127 2026 (print) | LCC HQ32 (ebook)
LC record available at https://lccn.loc.gov/2026001641
LC ebook record available at https://lccn.loc.gov/20260

1 2 3 4 5 6 7 8 9 KPC 30 29 28 27 26

Printed in the United States of America

Contents

Introduction 1

PART I

WHAT IS CONSENT?

"If You Can't Talk About Sex, You Shouldn't Be Having Sex": Abstinence Lite™ 7

I Am Taking Control of My Own Consent 11

Seven Patterns in Early Consent Learning 15

Interview with Meenadchi: Non-Violent Communication and Friendship Breakups 21

PART II

WHAT IS CONSENT NOT?

Consent Won't Save Us 35

Consent Is for Everyone 43

You Will Definitely Abuse the Power You Refuse to Acknowledge You Have 51

Interview with Kai Cheng Thom: What Consent Is Not . . . 53

PART III

WHERE ARE YOU IN THE PICTURE?

The Downside of Being a "Thank You for Telling Me" Person and That Time I Was Called a Greedy Bitch 71

How to Read a How-To Article 77

Commitment as a Relationship with Past Versions of Yourself 83
Interview with Janice Griffith: Sex Work, Autonomy, and Knowing Yourself 87

PART IV
SEX, TRUST, AND MAKING MISTAKES

How to Do Consent Without Sounding Like a Robot . . . 105
We Both Got Too High and Had Sex Anyway, and We're Fine 111
I Can't Trust Someone Who Can't Say No to Me 117
Utterly Unenthusiastic but Totally Consensual Sex 121
Against Pleasure 125
Interview with Andis Solomon: Polyamory, Communication, and Making Consent Hot through Dirty Talk 129

PART V
GENDER + SEXUALITY

Gatekeeping Queerness Doesn't Make You More Queer . . 149
If You Want to Make Someone Feel Good, You'll Figure Out How to Make Them Feel Good 153
My Sexuality Has Changed over Time 157
Virginia Woolf: Who Is She Writing for? (Or, for Whom Is She Writing?) 165

PART VI
BLAME, REGRET, PUNISHMENT, AND BUILDING COMMUNITY

Repentance Rituals and Cancel Culture 173
The People Who Will Cancel You Agree with 99 Out of 100 Things You Say 177

Personal Responsibility in a Post-#MeToo Feminism . . . 183
We Have to Stop Canceling Each Other So We Can Start Saving Each Other's Lives 189
Interview with Risdon Roberts: Cancellation, Transformative Justice, and Sex Work 195

PART VII
CREATIVITY, FINDING YOUR VOICE, AND PUTTING YOURSELF OUT THERE

Consent + Creativity: An Unexpected Link 211
FOMO as a Manifestation of the Pursuit of Perfection 217
Consent as a Path Toward Knowing Yourself 221
There Is Magic in Desire; Asking for What You Want Is the Spell 227
Something Bigger than Yourself 233
Interview with jo Valdés and bahar baharloo: BDSM, Kink, and Creative Sexual Expression 239

Acknowledgments 259
Index 261
About the Author 269

Introduction

How cool that you found this book! Welcome.

My name is Mia Schachter, and I'm an author, a multi-media artist, and an intimacy coordinator for TV, film, and theater. It's my mission to make consent education as digestible and widely available as possible so you can identify your desires, needs, and boundaries and authentically express them to others in your own unique voice. My studies in philosophy, neuroscience, gender, and visual and performing arts inform my approach to consent education, intimacy coordination, and creativity. Relationships are my life's work.

I define consent as an ongoing, practical approach to communication; it's a mode of checking in with yourself and others about limitations, capacity, and resources.

Consent is part of all realms of our lives, not just sex.

Consent is a practice of deep listening, not just for words, but also for body language, gaze, *prosody* (*how* you say what you say; everything in the sound of your speech besides the words; the sound of punctuation), and other forms of often unconscious information, and *acting based on all that information and being willing to adapt to it,* as opposed to continuing with your intention, goal, or motive.

Consent is a way to stretch your limits, take risks, and grow in a supported way. It's a path toward knowing yourself so that you can identify and express your boundaries, desires, needs, and capacity.

I think of it as a language and as such, something that can be embodied, meaning it moves from the head into the body. I think of embodiment as fluency.

Consent is *not* a checklist, rules, or a set of questions. It's not a one-and-done action, as if you could ask the questions and then be done. Consent isn't something that happens in one moment; it's ongoing.

Consent is *not* a way to control other people, such as, "I don't consent to you talking to your ex, or, "I don't consent to you wearing that outfit." I've also seen this when someone goes to a friend to talk about an issue they're having with another person. The person they're talking about will say, "I didn't consent to you talking about me with that friend." We simply cannot control other people. Using consent to justify doing so is antithetical to the ultimate goal of bringing consent into your life: empowerment, autonomy, and choice.

Consent is *not* a way to get out of doing stuff you don't wanna do, as in saying, "I didn't consent to that" when asked to have a difficult conversation or do your fair share of domestic labor. We do stuff we don't want to do all the time. We live in community, we have relationships, and we make commitments. Follow-through is a valuable trait in a person. We can't simply bail on others, on our lives' maintenance, or on ourselves because we just don't want to do the things we said we'd do.

Consent is *not* a tool of punishment. This one is so important. When we leave a situation or an experience with less-than-positive feelings, we will often feel a strong impulse to blame someone for those feelings. Binary thinking will have us concluding that the negative feelings are either *my* fault or *their* fault, so we will comb through the interaction or activity looking for some kind of error that we can label as a consent violation to pin our regret on the other person. When this gets out of hand, it results in trying to get that person removed from community, erased from our lives, or banished to anywhere else. We attempt to control other people by saying that anyone who associates with that person is complicit and tantamount to an abuser. This breaks my heart. Consent is such a beautiful tool for building lasting relationships and community, so when I see it used this way, it makes me very sad.

Consent is *not* something you can ever do perfectly. This can be a hard pill for some to swallow. "Then why even try?" you might think. But I hope that instead this can bring you some relief. Perfectionism impedes listening, and we're really trying to listen with this practice. We're sharpening our skills so we can adapt as needed, adjust to the person we're with and the situation we're in, and account for context, mood, or what we had for breakfast that day. This practice is ever-changing, like a river or a dance. It's not fixed and rigid. With repetition and fluency you find flow.

Consent is *not* math. There is no equation, no formula that can get you to the right answer, keep you 100 percent safe, or keep you from ever hurting anyone else. Consent is much more like literature or art: You learn to read and to interpret; you find your voice and then express yourself as authentically as possible.

Consent is *not just* permission. If you look up the definition of consent in a dictionary, you'll likely find a legal definition that conflates consent and permission. Permission is part of consent, often an important part, but it's not the whole picture. Reducing consent to permission would negate everything I've said consent is and isn't so far. I often say, "Permission is the tip of the iceberg."

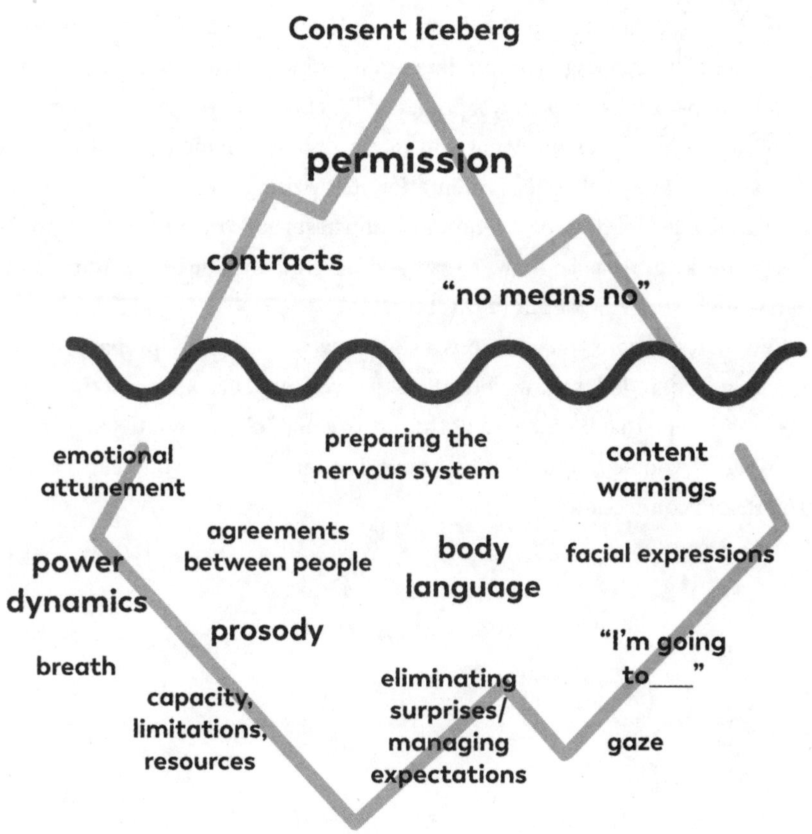

In this book, we're talking about relational consent, interpersonal consent, and perhaps ethical consent—so we'll go well beyond the legal definition. With consent as I've defined it, permission occasionally isn't even part of the practice. When I was working on my first book, *Unsolicited Advice*, at a friend's place in Costa Rica in 2023, she told me once I got there that her girlfriend was going to be moving in about a week into my two-week trip. I was surprised. In this instance, practicing consent would have meant better managing my expectations, giving me a heads-up and time to adjust to the change of plans before it was imminent. However, I don't think she needed to ask my permission for her girlfriend to move into her apartment. Permission was not part of practicing consent, in this situation.

You'll find in this book a thorough analysis of consent in many realms of life, from sex to friendships to creativity and art. You'll also encounter some ideas about consent that you likely have not heard before. Some of those conceptions might challenge your understanding of what consent is and isn't and how it can be used and even weaponized. This book is not a guide to consent for total beginners; it's not what you might find at a mandatory anti–sexual harassment training at college orientation. I'm writing on what I call "Consent 2.0," a much deeper dive, past required enthusiasm and "no means no," into the messy, murky gray space between yes and no. But you don't need to be more than a novice to get a lot out of this book.

No matter where you're at in your journey with consent, prepare to have your mind expanded. I think you'll find that consent isn't what you thought it was, and I hope that by the end of this book you'll have a new, deeper understanding of yourself, your desires, your limitations, and your capacity for growth and connection.

PART I

WHAT IS CONSENT?

“If You Can’t Talk About Sex, You Shouldn’t Be Having Sex”

Abstinence Lite™

“If you can’t talk about sex, you shouldn’t be having sex.” We’ve all heard this sentiment from authority figures in our lives or the media. But saying this doesn’t stop people from having sex before they can talk about it. People are gonna keep fucking; we know this. A not-so-controversial take would be that we need to *teach* people how to talk about sex before telling them it’s a prerequisite to having it. But I’d argue that we actually can’t know how to talk about sex before we *have* it.

Why is sex different?

What other activity would anyone say this about? “If you can’t talk about music, you shouldn’t make music.” “If you can’t talk about cooking, you shouldn’t cook.” This would be outrageous. So why is it different with sex?

It’s different with sex because sex is emotionally charged and physically and emotionally risky. We can get sick from sex. We can get hurt from sex. For these reasons, the risk of physical and emotional trauma from sex is high. But this is a risk many of us choose to take anyway. We do our best to learn the risks, mitigate them, and then decide how to proceed with informed consent.

It’s also different with sex because our culture has a lot of moral panic around sex. Often, those who decide how we teach (or don’t teach) sex and consent err on the side of what’s “safest” without dealing with what’s real, practical, or based on lived human experience. "If you can't talk about sex, you shouldn't be having sex" is like Abstinence Lite™. It's promoting *no sex* as the safest sex, without offering tools, skills, or practices for how to begin to learn to talk about sex.

But I don't really think sex is *that* different from cooking or making music. I see sex as a creative collaboration between two or more people, or between you and yourself. And like any creative act, it requires trial and error, exploration, play, and shaking off perfectionism and people-pleasing. When we are preoccupied with asking ourselves, "Is this right?" we forget to ask, "Do I like this? How could this be better? Would I prefer something else?"

Why do people struggle to talk about sex?

Another reason I don't like this "rule" of not having sex before you can talk about it is that it doesn't address *why* it's hard to talk about sex in our world. In conventional sex and consent education, we are not given much language to describe pleasure. Even outside of a sexual context, most of us have an easier time describing pain and discomfort than finding language to express our feelings of pleasure. We can say that pain is sharp, hot, acute, dull, prickly, raw, and so on. For pleasure we've got, what? Good, and various synonyms like amazing or incredible? Or maybe wow, yes, and more? These aren't very helpful descriptors of what our pleasure actually feels like.

I had been having sex for about ten years and was still struggling with saying words like "orgasm" and "wet," asking for lube or to use toys, or talking about test results. These are conversations that take practice. These words contain cultural minefields of connotations, associations, taboos, and stigmas. They can be loaded with shame, fear, and embarrassment. And we can't go around, above, or below those feelings. We can only go through them, which requires practice, which requires experience.

Recently, at thirty-three years old, I was having sex with someone in New York I had slept with a few times already. I had gotten an STI test recently, and because I was traveling, I had packed some toys for us. I had no problem saying, "I just got tested and I'm all clear." But when it came time to say that I'd brought some toys for us, my voice went high and giggly and I couldn't make eye contact. I got shy! Why? *I don't knowwwwwww!*

Because I'm a consent educator, people often assume I'm excellent at giving direction and feedback during sex, knowing my limits, and expressing my boundaries. But what being a consent educator really means to me is that I will always be finding new language, my body will always be changing—and so what feels good and what I need to orgasm will always be changing—and I will always be learning new things about consent, about sex, about my own body, and about how I am in a relationship. I will always find new boundaries, new limits. I will encounter new frameworks and vocabulary to communicate about sex. There is no right way to practice consent. There is no right way to have sex. There is no right way to talk about sex. There is no finish line to cross before we can say we are "ready."

Armchair philosophy

The philosopher Immanuel Kant distinguished between two kinds of knowledge: *a priori* and *a posteriori*. *A priori* knowledge is the kind of thing you can know in isolation, without direct experience, such as "all bachelors are unmarried" and "all circles are round." This is "armchair philosophy," which is to say it's things you can know without leaving your armchair (which I envision being in front of a fireplace, with a tobacco pipe on a side table and a lone candlestick dripping with a decade's worth of wax). *A posteriori* knowledge, on the other hand, is stuff you have to have experience with in order to know. This is most of being alive. Leaning too heavily on *a priori* knowledge often results in a small group of people making uninformed decisions for large groups of people they don't know, on issues they have no firsthand experience with (such as cis men making laws about abortion).

We cannot know about sex *a priori*. We have to do it; we have to engage with the creative act of it, with ourselves and with others, and then inquire deeply about our experience of it before we can talk about it. I'd break this down further into different sex acts and every fine gradation of them. You could ask me how I feel about penetrative sex, and then we could go one by one through various positions, through each of my partners I've done each of those positions with, how I felt about each of them, how long we'd been sleeping together at that point, and whether or not I'd eaten yet each day. I can tell you that I certainly didn't know how I felt about having anything in my butt before I had anything in my butt. I could've perhaps told you I felt curious and nervous, but not much more.

I believe you can paint before you can talk about painting, play tennis before you can talk about tennis, and write a novel before you can talk about writing a novel. You can learn as you go. One of the safest ways to do that is to do a little, then stop and reflect before doing more. Journal. Go slowly, take breaks, establish trust with the people you're doing these things with. Don't do them when you're drunk or stoned out of your mind.[1] How do you learn your limits without hitting them, or at least coming close? How do you learn what you like when you only speculate and theorize? We need hands-on, practical experience with things in order to discern and distill our feelings about them, learn what our desires are, and figure out what feels good, when, and with whom.

---

1 I don't think you *can't* have sex stoned or with a few drinks in you—we are adults, after all—but many people will tell you that if you've had anything mind-altering, you can't consent. I disagree. In part IV of this book, I write about making a drug-related sex mistake big time in my own life, one that I am still learning from. See "We Both Got Too High and Had Sex Anyway, and We're Fine."

I Am Taking Control of My Own Consent

ORIGINALLY PUBLISHED BY *SALTY*, 2020

I went to the doctor last week. My body was screaming at me not to go. I thought of my cat's reaction to her carrier because of her own medical trauma; when she knows we're going to the vet, her whole body spasms in resistance (unlike her calm, healing body against my abdomen right now, her purr penetrating to my bones). I was my cat that day, but I was also my own parent, determining that going to the doctor was in my body's best interest. I violated my own consent for the sake of my future self. It was a poignant reminder that I am in fact the chief violator of my own consent.

What does my body think when I don't listen to its very clear "no"? Am I betraying its already-tenuous trust in me? Will it get used to the violation and consequently endure or tolerate future violations from others? Will it scream louder at some later point to make sure its voice is heard?

My whole life I've battled what I now know to be gut-based chronic illness. My doctor told me at this most recent visit that in his thirty-five years of practicing medicine, he's almost never seen a more mysterious case–which on one hand makes me feel super special, and on the other hand makes me feel utterly hopeless.

I've been medically gaslit for decades. When I was six, I was fatigued, and my mom took me to get tested for anemia. Dr. Bob read us the results and said, "She's not anemic, she just has a lazy personality." When I was twenty-seven, I had four UTIs in a year and went to Dr. Dave, a motorcycle-riding punk doctor on the Lower East Side. He told me I was anorexic; he was not the first doctor to tell me that, as though it were the key to the locked vault of my health issues. ("Aha! I found it.") When I asked how he'd recommend that I eat, he said I should eat double cheeseburgers and milkshakes every day.

"I can't eat that much dairy," I said.

"See? You'll do anything to avoid eating." He paused—a pause pregnant with his own ego, gestating the most insightful medical question known to humanity: "Who else in your family has The Crazy?"

Later, as I learned about consent as a language and a practice, I was also learning to listen to my body, and I began to understand the depths to which I had gone to ignore it. The more I learned about this embodied form of consent, the more I saw and really *felt* the ways I had been ignoring my body in order to get things done. Now, as a consent educator, I talk in classes about getting and gauging consent with ourselves first.

There are a few things we can do to gauge self-consent. The first thing we need to do is learn what our boundaries feel like in our bodies. Then we need to parse out the difference between feeling uncomfortable (where we can learn, challenge ourselves, take risks, and try new things) and feeling unsafe (where trauma is possible if not likely). For a lot of us, our wires get a bit crossed about the difference between the two because of our upbringing and trauma. For example, many of us will come out of COVID-19 with fears of crowds and enclosed spaces long past when the danger is present. Uncrossing these wires takes a lot of patience and compassion with ourselves.

We can also prepare our own nervous systems. When I knew I had to go to the doctor, I did some breathing exercises. When I was waiting to be called in, I paid attention to the feeling of my feet on the floor, and I put a hand on my belly and breathed into it. I reminded myself about all the times I've gotten to the other side of a bad doctor visit. I went over ways to stand up for myself if I needed to. Consent can often come in the form of a warning instead of waiting for permission to be granted or explicitly asking for it when we've already agreed to a certain relationship, such as doctor and patient. We see that with content warnings on media that might be upsetting, such as movies that have content not suitable for minors, or when the dentist says, "You're going to feel some water. It might be cold." Preparing the nervous system can help us get through things that we know we have to do, but we don't want to do.

I want to be very clear: I don't believe that if someone has fuzzy boundaries or is not experienced at holding them, they are to blame for their own trauma. But to overlook the ways we teach our bodies that we are not going to listen to them is masochistic and a form of self-harm. We reject our bodies daily. We tell them that their insight is not welcome when we prioritize our intellect over our emotions. We tell them that their experience of gender and societal norms is dangerous, and they should be quiet. We tell them that other people have it worse, and they should stop complaining.

The separation between our minds and bodies serves capitalist goals. There's not much profit to be made if I like myself the way I am, so capitalism splits us from ourselves and then sells us things to repair the damage. I often think of that song from *Hedwig and the Angry Inch*, "The Origin of Love," about Aristophanes's theory that we've been split from our soulmates and wander the earth trying to reunite with them. But I think of the two halves as my own mind and body, wedged apart by marketing and media that tell me I can be whole if I pay for "necessities" like makeup, razors, tweezers, straightening irons, food supplements, diet pills, and toxic chemicals with which to beat my body into submission. We're sold this dualist tug-of-war that keeps us from knowing the feeling of our boundaries. We can't always predict what our boundaries are or will be, but we can know the feeling of hitting one of them, so we can regulate our nervous systems and speak our needs. Recognizing my healing in the form of reconnecting with my body—so I can act from my gut—is an act of self-love. And that is a daily revolution that I'm committed to for the rest of my life.

Seven Patterns in Early Consent Learning

I've been teaching consent for about six years now. What follows are some patterns I've noticed in myself and others as we have moved through the beginning stages of our consent education as adults in a deeper, more comprehensive way, beyond "no means no." I don't intend to suggest that you should try to avoid these patterns but rather to demonstrate that they are common. I think there is great power in naming things, and my hope is that by identifying these patterns, you can feel less alone and experience more choice as you navigate them.

1. People get "no-happy."

When people aren't used to saying no, it can feel thrilling, which can lead them to just say "no, no, no" to everything. The result is stifled growth, isolation, and massive FOMO.

After I first practiced saying no as part of the orientation at the Cuddle Sanctuary in Venice Beach with founder Jean Franzblau, I spent ninety minutes crying on the pile of pillows designated for people who want to be left alone. I was inconsolable. If you, like me, felt overwhelmed at the unfamiliarity of "no" in your body when you first learned about consent, you may feel your pendulum swing far in the direction of opting out of all kinds of things. But eventually I had to reconcile wanting to say no with what I know to be good for me: getting out of the house, going for a walk, exercising, seeing friends, meeting new people, exposing myself to new ideas, art, movies, and theater, being amongst the trees, vibrating amongst my spiritual community to the same prayers my ancestors have said for thousands of years in Shabbat services. Getting off the cozy couch with a cat on my lap often requires a little push, a little discipline, or remembering a commitment a past me made to a future me. Getting going sometimes creates some discomfort and frustration, but ultimately I choose a life full of growth, expansion, exploration, love, joy, and connection over a squishy seat and a living weighted blanket every single night.

For some, this no-happy phase is really crucial. For those of us who've reached burnout, who might have been in denial about a disability or chronically unrealistic about our energy, spending some time saying no to every invitation and vegging out on the couch until we're sick of ourselves and have cabin fever might be a necessary step in our healing. If this is you, take your time. But I hope you eventually find equilibrium.

2. They say, "All my friends have been taking from me. I need to cut them out."

This is a way to use consent to bypass the hard work of setting boundaries. Relationships are collaborations. It's valid to cut people out of your life if they demonstrate that they can't have difficult conversations or if the relationship can't withstand conflict. But before you do that, set boundaries. Ending relationships without attempting to shift them first results in immense amounts of grief and isolation.

Recently in my classes, I've started asking people to write down on the first day, "I will not end any friendships until this class is over." I do this because over several years of doing this work, I've had a few too many students come to me and share, rather excitedly, "I ended a friendship with someone who just takes, takes, takes and doesn't give anything in return!" They're often proud of themselves. While only you know if you need to get out of a friendship—and perhaps reading this book or taking my class has led you to see that there truly is nothing that can be done to renegotiate the dynamic—it saddens me to hear that someone has ended a relationship with a *snip* before or instead of trying to do the work necessary to navigate conflict, repair ruptures, and set and hold boundaries with their friends, partners, and family. Cutting people off can be necessary in certain circumstances, as a last resort, but I'd caution anyone against doing it before trying to preserve the connection.

3. They think, "Everything is nonconsensual."

You didn't opt in to the world as we know it with all its oppressive systems; this is absolutely true. While there is a philosophical argument to be made here, simply saying "everything is nonconsensual" is neither practical nor serving you. We can find lots of things you didn't opt in to, such as being born. Thinking this way results in increased hypervigilance, because everything and anything could be a violation—which leads to increased stress, which leads to illness. This kind of thinking is disempowering and strips you of autonomy.

This line of thinking also asks consent to do and hold too much. In this book, I argue for a model of consent that supports autonomy, freedom, pleasure, joy, and connection. The "everything is nonconsensual" train of thought takes us down a depressing rabbit hole in which we have zero agency and our entire lives are happening *to* us. This does not help us reach autonomy, freedom, pleasure, joy, or connection.

4. They point the finger of blame everywhere but at themselves.

It's easy to learn about consent and recognize the ways you've been hurt or violated. It's harder to look at the ways you've crossed your own boundaries and violated your own consent—or crossed *other* people's boundaries, violated their consent, made them uncomfortable, held power over them, or pushed them past their limits. None of us are immune to this kind of behavior.

In a culture stuck in black-and-white thinking, reinforced by a deeply flawed legal system stuck in its own innocent-guilty binary, the impulse to blame is forceful. We often fall prey to thoughts like, "If it's not their fault, then it's my fault—and it can't be my fault, so it must be their fault." We punish others to avoid punishment ourselves. But this sort of thinking does not help us heal, find resolution, prevent bad things from happening again, or build lasting relationships and community.

5. They think learning about consent is going to help them avoid things they don't want to do.

In our interpersonal lives, consent is not about avoiding stuff that's hard or uncomfortable. If it were, you'd stop learning new things, challenging yourself, and exploring with curiosity. Consent is about empowering yourself to move through hard things as safely as possible.

If you're only thinking about consent as a concept relevant in sex, this point might rub you the wrong way. If you don't want to do anything sexually, you absolutely shouldn't. But of course, I have a caveat to this: You may find that you want to push your limits, try new things, or uncover or create new desires for yourself sexually. Stretching yourself in this way isn't comfortable. It likely will come with some mistakes, misunderstandings, risk, and possibly some pain, whether physical or emotional. You may feel yourself torn—part of you really wants to know what something is like, but part of you really *doesn't* want to know, or fears it may hurt or that it might leave you feeling embarrassed. Consent can escort you through this exploration, support you in facing fears, help you negotiate with someone you're experimenting with, and give you tools to plan for what to do if and when something goes awry.

6. They stop trusting other people to say no and they fear that any display of a preference or desire could be coercive.

When some people first learn about consent in the way we've been discussing it, they get really nervous that people don't feel able to say no to them. They sometimes fear that people will feel pressured by them merely asking a question at all, or they feel it's 100 percent their job to make sure that other people can say no, forgetting that all relationships are (at least) a two-way street. This misconception comes, I think, from the typical understanding of consent as merely asking, "Is this okay?" or being able to freely say yes or no, as opposed to the much more holistic and comprehensive way in which we're talking about it in this book. In relationships where there is trust, you can begin to *trust* that your friends, lovers, family, coworkers can say no to you. Consent is not any *one* person's responsibility; it is shared. This fear that others can't say no to you often comes from *your* inability to say no, so practice saying no in your own life to build trust in others. *You are allowed to have needs!*

Your excitement and enthusiasm are not coercive. While someone's feelings may create a sense of pressure for someone else, it's important to be able to distinguish between *feeling pressure* and *being pressured.* The difference is blame. And not all pressure amounts to coercion, either. Coercion would come with punishment or retaliation, while pressure could be something more along the lines of saying, "Please, please, please." It's okay to be excited about a request when you make it. You don't have to neuter your emotions in order for someone else to be able to freely give consent.

Real time constraints are also not coercive, even though they may create real pressure. Deadlines, due dates, having to pee on a road trip, biological clocks, impending fires, hurricanes, medical emergencies . . . these are all real time constraints. Acknowledging them and contending with them is not the same as putting pressure on someone else.

7. They overuse the concept of consent, asking it to do and hold too much by haphazardly applying consent where it doesn't belong.

I know I said that these patterns aren't necessarily to be avoided, but this one is different. Using the concept of consent where it doesn't belong is damaging, reckless, and dangerous, and it contributes to severing relationships and communities. Disagreeing with someone is not violating their consent. Making a snap judgment in a risky situation because you think you're choosing the safer option is not a consent violation. Calling things consent violations when they are not is a conversation-ending move. It puts the other person on the defensive, giving them no choice but to defend and grovel, and they are suddenly not allowed to have any needs themself. Consent belongs in the realm of agreements. If you agree to take a risk, you are responsible for your own feelings that come up as a result of that risk. You may experience regret, pain, or shame, and you may wish you hadn't taken a risk. That is *no one's fault.* Not even yours, but certainly not anyone else's. When we agree to take a risk, we agree to the unknown. We cannot tell the future—not what's going to happen nor how we will feel. If you wish you hadn't taken a risk, that's great information for you about how to make choices moving forward. Going over the experience with a fine-toothed comb trying to find where someone else's "consent violation" led to your icky feelings, instead of taking responsibility for agreeing to being in that situation despite the risk, is a gross and egregious misuse of consent.

Discomfort can easily be mistaken for danger. The terminology of boundaries and consent gets misused to stave off discomfort when people say things such as, "I don't want to talk about race. That's my boundary," or, "I don't consent to talking about trans issues." Someone might be feeling uncomfortable for any host of reasons without a consent violation being one of them. I talk more with Meenadchi in the next chapter about what happens when the only language we have is "consent violation."

Interview with Meenadchi

Non-Violent Communication and Friendship Breakups

Meenadchi is a somatic healing practitioner, TEDx speaker, and communications expert whose work centers social change and embodied transformation. Using a blend of Family Constellation Therapy and Non-Violent Communication, Meenadchi supports individuals and changemakers in reconnecting with the intuitive wisdom of our bodies so that we can co-create intergenerational healing by changing the way we speak to ourselves, each other, and the universe. Meenadchi holds a clinical license in occupational therapy and has historically served communities impacted by gender-based violence, complex trauma, and serious mental illness. She is the author of *Decolonizing Non-Violent Communication* (2019).

Mia: Can you explain what NVC [Non-Violent Communication] is to you and what your approach is? And maybe how it's different from the original book that I read, which you once told me to throw away and burn.[1]

Meenadchi: Yeah, yeah.

[Laughter]

Meenadchi: So I was introduced to Non-Violent Communication in 2002. And I loved it. There were pieces of it that felt wonky and weird. There were

1 The book was Marshall Rosenberg's *Nonviolent Communication: A Language of Life.*

pieces of it that really worked. And it was a really helpful tool later on, when I was doing a lot of work in rape crisis advocacy and suicide prevention stuff. Having a framework for questions like, "How do we listen deeply? How do we listen well? How do we hold space?" was really, really important.

But there are pieces of conventional Non-Violent Communication that just don't work. They just don't work anywhere. And so in 2016–2017, I started developing my own framework of decolonizing Non-Violent Communication. How do we use these tools in a really effective way? And what is the weird stuff within Non-Violent Communication that has its roots in systemic oppression, in unacknowledged, unaddressed systemic oppression? And how do we take that out of it?

So for me, decolonized Non-Violent Communication, or DNVC, is really about listening to our bodies and bringing our authentic voice into the world. Because our authentic voice, our authenticity, is the most nonviolent thing that we can contribute to community, to care for society, and that takes a lot of self-awareness. It takes a lot of self-awareness, because we have bodily reactions when we're pissed, when we're hurt, when we're sad. I think the most common one is when we are sad—lashing out is a very common response, or shutting down, because our body is doing things to protect itself. Which then creates problems in relationships, right? We get reactionary with each other, we push each other away, that kind of thing. But when we can name those feelings—"I'm sad, and I really want connection," or "I'm angry, and I don't have capacity for connection"—when we find that self-awareness, when we strengthen those skills, it allows us to come back to each other, I think, in better, more authentic ways. So decolonizing Non-Violent Communication is about listening to the body and developing an emotional vocabulary so that we can communicate our needs, and then staying within our capacity so that we can build the connections and relationships we want to build.

Mia: Awesome. There's so much in there that I feel is also necessary for consent to be practiced in an ongoing way, particularly the "listening to your body" piece. I call that *full-body listening,* which is not just listening to your body but also observing someone else's nonverbal cues and taking that as equally important information—possibly more important information than the words that they're saying. I mean, the best example is when someone's visibly upset and you say, "Are you okay?" And they're like, "Yeah, I'm fine," you know. And the words are just completely incongruous to the way that they're expressing their emotional state. And then, as the person in connection with them, you're tending to all of that, and even maybe also tending to the fact that they maybe aren't so aware of how they're feeling. And so they're telling you they're fine, or they're actively lying because they want you to think they're fine, or they don't want to ask for help. So how do you incorporate all of that into your approach?

Meenadchi: Yeah. I feel like that's where the nuances of consent start to get really tricky. I can think of times when I have offered to show up for someone when they're in a bad state—I've offered to fly out somewhere, I've offered to drive somewhere—and I will say, "I could come be with you, would you like that?" And they'll say no. But I'll think, Is that really what you want to say? You know what I mean? Also, you know, I'm an Enneagram 2, Cancer sun sign. So like, hyper-helper, and that "helping" identity has historically been a big part of me.

Mia: Yeah, me too. I'm also a Cancer, for the record.

Meenadchi: So there have been times when I was overrunning consent by showing up, and it wasn't wanted, but also times when I was tuning in accurately to something that was necessary. I remember one time, with someone that I loved, I just got this intuitive hit, and I was like, "I'm gonna cancel my meetings today and I'm gonna walk over to your place." And I walked over and they were just getting off the phone. In that moment—I did not know this beforehand, but in that moment they had found out that someone that they loved dearly was dying, and that was hard . . . oh, I'm crying . . . and I just showed up outside. But these are all nuanced situations. These are edge places, because somebody else would not have liked that. You know what I mean? Somebody else would have liked the space—like, don't be up on me like that. And sometimes we don't know until we do it wrong.

Mia: You know, I've been reading this book called *Sexuality Beyond Consent* by Avgi Saketopoulou, where she talks about how the whole idea of affirmative consent is kind of based on this false premise that you can ever fully know yourself. And I studied philosophy in college, and so much of what I was most interested in was about the sort of faultiness of the process of introspection and perception, and how no two people share the same exact reality. And so, what does that mean for us in relationship? What does that mean for our sense of justice? I think a lot about the concept of risk and growth, and challenging yourself and exploring your curiosity. There are so many aspects of the most basic kind of consent education that suggest, implicitly or explicitly, that unless you are 100 percent sure about something, don't do it. And that doesn't account for something that I'm curious about but maybe makes me nervous, or a challenge I'd like to take on, or a risk that I'd like to take, and maybe a risk I'd like to take with you.

You know, relationships are risky. Sex is risky. A lot of these things in our lives are risky. We can't see the future. I can't fully, fully know how I'm going to feel, or how I'm going to respond, or what I'm going to want or not want. And so part of what we do in relationships is to agree to the risk. So, showing up for a friend when they say no—I mean, that's not exactly the same kind of agreement that I'm talking about, but there is maybe an agreement that I'm making internally: I'm taking a risk here that I might upset my friend, but I am using as much information as I possibly can about them, about where they're at, about who they are. And I'm gonna take that risk. If they get mad at me, I'm prepared to handle that. But it's in line with my integrity right now to show up for my friend. So I'm just thinking about NVC, too, and what you're saying about listening to your body and your intuition, and how sometimes that means—interestingly and with so much complexity—ignoring the words that someone is saying to you.

Meenadchi: Yeah, and I was thinking, as you were speaking, about how everything we do is an action to meet our own needs. But the question is, Am I showing up because I have a need to be wanted, or I have a need to be helpful? Or am I showing up from a place of real, true interdependence, where I sense your need for care, and I'm being present for that. They're two different things, and I think that it's a really beautiful thing when we're able to tap into the latter. But we need to have the self-awareness to even track that, and especially during moments of heightened emotion, during moments of crisis, during moments of emergency, we have to be practicing that self-awareness beforehand. Even just having conversations around ideas like consent not always being enthusiastic; sometimes it's a thing that I'm just going to try. But if we don't talk about that beforehand, if we aren't even aware that that is an option, then we get to a place where we're making a choice because we have to, because we're being pushed to make a choice—whatever it is, we're making a choice. And then it feels like we're sort of splattered up against the ramifications of that choice and are trying to make sense of it.

And so I think that with both consent education and DNVC, it's important to understand your needs and do the work ahead of time . . . . I don't think we can actually ever prevent conflict from happening. But I think that as we build muscles for awareness beforehand, it can sometimes create guardrails for when we're climbing up out of the mess, so that we have a few different things to hold on to, to pull us up.

Mia: Right. Yeah, the idea of the guardrails is really interesting. And also, what you're describing is like the prep work in intimacy coordination. Like, on the day of shooting, if you've done your prep, it goes really smoothly, and if and when mistakes happen, you know you have those guardrails to catch you.

I was talking to a colleague the other day about the language of guardrails, and how sometimes the guardrails are the vocabulary itself, right? And if the only vocabulary that we're providing is very black-and-white terms, very binary terms, then terms like "consent violation" get stretched to encompass way more than they actually can, and then everything becomes a consent violation if it doesn't feel good. And then, as a result, you're collapsing such a wide range of human error or miscommunication or confusion into this very binary concept of like, I either consented or I didn't, or it was either consensual or it wasn't—and I'm not even talking about a sexual context. I think I'm really just talking about, you know, if something happens between us that one of us doesn't like. And I feel like the only language I have to say, "Hey, I didn't love how this happened," is "you violated my consent," which I don't think I actually mean.

Thinking about it in terms of NVC, I don't think that is a non-violent way to engage in moving through conflict, because it's a conversation-ender. All you can do, if I say you violated my consent, is try to figure out where you went wrong and apologize to me, or explain yourself, or defend yourself. Whereas if we have these larger guardrails, like the language of risk—"We took a risk together; I don't love how it went let's talk about it"—I feel like that keeps us connected. "Let's figure this out together."

Meenadchi: Okay, so two things. One, the piece where you talked about people saying, "you violated my consent," and how you don't feel like that's a very non-violent way to approach things. I don't use that language. I don't ever label anybody else's behavior as violent or non-violent. I trust other people to show up the way they want to show up, and then it's my job to show up authentically in response to that. Because when you're just getting introduced to consent, and when we're just getting introduced to healthy communication, there's often this experience of five million light bulbs going off, like, "Oh, my god, I didn't realize that I had a choice, and I wasn't given a choice." You know what I mean?

We're suddenly registering all the moments in our lives where we weren't given enough options or where choice wasn't made available to us, and it can bring up this volcano of grief or frustration, all of these really, really big emotions. And then we get into finger-pointing land: "My parents didn't tell me how to do it; society didn't tell me how to do it. This was what I should have been given." I think that, frankly, truthfully, speaking for both of us, a lot of our work started there [*laughs*]. You know, there was a sense of *we have to change this* because the way that this was given to us wasn't right, and it wasn't working. And I think that we've also changed in how we hold the work. We're at different places. We've had different life experiences. And the things that I care about the most are moments when I sort of cross my own boundaries of consent, because self-responsibility has become an access point of like, "I cannot control everything around me. But I can control this. I can be responsible for this."

Mia: Yeah, yeah, yeah. My work was very much born out of 2017: Me Too blew up, articles about Harvey Weinstein came out, Matt Lauer, so on and so forth. And I remember even then, in 2017, I was thinking ahead, like, How are these men gonna reenter society? How do we facilitate that?

Who's gonna do that? What does that look like? What would it look like for someone to apologize, and for the majority of people to be like, "That is sufficient, and you can come back?" I started writing a play about it that I never finished, and I think I see those seeds in my work today.

But I think where a huge shift has taken place is . . . the impulse to do the work was to change how men behave, right? It was to change how perpetrators behave—and I'm not saying that those are always the same groups. But then I think I got to a point where it's kind of like the *opposite* of autonomy and liberation for me to feel like my safety is contingent on anyone else changing their behavior. So even from a really early stage, I was focusing on the question, "How do you get to know yourself?" And how do you get to know your limits and your boundaries, and your needs, and your desires? And then how do you communicate that authentically? So it was always about looking inward. And I frequently have to kind of stop myself from putting my ideas out there in a way that they could get interpreted as saying, This is how *everyone* should be acting in relation to other people. I can only control what's in me and what I let out, how I choose to express myself. And, you know, that work is a lifelong excavation project.

Meenadchi: Excavation feels like the word.

Mia: That's funny that you say that, because as soon as I said it, I was thinking, it's really more of a simultaneous excavation and creation. Like I'm both actively choosing "this is who I want to be" and accepting "that's who I've always been." And so how do I co-create myself alongside my fate, or destiny, or whatever.

Meenadchi: These moments of shared experience, or presumed shared experience—like for me, that moment just now felt like a really resonant sweet spot, and it just kind of felt good to sit in it. And I think about moments where consent is present . . . . One of the things that I love in so many of my most intimate relationships are the moments where we actually don't have to say anything. I often say that, you know, the less I have to explain, the more there is to talk about. And I'm just thinking about that in the context of the work we both do, because there are also times when it doesn't matter what the words are—we just cannot find our way to each other, because something energetically is off. Speaking of the binary, statements like "I will do this," or "I won't do that" are sort of like the clean places to be when we know we're not able to be fluid with each other. In those moments, it is safer to just say we are only going to talk on these days, or from this time to this time—whatever container is necessary. But so much pleasure can be experienced when we're able to be in a fluid state.

Mia: Yeah, and a word coming up for me in relation to that is *trust*. Navigating messy territory requires a lot of trust. And I'm not gonna do that with everybody, you know? And so there are instances of conflict where I'll choose to not address something that is maybe bothering me. And instead, I'll choose to take space. I don't mean indefinitely—I just mean, I'm kind of activated, and I need some time away, or whatever, and then I'll come back. Whereas with other people in my life, there's more trust, and I want to try to navigate this conflict, even if it means that we're getting activated, and even if it means we're getting heated with each other.

I originally wanted to talk to you about friendship breakups, because I'm curious how our work intersects in that arena. I think so much about how consent is such a beautiful tool for connection, and building long-lasting relationships, and getting through conflict. And how sad it makes me when it instead gets used like "well, consent was breached, therefore we can't be in each other's lives anymore." Or, you know, when it's used to sort of bypass setting boundaries or having difficult conversations, which are important to having long-lasting relationships. And I've lost relationships where that wasn't something that the other person was willing to do—like it was too uncomfortable or too challenging, or they maybe didn't feel the trust.

Meenadchi: Yeah. Didn't feel the trust, or it wasn't worth the time in that moment, or there wasn't capacity. When you use the word *trust*, I think about the word *capacity*, about how much we're all holding, which then shapes how much [energy] I can put in this direction or not? And I think that for me, friendships are gold. They feel like a thread of gold that is, like, part of this weave, this stitch, that is actually kind of the primary bond—beyond blood family, beyond romantic relationships, or whatever. Friendship feels like this really incredible, important bond. And I remember when I started really understanding that friendships can go away and that they can break—which for me, as a Cancer, was incredibly weird. I was like, What do you mean? Why?! [*Laughs*]

Mia: Yeah, what? But we could be friends forever. We could just be friends forever. Why would we not?

Meenadchi: Yeah. And since then, I have met people who think more along the lines of, you know, some friendships are for a season. I have one buddy who describes herself as being like a skittish cat when it comes to friendship and intimacy, and there's ways I think that I am skittish. Now I'm slow to call somebody my friend, because I'm like, What does that really mean? How long are we really going to be friends? Again, because I don't know that hard conversations always guarantee a strengthened outcome. So I don't know that I can say anymore that it is important to have hard conversations. I don't know what is important these days, when it comes to that [*laughs*]. I think that it is important to have the skill to have hard conversations. I think that is something that I can firmly say. I think it is important to have different skills. And then you can decide which relationship merits using them or not, but I think that if you don't know how to have a hard conversation, or don't know how to sit with discomfort, then there's a big loss waiting to happen, because then we just don't know what could have been.

Mia: And again and again and again, you know, not just one time. I had to have a difficult friend breakup that was really heartbreaking for me. And I had this whole belief system and this stuff around communication and consent that was very much tied to my values; I had made commitments to myself because of ways that friendships had ended in the past, where I was left wondering what the fuck happened. And so I had made the promise to myself that if I wanted other people to have difficult conversations with me and be willing to do that, then I also needed to be willing to do that with other people. And navigate conflict, and try to move through it, and so on and so forth.

And then I ended up in this situation, where I was talking to my therapist about just feeling like I couldn't be in that friendship anymore. It feels so controlling to me, you know. And when I thought about what I could bring to this friend—like, this is what I need—there was no way to divorce what I needed from asking them to change, in so many ways. And I thought, if I need you to change in all these ways in order for us to stay friends, I think we're just not compatible. I don't wanna ask you to change. I'm not okay with that. You're gonna reach whatever conclusions about your own behavior in your own time. Every time I would run through the conflict conversation in my head, I was like, if you need me to change and I need you to change, then we probably shouldn't be friends. And yet I requested a conversation. I was ready and willing to do that. I have loved this person for years and that conversation was dodged and avoided, and I had also been privy to so many conversations that they had had with other people in their life that were going to be similar. I had a lot of evidence that this was not gonna go well, and that it would ultimately just be a situation where they were gonna tell me that I was wrong in so many different ways.

And so I talked to my therapist about it. And I was like, "I just feel like it's not really in line with my values to step away from this friendship without having the conversation," and she was like, "Well, you have many values, and one of those values is your own safety and security. And it's sounding pretty clear that going into that conversation, you don't really feel like it's a safe thing for you to do, so I don't see it as out of line with your values to not have it." And so I think sometimes values are in conflict. You can prioritize some at the same time, but sometimes prioritizing my authenticity reduces my impact, even though both authenticity and impact are my values, or increasing my impact means that I have to sacrifice some authenticity in this moment. So in this instance, my own commitments to myself around relationships and friendships and connection and conflict had to shift, to incorporate the nuances of this particular dynamic—which is hard to stomach, you know. I felt like a hypocrite.

Meenadchi: Hmm! I have a different way of thinking about authenticity. I think about what is the most effective thing to do, and what is the most important. I think one of the things that I strive for and also try to teach is how to maintain my authenticity and my sense of dignity while I'm communicating in a way that the other person can hear me. Because the point of conversation, the point of anything, is to be effective. And another thing that I like to ask people is, Is it important for you to hear yourself? Or is it important for the other person to hear you? What is more important to you? And if it's important for the other person to hear you, then we have to put our words in a way that they can hear us. And so then the question is, What are the words they need to hear? And how do I communicate that in a way that keeps me with my dignity and my sense of authenticity? [. . . .] But something I realize about myself is that when I'm talking to people who I know don't respect me and don't value what I have to say, it's a lot easier for me. Because I don't go in asking them to respect me. That's not the reason I'm here, right? I'm here because there's a particular conversation that needs to happen. There's a particular end goal. There's some functional thing that I want to move toward, and I need this person's participation. Which then frees me up, because then I hold my own sense of dignity internally, and I'm really just listening for what I need to say, how I need to move in order to effectively navigate this conversation with this person.

We all have a need to be seen. We have a need to be valued. We have a need to be heard. The relationships where we rely on the other person to bring that to the table, where I really want to be seen by you, I really want you to meet that need for me—I think in those moments, yes, it can be incredibly tricky. Whether we register it or not, we're navigating this feeling of, I really want you to hold this, but you don't know how to hold this. And now, I don't know how to hold this when I'm with you, because I'm used to you being able to hold it. It felt good to be seen by you, and something has changed, and you don't know how to see me anymore. And then all these emotions come up. And then I think it becomes harder for me to have that conversation.

When I'm having conversations with people where I don't need them to respect me or see me, I'm able to walk in with a sense of dignity that allows me to stay in my authenticity, like strategically. What do I need to say or do to move the needle? But in conversations with people I'm accustomed to being more vulnerable with, I don't have to think so much, I'm accustomed to that quality of fluidity, right? But if that fluidity isn't there, I need to shapeshift—which feels inauthentic if I'm not accustomed to shapeshifting with you. I know that I know *how* to shapeshift and still maintain my authenticity, but I don't do that in every relationship.

Mia: Yeah, I really resonate with that. And that's something that comes up a lot in my classes: the concept of *masking*, whether it's autistic masking or various other kinds of masking. You know, I think people bring up code-switching as a kind of masking, too. And I often ask a similar question about authenticity, because communication can take a lot of energy and time. If I don't want to have to have this conversation again and again, I do have to incorporate what I know about how you will best hear me. And are there ways that I can do that while I still feel authentic, and I still feel like I'm showing up as myself. But I'm also accounting for the fact that we're in relationship. We're gonna have to find the space between us and meet there. So you know, I can't simply say something the way that I want to say it, the way that feels most authentic to me. I care about you, and I also care about not having to have this conversation forever. So I'm gonna try to do it in a way that includes how I like to communicate and how you need me to communicate with you, and also in a way that feels authentic and in line with my values.

PART II

WHAT IS CONSENT NOT?

Consent Won't Save Us

Last year, I started telling people I'm a writer when they ask what I do for work. I used to say I was a consent educator, but the patterns in people's responses have made me increasingly uneasy over the years. Immediately, most people would try to put distance between us, indicating that my work couldn't possibly be relevant to them. They'd say, "I'm pretty good with that stuff." Or I'd feel them put me on a pedestal, expectations flooding in of what I must be like in various contexts. A standard of perfection materializing out of thin air. When I say I'm a writer, people suddenly see me as an artist, and my work as something to be interpreted rather than factual, expert guidance.

Learning about consent changed my life, and I'm devoted to sharing what I know with as many people as I can, but there are several misuses and misunderstandings of consent that have made me wary of continuing to teach it. So many people think consent only relates to sex, and just mentioning the word "consent" can cause people to shut down or get defensive because they feel they're being accused of doing something wrong. Some people worry that they would learn they've done something wrong if they were to take a consent class. However, the issues leading me to want to move away from consent education are a bit more subtle and more sinister.

1. Consent is used to avoid healing work and growth.

When consent becomes about figuring out who to blame for something that went wrong, punishment becomes the end goal. The blame game becomes a distraction from the work of healing and growth that will need to happen whether or not the person who caused harm is punished. Often this quest to place blame looks like combing through an interaction or set of interactions to find the moments where consent was violated or didn't take place.

Consent is not a way to avoid doing stuff that you don't want to do or that makes you uncomfortable, such as growth, healing work, repair, or moving through conflict. Rather, it's a way to bring more awareness and more choice into the decisions you make so that you can move through discomfort—and even through danger and things you explicitly don't want to do, but choose to do anyway—with care, supporting yourself along the way.

I'm reminded of a common misunderstanding regarding therapy. For some, therapy is about finding the locus or cause of their trauma. They think, "If I can just figure out *why* I'm like this, everything else will fall into place." But finding the *why* doesn't rid you of the issues that resulted from the traumatic event or events. The trauma is in your body. If you have angry outbursts, or you shut down under stress, or you dissociate during sex, figuring out what caused these reactions in you doesn't exorcise them from your being. You will still have those habits whether or not you ever figure out when and why they originated. You will have to do the work of healing—building new habits, identifying your triggers, and learning self-regulation—no matter what. You can start that work now, before you know who or what is to "blame." This can be therapy, EMDR (Eye Movement Desensitization and Reprocessing), movement, actively metabolizing grief through ritual, and seeking out various forms of support, often from professionals. There are some very healthy ways to express anger. Two of my faves are journaling and singing. All too often, I see people shirk this responsibility to heal (because we are the only ones who can decide whether or not we heal or seek support in healing) and believe on some conscious or unconscious level that figuring out what went wrong or whose fault it was will make the hurt go away or get them around having to do the healing work. It won't. Similarly, simply punishing or banishing the person who hurt you won't heal your wound.

I get accused of victim blaming for this take. But it seems pretty obvious to me that there are things within my control and things that aren't. If my porous boundaries, my people-pleasing tendencies, my unresolved trauma and quick stress responses, my lack of confidence and low self-esteem, my inability to speak up for myself, or my poor communication skills keep getting me into situations where I'm being taken advantage of, used, manipulated, pushed around, and even violated or abused, I can keep cutting these people out of my life—but ultimately, I'm going to need to work on myself. My ability to learn and grow and strengthen my skills is within my control; whether or not other people are punished, learn from their mistakes, or even ever understand how they hurt me are simply not in my control.

2. Consent is weaponized to justify prejudice and judgment.

Often when we are uncomfortable with something, it shows up in the form of fear. This can feel like a boundary, but it's not; it's a phobia or prejudice. When someone pushes on our fear, it can feel like we're being attacked. We're not. We're being *challenged*.

It's easy to hide behind ignorance and call the fear a boundary in order to bypass the discomfort. This way, you don't have to educate yourself, call in other people, or challenge your beliefs. Bypassing all that is convenient, because that stuff is *hard*. But pushing through discomfort is how we learn, grow, and expand.

Amongst liberals, the more moderate left, and especially cis white women, we often see this in the form of transmisogyny and exclusion. We see it in the form of fragility around topics like race, gender, religion, money, or politics—for example, when someone will avoid a hard topic or being called out/in by saying, "I don't want to talk about that. That's my boundary."

But we also see this amongst people who spell "folks" with an x or insist that the word "bisexual" is transphobic. Queer people will argue with other queer people about whether straight people can use the term "partner" for each other. Trans people will argue with other trans people about whether using the term AFAB or AMAB ("assigned female or male at birth") is bio-essentialist because it continues to draw attention to genitals. White Instagram users will comment on Black content creators' posts about race, accusing them of making content that's not accessible enough to people who are neurodivergent.

This sort of thing causes divisions between people who are mostly in agreement, people who should be working together and could be building bridges but instead tear down the ones that already exist. I once had someone email me to tell me that the terms homophobia and transphobia were ableist toward people who have "actual phobias," like of birds and spiders. I began to draw the line after enough of this absurdity. As I'll discuss later, the people who are most likely to cancel you will agree with ninety-nine out of a hundred things you say.

When consent gets weaponized as a tool for control, it loses its ability to open space for creativity. Consent helps us build a structure in which to play. Its creative constraints actually open up our ability to explore, to try new things, to fall down and try again.

3. Consent becomes rules.

When consent becomes a list of (subjective and personal) rules, and then people break those rules (even though the rules are often not spoken), love and respect are withheld. Patience decreases and, as a result, connection does too. These rules might sound like, "If you go to that music venue, we can't be friends because the owner treats his employees poorly," or, "Everyone should ask consent before venting to me," or, "The shortened version of my name is reserved only for people I've given permission to use it," even if this has not been stated previously.

Consent is a beautiful tool for connection and for building long-term, sustainable relationships. When consent gets used in this overly intellectual way and gets set up as essentially a series of tests and traps, we lose connection. We lose community and family. We lose our own histories, rituals, cosmologies, and lineages. If consent is wedging us apart, creating barriers to connection, you're doing it wrong.

4. Consent is seen as a foolproof, catch-all panacea.

Consent helps us navigate relationships, boundaries, desires, needs, wants, conflict, and more. Consent consists of more than one tool, certainly, but it's not a complete toolbox by any means. It's a harm-reduction strategy, not a harm-avoidance or harm-elimination strategy. Consent is not a panacea that cures all negative human interaction and keeps us totally safe. Life is full of risks. Love is full of risks. Sex is full of risks. Crossing the street is full of risks. Did you wake up today? Awesome, congrats. That's not a given. We can mitigate risk, but safety is subjective, relative, and deeply personal. Trying to get consent to protect us all, at all times, in every way is asking it to do too much. If consent is maybe a hammer and some nails, but we're asking it to be a screwdriver and a level and screws and an X-Acto knife and a ruler, we're going to end up with some pretty shoddy furniture. Good luck fucking on that bed!

5. Consent teachers are viewed as "symbolic exemplars."

I told my rabbi a few years ago about a recurring struggle I was facing with new friends and especially people I'd met through my work. I was getting pedestalized, and there's only one direction to go from a pedestal: down. Inevitably, someone who put me up there would discover that I was merely human, and they would experience this as a betrayal. They'd feel duped and lied to. I wasn't who they thought I was, or who they wanted me to be. I had become a symbol to them, a leader, a guide, even a guru. Pedestals are precarious by nature, and I felt constantly on edge. It felt like a tightening of the grip around my proverbial throat, and I found myself scrutinizing everything I said, combing over past conversations looking for instances of transgression with my language, ways my message could be misinterpreted, and anything someone might call hypocrisy. I felt I had to be perfect at consent, which also meant I could never be perceived to be flirting or even interested in someone sexually or romantically unless they had no idea what I did for work.

"Ah yes, the symbolic exemplar," my rabbi said. Of course he knew this feeling. Therapists experience it, too. I couldn't help but think, "It's lonely up here."

When you teach consent, people expect that you must be excellent if not perfect at it. But consent is relative, subjective, fluid, interpersonal, and subject to endless, constantly moving variables, including the variable of time. As such, it's not something anyone can ever do perfectly. Math teachers occasionally get wrong answers; English teachers occasionally misspell; History teachers mix up dates. I'm a writer, and everything I write is riddled with errors. Perfection is not the goal.

6. Consent gets used to control others.

Much is beyond our domain,[1] such as what people say about us when we're not around. Consent simply does not apply to much of our lives, and yet many of us try to stretch it to do so. We can't control where people look, for example, and yet my neighbor told me to tell my dog sitter not to look into her apartment when her door is open. Huh? I can't control that, and neither can she. We simply can't control what other people do, where they go, who they talk to, or what they say. I can't control where your eyes go, or what you think when you look at me, or how you interpret this book. Here's a scandalous one, are you ready? I can't even control if someone thinks about me when they masturbate.

Here are some examples of how people might say, "I didn't consent to that" or, "You need to ask consent before you do that" in instances where consent simply does not apply:

- I've processed something that happened between me and a friend with a different friend. The friend I'm processing about tells me they didn't give consent for me to talk about them when they're not around.
- I tell a story that upsets or triggers someone. They say I should have asked consent to tell the story.
- Someone initially says yes to something out of a desire to people-please or because of a fawn/appeasement trauma response, rather than because they actually wanted it. Later, they accuse the other person of pressuring them simply because the person was excited about what they were asking.
- Someone agrees to something that they later regret. They then retroactively look for where the other person didn't explicitly ask for permission or where they could have practiced consent more thoroughly in order to pin blame on the other person for their feelings of regret.

Here are some examples of things we can't "consent" to:

- the person at the table next to me at the coffee shop watching a TikTok without headphones
- the music at the coffee shop

1 Matthias Schwenteck provides an explanation of Betty Martin's definition of the term "domain" in his video "Relating – Domain, Boundaries, Limits II," posted November 20, 2018, YouTube, www.youtube.com/watch?v=kh-83sFIpLw.

- what other people say about me
- daylight saving time
- being born
- the sky being blue
- what day of the week trash day is

We simply don't get asked for permission for most things in our lives; if we did, we'd be spending all our time trying to reach consensus about things like where the curb should be red and which plants belong in the median.

7. Consent is seen as math.

There is no foolproof formula or equation you can follow to do consent right, to make sure you never hurt anyone and are never hurt. Consent should be approached less like math and more like literature or art. In an art class, we learn to interpret, become aware of our lens, find our voice, and then express ourselves as authentically as we can. I recently taught a consent class at a college, and a boy who came with three others from his fraternity raised his hand and said, "The way you're describing this, it's much more like a dance than I've ever heard anyone teach it before." Yes! Exactly. I felt so proud and so hopeful.

All too often I see consent get used to justify ending relationships before tough conversations are had or anyone attempts to set boundaries. But what I see most frequently, and what makes me perhaps the most uneasy about this work, is that the very people who cry "consent violation" most often tend to be the same people who refuse to look at the ways their own consent practices could be improved and the ways they, too, participate in harm. Thinking that everyone is always out to get *you* is a great way to avoid looking at your own behavior.

⁂

Consent has served me well. But for a time, it also made me rigid, judgmental, and self-righteous. It led me to end relationships without trying first to set boundaries and navigate conflict. It led me to draw hard lines between what was and wasn't okay, in ways that ultimately cost me a lot of love and connection and led to immense grief and regret. The more I've prioritized connection, the more I've had to increase my patience and my tolerance for activation. As a result, my relationships with my family, my friends, my work, and myself have been greatly improved, as has my mental health.

I'm leaning into my work as an artist and away from my work as an educator. I want my work to be interpreted, not taken as fact from "an expert." I hope it's clear from the work I do and my writing thus far that I believe consent is a powerful tool for self-discovery and growth; that it is somewhat sacred in how it allows us to connect, be present, and listen; and that it can foster creativity and flow. I hope to convey and preserve that in my work, moving forward. I hope to support people in getting beyond the idea that consent is a fortress and toward a model of consent as a flexible, ever-changing structure in which we get to bop around like the silly goobers we are, looking for a good time.

Consent Is for Everyone

I get a few different reactions from people when I tell them that I teach consent.

1. "Oh, like, to kids?"
2. "Wow, that's so important. Men really need that."
3. "I'm pretty good with that, I think."

I teach consent to adults in a variety of classes tailored to different groups: artists, mental health practitioners, people who identify as people-pleasers, people who want to teach consent, people in the TV and film industry, and more. You could probably call me a little obsessed with consent—a consent nerd. Consent is enormously important to me, and yet I would never suggest that I'm done learning about it or "pretty good at it." To each of these reactions, I would say, "Consent is for everyone."

1. "Oh, like, to kids?"

I specifically don't teach children. It's not my wheelhouse. I don't know how to get a kid to brush their teeth or do their homework while teaching them that they can say no and have autonomy. That all strikes me as impossibly confusing! I've trained several people to teach consent who want to work with kids, and I'm close friends with a wonderful consent educator named Sarah Casper who wrote a book of consent lessons for kids.[1] I refer people to my students and Sarah if they want help with teaching consent to kids.

---

1 Sarah Casper, *The Kids and Consent Curriculum: 25 Whole-Classroom Lessons to Teach Boundaries, Collaboration, and Respect* (PESI Publishing, 2024).

I don't know many adults who received adequate (or any) consent education as kids, which makes me curious why someone wouldn't think that learning more about it as an adult would be a good idea. I have a hard time understanding how someone wouldn't light up and get excited to learn more about consent, but as I said, I'm a consent nerd, and I don't expect the same reaction from anyone else.

Recently on TikTok, I talked, as I usually do, about consent education as a field and particularly the way that many consent educators have moved on from the idea of enthusiastic consent because we see how it's not working and in fact often causing a lot of issues for individuals, couples, and communities. Someone commented that "enthusiastic consent is a good starting point for kids," to which I replied that my work isn't for kids and I'm not talking about children. They replied, "You said, 'consent education,' which implies it's for kids."

Weird, right?! Presumably you, reader, are not a child. The idea that even the term "consent education" suggests a focus on children and excludes adults causes such a striking barrier to learning and growth for adults. This also feels so counterintuitive because typically people assume that my work focuses on sex. It doesn't, but if we both think that any mention of consent refers to sex *and* that all consent education is for kids, we're both not teaching consent to the majority of sexually active people *and* not teaching kids consent beyond sex.

2. "Wow that's so important. Men really need that."

I almost exclusively hear this one from cis women, which is to say that trans men, trans women, nonbinary people, and cis men understand that consent is something they, too, need to be learning about, practicing, and engaging in with others. Those groups don't feel that consent doesn't apply to them or that they're exempt from practicing it.

I think this largely comes from a hugely problematic myth that cis women can't sexually harm other people, can't commit sexual assault or rape, can't push boundaries, can't violate consent, and can't be "the problem." These very beliefs cause cis women to do exactly those things. When they decide that consent is *someone else's responsibility*, they exempt themselves from looking at their own behavior.

Moreover, when you decide that consent is someone else's responsibility, *you give up autonomy*. Consent is a *shared* responsibility. A communal effort.

It's not how men keep women safe, it's how we all keep each other safe. It's a two-way (or multiple-way) street.

When you take consent and sex out of a cisheteronormative framework and look at queer relationships, this becomes not only crystal clear but painfully obvious. When two cis women, two trans women, two cis men, two trans men, or two nonbinary people have sex, are they not practicing consent in an ongoing way? Are they not checking in with each other? Asking for what they want? Sharing what they like and don't like? Asking permission? Hearing no? Stating boundaries, respecting them, maintaining them? Of course they are. And whose responsibility is it? Both of theirs.

I've talked a lot in this book about binaries. Binaries suggest that that are two options; if it's not one, it's the other. Either, or. There are countless ways this hurts us, from very personal ways in our private lives to larger, systemic ways like in the criminal justice system. Here, I'm looking specifically at the gender binary.

When we talk about consent exclusively as something for cis, heterosexual couples, all other relevant binaries snap to the gender binary. We have men and women, and then men become perpetrators and women become victims. Men are guilty, women are innocent. Men are wrong, women are right. Men are bad, women are good. Men need to get better at hearing "no," women need to get better at saying "no." Men need to practice consent, women need to practice boundaries.

I've experienced some pretty bizarre breaches of consent with women (as well as nonbinary people who at one point identified as cis girls or women) in interpersonal, professional, and sexual contexts. I chock this up largely to their belief that they couldn't possibly do such a thing.

Meanwhile, so many men I've personally known and many I've worked with have shared stories of being assaulted, but many of them don't know that this is what happened to them. They have told me about how their lives changed after a particular sexual encounter, how they didn't want to date after that, how they started to drink more, became reclusive, or avoided certain places, people, or situations.

Now, I don't believe anyone can define for anyone else what happened to them. I can give a personal example of this. When I was nineteen, I dated someone a few years older than I was. When we decided to have sex for the first time, I told him I wasn't on birth control and handed him a condom.

We made out a little, he got hard, he went down on me, and then he inserted himself inside me without a condom. I dissociated, watching it happen from above, and convinced myself that he must know something I didn't know *or* he must not know that precum can get someone pregnant. We also had had no conversation about STIs or whether we had gotten tested. As he got close to orgasm, he pulled out, put the condom on, went back in and finished.

There are people who would say this is a rape. It's akin to "stealthing" (which is classified as rape in the UK but not in the US), but it's not quite stealthing because I don't think he meant to trick me or hide the fact that he wasn't using a condom. It could be defined as rape because he had a kind of sex with me that I did not agree to. However, there was no force, no coercion, I didn't say anything, let alone "no," when he did it, so I classify it as a sexual assault but not rape.

I was deeply traumatized for years to come, nonetheless. I had panic attacks during sex until I was twenty-three; I'd often push through pain, discomfort, or having to pee until I couldn't stand it anymore, push someone off me, and start apologizing to them. People were usually confused and asked if I was okay. For a long time, I wrote it off as a weird thing that had happened. It took me ten years to realize that what I had experienced was dissociation and to call it assault. This is all to say: I needed support in understanding and healing from this experience regardless of the definition or label I assigned to it, but I think it's important to distinguish for myself what I believe occurred and call it such, instead of listening to people who want to label it as something else on my behalf.

I think *you* get to decide how you want to describe an experience. So if any of these men don't feel they were assaulted—even though that's what it seems like happened, from what they're saying—I don't believe it's my place or anyone else's place to insist on a label for what they went through. However, in my experience with some of these men, helping them see that *perhaps* they were assaulted, or that many people would define what they're describing as an assault, has brought them so much relief. It's given them the language they needed to seek out more tailored support in healing, whether that's a therapist, a somatic practitioner, or even a helpful Reddit thread.

Men don't see themselves in the narrative of sexual assault as anything but potential perpetrators. Many people think cis men *can't* be assaulted

CONSENT IS A SHARED RESPONSIBILITY

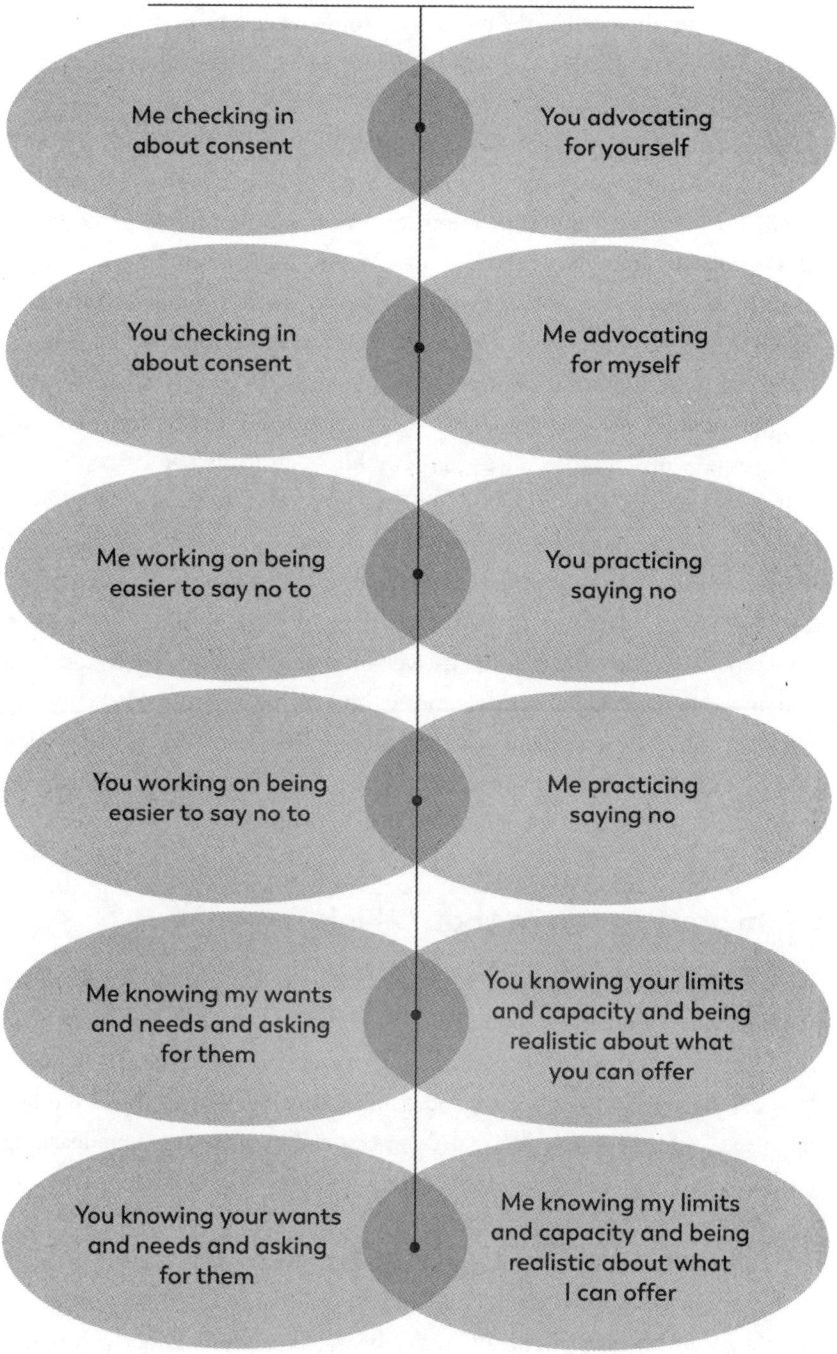

because of their anatomy: If they got hard, they must've wanted it. This ignores unwanted arousal as well as the many ways someone can be sexually assaulted without sex. A butt squeeze, an unwanted kiss, or a grope all constitute sexual assault—or harassment, at the very least.

From time to time, I've gotten the question from men, "What do I do if she says, 'You don't have to do all that consent stuff' when we're hooking up?" Usually they've heard this from a new lover during a first hookup. My knee-jerk response is, "Run. Get the fuck out of there. *You* are not safe." I've heard too many stories of a woman saying, "Don't ask, just do whatever you want" only to hear later from her or her friends that she was assaulted because of something he did without asking—even though that's exactly what she told him (not) to do. But usually I say, "You tell her, 'I'm doing this *for me*.'" Typically their eyes go wide and they release an "Ohhhh . . ." as it sinks in.

If someone tells you, "You don't have to do all that consent stuff," they're telling you that *they do not know how to do consent.* They will not be practicing consent *with you!* They will not check in with you, gauge your reactions, or respect your boundaries. It's a huge red flag for me that tells me that person is not safe. Because men see themselves only as possible perpetrators and women see themselves only as possible victims, men very often don't consider their own safety needs during sex, and women feel that they get to decide whether or not consent happens at all. But consent is not something men do *for women.* Consent is for all of us. Men, protect yourselves.

3. "I'm pretty good at that, I think."

This one is so weird, you guys. I teach consent for a living, and I would never say, "I'm pretty good at consent, I think." I'm never done learning about consent. That's one of the most beautiful things about consent to me, that you can always go deeper, learn more, try more, play. This reaction confuses the hell out of me, because it tells me that this person thinks they're done learning and growing. They've achieved some sort of nirvana of human interaction and have nothing left to work on.

I've heard from past students that originally they understood consent to be about how to treat other people, but they've learned that it's also about how they want to be treated. When I've heard, "I'm pretty good with that, I think," I have to wonder if I'm talking to someone who thinks that consent is something we only do so we don't rape people—and who amongst us (other than seriously sick people, who are the minority) thinks of themself as being capable of raping someone?

But this is such a limited view of consent. So uninspired, so bleak. It's a totally negative framework in which consent only applies to things we should *not* do, instead of including all the wonderful, beautiful, fun things we *get to* do. Consent isn't just about being able to say, "Don't do x" and "I don't like y." Consent encompasses asking for what you want, getting specific and creative, trying new things, pushing your limits, finding new desires you didn't know you had, learning about yourself in different situations, finding your own boundaries, and so much more.

⁂

In 2017, when the #MeToo movement went viral and became a global sensation (after many years of hard work that had already been done by Tarana Burke), we saw a rise in misandry—an unexpected outcome. Misandry, or the hatred of men, unfortunately doesn't do anything to inspire men to learn or to change. It positions men as the problem in a society that sculpts them. While some men are exceptionally problematic with no hope for growth, and others complicit but *with* hope for growth, many men actively seek to do better, be better, and unlearn cultural, sexual, and gender norms. The impact of misandry on a woman also has to be considered. When a cis, heterosexual woman adopts misandrist views, she typically begins to believe that her safety and wellbeing in romantic and sexual relationships is *contingent on men changing.* To me, this is antithetical to the project of women's—or anyone's—empowerment. To say it slightly differently, I find it incredibly *disempowering* to believe that my safety is contingent on *other people changing.* This strips me of agency. I become powerless to create conditions in which I feel safe/r.

I hope to add to the consent conversation a mandate of personal responsibility. We have to take responsibility for choices we make, even when we don't like the outcome, and this includes our choices around sex, love, and romance. We have to venture to know ourselves, to remove the veil that allows us to remain opaque to ourselves, and we have to be willing to be honest with ourselves first and foremost, so we can be honest with others. We can never fully know ourselves, because we can never clearly see our subconscious and everything that makes us *us*, nor are we static, unchanging beings. But we can commit to continuing to try, to peel back the onion, to lift the curtain. This is how we begin to share the load, to contribute to the communal effort of consent. Consent is everyone's responsibility.

You Will Definitely Abuse the Power You Refuse to Acknowledge You Have

Power dynamics are *dynamic*. They are constantly shifting and changing, and they are not always intuitively comprehended when someone accrues more or new power. They take time to understand and are extremely complex. There's never only one power dynamic in place; even within an obvious power dynamic like the relationship between a boss and an employee, there are other power dynamics at play, including identity, experience, age, positionality, and background. Many power dynamics are relative, subjective, or based on values. In fact, a perceived power dynamic can reveal someone's values: For example, one person may value youth while the other values experience. Or one person may value a college degree while the other values someone's ability to educate themself and stay away from institutional education.

You're more likely to abuse a power dynamic if you don't believe you have any power. You will definitely abuse power you refuse to acknowledge you have. You might find yourself ignoring the evidence of your impact or effect on others. This often sounds like:

"How could they find me intimidating? I'm nobody."

"I don't have that kind of influence."

"How is that my responsibility?"

"But I'm a 'nice person.'"

We can't mitigate the effects of a power dynamic if we deny we have any power. This is why confidence is a crucial part of consent. If I've locked myself into the belief that little old me could never have power over anyone or anything, when someone comes to me with concerns about my leadership, my reach, my influence, I will dismiss them out of pocket in order to maintain my narrative that I'm powerless. If I can embrace the possibility that I could have influence, that others might look up to me or respect me as an expert, I can inch my way toward mitigating the effects of that influence.

Here are some questions for reflection:

1. When have you not given someone all the space you could have to say "no" to you?
2. When have you crossed someone else's boundaries in order to get something you want or need—or perhaps not checked in about what their boundaries were?
3. When have you ignored cues of discomfort in yourself or someone else because of a need, a desire, or a goal?
4. When have you not updated the (implicit or explicit) agreement you have with someone for fear of things changing?

Interview with Kai Cheng Thom

What Consent Is Not

Kai Cheng Thom is an award-winning writer, performer, and creative arts facilitator based in Tkaronto/Toronto whose work delves deeply into the themes of revolutionary love, transformative justice, and healing from collective trauma. Kai Cheng's work has received multiple literary awards, including the Stonewall Book Award, the Publishing Triangle Award, and the Dayne Ogilvie Prize for LGBTQ2S+ Emerging Writers.

Mia: I love your take on consent, and I have felt like there's such an alignment here in moving past this 50/50 question of *yes or no, is this okay or not okay?*—well beyond that. In the diagrams that you and I both make in our work,[1] there is all this sort of gray space between yes and no, and even asking, "What is that process like internally?" You know, making a choice, feeling *choiceful*, maybe—is that real? Is that an illusion? That's really meaty stuff for me. And I also really appreciate the ways that I think you see, as I do, this language and these concepts being sort of co-opted to tear communities apart, and hurt people, and tear them down. So today I wanted to talk to you about what consent is *not*.

---

1 We both make infographics that help visually demonstrate the concepts of consent that we teach and write about. Kai Cheng has one I particularly love that shows a spectrum of consent, which includes "willingness" (as opposed to "wanting"). You can find those on her Instagram, @kaichengthom.

Kai Cheng: Yeah, I love that. I'm so excited. It feels super edgy and really exciting. And then I just wanted to shout you out back—I'm really lucky to get to know such cool consent and sex educators, and when I came across your work, it was like, *bam*! It's like feeling your brain expanding in response to someone else's work. These diagrams that you make, they're also mental models, and they're embodiment models.[2] I just feel like when you combine images and words, it creates so much more space to do practice differently. So yeah, thank you. I just really value what you do.

Mia: Thank you, I love how you put that. I'm really gonna hold on to that. Okay, maybe it would be good to hear your definition of consent, and then what you think it's not.

Kai Cheng: Okay, well, I'm always afraid of the "how do you define consent" question, because I sort of believe that something that consent is *not* is one single thing that applies to every [situation] where a choice might be made.

Mia: Absolutely.

Kai Cheng: But I'm just gonna go with tried and true. The definition I really, really like is from the somatic sex education field, which is my home lineage of practice: somatic healing and transformation, all that kind of stuff. Somatic sex education is kind of connected to queer history, and the history of the AIDS crisis, and sex worker movements. And we tend to use an empowered choice-and-voice model—practicing consent as an opportunity to create an expansive space where people get to notice the feelings of *yes, no, maybe, I changed my mind* inside themselves and then to voice that, to articulate what is happening for them—whether that is through actual language and voice, or gesture, or some other form of expression. So, consent is a dynamic process, it's about the *yes, no, maybe,* it's about getting to voice things, and then it is about trying to cultivate empowerment—which is not to say that everyone is always empowered, or should always have to feel empowered, but that it's kind of a general orientation to consent as a process, a verb, a practice. Does that make sense?

---

2 See, for example, the "consent iceberg" graphic on page 3 and the "consent is a shared responsibility" diagrams on page 47.

Mia: Totally, yes. That's very aligned with a lot of the things that I say, but I'm gonna look back at some of the language that you're using, because I think it's really helpful. And yeah, I talk about consent as a practice, I like the word "process," and I also like what you're saying about it being the act of engaging with what's going on internally, and the expression piece. Because so much of that just immediately undercuts this idea that consent is a thing that happens in one moment, that it's a thing that you can give and take back like a poker chip or something. And then it also gets right at the heart of what I'm talking about consent *not* being, which is this tool to control other people, or to get out of doing things that might make you a little uncomfortable. You know, "I didn't consent to that difficult conversation," like that type of thing.

Kai Cheng: Right, like, "I didn't consent to you having these feelings about me?" [*Laughing*]

Mia: Exactly, "I didn't consent to you talking." [*Laughing*]

Kai Cheng: "I didn't consent to you not liking me." [*Laughing*]

Mia: Yeah, "I didn't consent to you talking to someone else about me." Like, that to me is just such a gross misuse of the word "consent." And it also makes me really sad, because the way that you defined consent just now, and the way that I try to define it in my classes, it's such a beautiful thing, and it's meant to help us be more connected to ourselves and more connected to other people. And so then when I see it get used to do really negative things, or split people apart, I'm just like, "Oh no, where have we gone wrong?" As a consent educator, how do I make sure that people don't leave my classes thinking that that's what this is?

Kai Cheng: Oh gosh, thank you. You're doing the holy work here. Holy in many senses, perhaps. [*Both laughing*] But I'm super grateful to hear you talking about it this way, and to hear that our weird little field is also starting to shift around this. Because it's not workable, nor is it desirable to be in the space of consent as contract, consent as obligation. Consent as weird domination from the bottom, it's . . . Yeah, it's a lot.

Mia: Yeah. Well, not that we have to solve this problem right now, but what have you found helps or works to keep an understanding of consent in the realm of how you're defining it, in this really positive and connective way?

And how do you steer people, and even yourself, away from . . . I notice in these moments when I'm really activated, or I'm really stressed, or when I've been really sick in the past, where I'm like, "No one's doing enough," and I'll catch myself kind of being like, "Well, where did they screw up so that what happened isn't my fault?" You know, I don't ever want to be like, "Well, those people do that, and I *don't* do that because I'm one of the good ones." How do you combat that urge to use consent that way, or how do you help other people combat it in themselves?

Kai Cheng: Totally. I think as soon as we start to be like, "I'm one of the good ones," that's when we lose our grip on how to be generally good. I guess the first thing that comes to mind is that I really love the orientation to consent as being its own direction toward pleasure, joyfulness, expansiveness, freedom, self-sovereignty, relationship. It then becomes a creative tool, a philosophy, a practice—it's all those things, right? As opposed to using it as a tool to prevent, block, not do, restrict. And I think, unfortunately, dominant cultural and even subcultural understandings of consent are that consent is the tool to not do something wrong. If you do something consent-based, then you are not in trouble, you are not being the perpetrator, you are not-not-not-not-not-not. And then it's automatically becoming very fear-centric, and a-relational, because then I'm not thinking about the other person as much as I'm thinking about not being in trouble. And then it's also not being as much in contact with myself, because I'm pushing away all these parts of myself that could get in trouble, right?

So, it's more about consent as this connective tool for trying to be very conscious, on a body level and an intellectual level, of my desire. What do I really want? What do I really value? And what about this other person or other people, if there are other people involved, what do we really desire? What do we really want? How are we different? And then this last piece I'll throw in is something that I really value from the work of Betty Martin: this concept of domains, which is the idea that consent supports us to know what is ours, what we have a right to and a responsibility for.[3]

---

3 Betty Martin created one of the modern foundational models of consent, called "The Wheel of Consent." This model helps answer the question, "Who is an action for?" by helping to distinguish between offers and requests. She offers trainings through her school, The School of Consent.

We could problematize this language, there's a lot of ways that we could debate this, but I think in practice it makes things clear. I don't think I should use my consent practice to try and tell people what they should be thinking, feeling, or doing. Like, if I want them to do something, I should be honest about it, and just say, "I want you to do this," but I don't think I can be like, "I consent or don't consent to you living this way." And I think an obvious example for a lot of progressive people is, you know how conservative Christian folks will sometimes say, "Well, did Jesus consent to you having sex?" It's using this idea of consent to try to take someone else's freedom away from them. And maybe I could have avoided saying all of this by just saying, I like it when consent is about creating more freedom. Not less.

Mia: Yes. I love that you're using the words create and creative. There's a whole section in this book about consent as a window to creativity. And then also looking at sex as an art form, a collaborative art form. But that's interesting that you went to "domains." I love that concept, but I did think that you were going to "willingness."

Kai Cheng: Oh, yeah, I also do like that.

Mia: Yeah, me too! I've talked about it, but I'd love to hear it in your words.

Kai Cheng: Totally. I love this "willingness" thing, it's such an interesting gray space. So willingness to me is when we are choosing, actively choosing, to do something that doesn't bring us immediate gratification or pleasure, or have an immediate personal benefit. It's for someone else. The action we're doing is for someone else, or the interaction that we're having. And then there's . . . I like to think of willingness as having a potential payoff in the future. Or an unknown kind of benefit, which is more relational, right? Like, I am willing to give someone, I don't know, a blowjob, even if I'm not dying to give them a blowjob. I personally might not want to in that moment, but I'm willing to because I love them, or I care about them, or I don't know, I want them to pay me $5,000, or however much . . . [*both laughing*] that's actually honestly a lot. I would never have charged that much, but . . . [*both laughing hard*] but I've gotten really good over the past few years . . . .

Anyway, willingness is about the field that then allows me to do something for someone else in a way that doesn't harm me or take away from my freedom.

Mia: Yes, totally. And I think, expanding this into community, often I'm willing to do something for my community that I have no personal desire to do, but it's gratifying in some way because I feel like I'm contributing, I feel like I'm part of a group, I'm helping the greater good, whatever. But what it also brings to mind, and I think we're sort of touching on some really big philosophical questions here—I studied philosophy in college, so . . .

Kai Cheng: This explains a lot [*laughs*].

Mia: I bet.

Kai Cheng: This explains so much [*both laughing*]. Okay, perfect, perfect.

Mia: It's funny, because when I chose it in college, I was like, this is such a bullshit major, I'm never gonna use this for the rest of my life. Anyway, I think one of the questions that this brings up for me is, is altruism real? Is there anything that is not also personally benefiting you? And I have thoughts on that. And then there's also this question of, Do we have free will? Do we have choice?

Kai Cheng: We are just bringing in the deep ones, eh?

Mia: [*Laughing*] It's big stuff, because the biggest hypocrisy of my life is that I simultaneously believe that we have very little free will and control over our choices—our paths are largely carved for us—and, at the same time, that it's really important to take responsibility for our choices. I don't even try to totally reconcile that. I just try to hold both of those things to be true. And then the third philosophical question is, Can we ever fully know ourselves? We can try, and we can work toward that ever-moving goal, but can we ever fully know who we are, what we want, how we feel?

Kai Cheng: I love that. It's a mystery. I don't think we're gonna be able to figure that out in the next twenty minutes.

Mia: No!

Kai Cheng: But what I really like about that, I think it's sort of like . . . consent is just this deeply troubling mystery. And it's also so exciting for day-to-day life. But I think that maybe because we connect it with fear and an attempt to get away from punishment, we forget that it is a mystery, and instead we think about consent as something that has a clear answer. And for sure, I think there are cases where it's really clear—you shouldn't violate somebody, you shouldn't attack somebody, these important things—but we're not gonna get to this place where it is really easy and everybody knows. It was driving me really, really up the wall when people would make these posts on social media, like, "Ugh, I don't understand people who do consent violations; consent is so easy, it's just really simple." I'm like, man, you're just making me feel like I don't want to interact with you, because I *don't* think consent is easy, and if you do, I'm worried . . . [*laughing, but uncomfortably*] . . . that I'll do it wrong in your eyes, and then I'll be wrong.

Mia: I agree.

Kai Cheng: And maybe this comes full circle, but I guess what I'm saying is I think that we are actually more skillful in embodying consent when we acknowledge that it touches these existential questions that will never have a clear answer.

Mia: Right, right. Yeah, I completely agree. Some of the things that I say that consent is not—one is a tool for punishment, a way to control other people, but I also say that it's not something you can ever do perfectly.

Kai Cheng: And it's not math.

Mia: I think that there's this approach to consent that you're describing that's like, if I just know the formula or the equation, and I just do it correctly, then I will find the one right answer, and I'll be able to never hurt anybody, never make anyone uncomfortable. I'll never get in trouble, I will never be hurt, I will always be safe. And to go back to this word "creative," I think consent is something for us to approach as an art form, or literature, or something where we're interpreting. We're practicing our interpretation skills and our self-expression skills.

Kai Cheng: Oh, really beautiful, I love that.

Mia: Thank you. Thank you. It's not, "Do the process and then you get the answer." It's this very different way of engaging, it's closer to something you would learn in a literature or art class than in a math or science class.

Kai Cheng: Yeah, I think this is profound. Consent is an art, right?

Mia: Yes!

Kai Cheng: We come back to creative process. I don't want to knock this too much, because I do think there's utility in it, but there are consent practices that are literal math, you know? You're like, am I three fingers up for this decision, out of a maximum number of ten? You can be zero to ten, and then it kind of shows where you are. But, yeah, I think consent practices give us so much information that is beyond the quantitative.

Mia: Yes.

Kai Cheng: It gives us a texture of who we are. And that's so, so different from the "yes or no," 50/50 model you're talking about. I do want to say one more piece which feels really important to name in a conversation about what consent is not, and that is the idea that consent is *enthusiastic* and *informed*. You know, this kind of college-campus model of consent. Sex workers were calling that one out right away. The word *enthusiastic* just completely deletes *willingness*, which is a whole section of people's agency. But then also, this idea of consent being explicit and informed—you can't really be fully informed about something before it happens, particularly something as systemic as human interaction.

Mia: Absolutely. Yeah, I really love how you're putting that. I talk about that as "abstinence lite," because I don't think that we can tell people, "If you can't talk about this thing that you've never done, then you shouldn't be doing it." How do you learn without doing? But also, this point about enthusiasm—I don't want to harp on it too much, but it's really been interesting to see the ways that lots of people who do this work professionally are so tired of this "enthusiasm" requirement, for so many reasons. It's not just that it deletes willingness, but it also has led to a lot of people thinking that what happened to them was rape, assault, nonconsensual, because they weren't "hell yes" about something, when actually willingness may have been present, or curiosity may have been present, alongside some nervousness. There's just way more going on, and I think that that blanket requirement of enthusiasm has, unfortunately, accidentally created a lot of confusion and misunderstandings. What you're talking about, this "campus" education, I call bumper-sticker education.

Kai Cheng: Yeah, that's also really good.

Mia: Thank you. Yeah, where it's like, let's embroider it on a pillow, and then we're good to go, you know?

Kai Cheng: I mean, no offense to anyone who cross-stitches social-justice slogans, but it's not a good way to teach complex, layered processes like consent.

Mia: It is not. We're not teaching people how to do these things, and I think when you say, "Anything other than a 'hell yes' is a 'no,'" it removes agency. It actually takes away your agency to say, "If you weren't feeling these exact feelings, or didn't do this exact process, then what happened to you is not what you think it was."

Kai Cheng: Oh, yeah, and I mean, I think this makes sex kind of terrifying. If you really care.

Mia: Totally! [*Both laughing*]

Kai Cheng: There are so many moments in sex with delightful, loving, sweet partners where it's awkward, smelly, bad, uncomfortable, even momentarily painful or something, and I'm like . . .

Mia: Yes!

Kai Cheng: So what is this, then? What territory is this, if it's not consensual? It falls into this realm of "not okay." It might even fall into the realm of assault. And this is terrifying. I am terrified for, particularly, people who are less experienced with sex—so, often adolescents, but also adults of any age can be less experienced. And then, they hear this idea that if they're not doing it perfectly—not being perfectly pleased, perfectly pleasing others—then they're in assault territory? This is not helpful. It does not prevent assault, and I think it actually might make people even more vulnerable going into . . .

Mia: Right.

Kai Cheng: Anyway, it really gets my goat, this whole thing.

Mia: I think this thing that you're saying, that it might even increase vulnerability, is so real. Because when you're in that perfectionist mindset and that people-pleasing mindset of, "I just want to make sure that you're safe, and you're pleased, and that you're okay," you're not listening. You're not listening to them, and you're not listening to yourself. We need to move away from questions like, "Am I doing this right? Is this good?" and toward questions like, "Do I like this? How do I feel right now? How is this for you? Much more in the moment, what is happening right now? Do we want to change anything?" These are much more open-ended questions that get us out of that perfectionist headspace.

Kai Cheng: Yeah, yeah, and maybe because it's so edgy, I feel this need to speak to this other thing, which is that when we are in the gray space of exploration, and something is uncomfortable—or bad, or painful, or triggering, or whatever—it's totally possible that we could have a really, really negative, painful, even traumatic experience within this gray zone of willingness. Did I want that? Was it really bad? There is this total possibility that we can be consenting, to some extent, to something that is hurting us. I mean, under capitalism I consent to do jobs all the time, and they're definitely hurting me in some ways—and I love them, you know, sometimes, but also not all the time. I think something simple we can tell people that makes it much easier to embrace a complex model of consent is that your pain and your discomfort always matter. No matter what.

Mia: Yes. I think it's really important. I know that sometimes I say things that can push buttons when taken out of context. I am aware of this. And certainly, if you have a negative experience that leaves you with any kind of negative feelings or trauma, you deserve help. There should be resources that can help you find affordable and accessible help and make sure that you're not stuck there. You're not broken; it doesn't have to become part of your identity that something happened to you that was bad or traumatizing. I'm curious, though, I've now heard you say a couple times that we're talking about edgy stuff—can you be specific about what is so edgy? [*Both laughing*]

Kai Cheng: It was edgy for me because I have grown up with deep conditioning, first, by Christianity, and second, by the social-justice culture of

North America of the 2010s. And still, to some extent, the 2020s. I was first educated in consent through the "campus" model. I actually first got into workshop-based consent education through my undergraduate college's local sexual assault–response student group. And so, because it was also a student-run service, there were no administration people around. It was very, very radical, in some ways that were great, and in some ways that were very questionable. No fault of anyone in particular, just some collectively bad decisions, you know? And when I say "edgy," I guess I mean two things. One is that I genuinely do care about hurting people's feelings. Like, when people listen to you and me, or they come to a workshop of mine, and they feel attacked, put down, disregarded—I really care about that. And then the other piece is that I'm afraid of being punished. I am saying things that are against the orthodoxy with which I was raised in activism, and I am afraid that if people get triggered by what I say, they'll punish me. And so I notice I'm always tracking the Overton window of the conversation in the communities that I really care about, trying to sense where the edges of that Overton window are.

Mia: Yeah, that's interesting. I'm thinking about this concept of domains, and what I can and can't control, and I'm hearing you say that you care about how other people feel about something that you've said, or in a class, and I wonder how you balance that concern with knowing what's not your domain.

Kai Cheng: Oh, this is juicy. I love it! Yeah, it's an ongoing struggle for me. I am a people-pleaser by reflex, and it's my trauma. [*Both laughing*] It's sad, but true. And I desperately want people to be happy with me, which is probably why I've gotten into the careers that I've gotten into, right? I don't think that's bad—I think it's good and bad—but I think where I'm at right now is that I'm really sick and tired of censoring myself and shutting down my own agency in the name of trying to please other people. And then I just can't help but notice how this is also an attempt to control them: I'm trying to please them so they won't punish me. And then the reverse is also true. I am really tired of people attempting to control me with their moral claims. So I don't like that, either, and so going to the edge, wherever that is, is also important to me. And then how I balance that is, genuinely—it's not rocket science to not be an asshole, you know?

Mia: [*Laughing*]

Kai Cheng: We live in a community, and there's this funny thing about free speech or free expression, that it doesn't mean that it doesn't have consequences. Well, what I really understand from that phrase is not that people should get to punish you whenever they want for your speech, but that we should acknowledge that our speech affects other people's feelings. There is a shared domain where my words touch people's feelings. And that doesn't mean that I shouldn't say things that I believe in if they might be hurtful to people, or that I shouldn't question myself if I get critical feedback, but I do think it means that I want to care about how my words affect other people. So maybe it's the way that I say something, or the way that I acknowledge other possibilities or perspectives. I want to be relational with this free-expression thing.

Mia: Well, right, that's exactly what consent is for, relating and building relationships, and to care about how you impact people is a huge part of that. And I come up against this people-pleasing thing—I can't go into your mind and make sure that you are okay, and not mad at me, and that you understand the concepts in their fullness, and that nothing I'm saying is being taken out of context. I can't control that, and I also can't control whether or not people attempt to punish me. I recently found a Reddit thread about me, where people were saying that I deserved to be in prison, and I should be deplatformed, and they were reporting me on social media. This was, like, two years old.

Kai Cheng: Wait, why should you be in prison?

Mia: I don't know. For things I've said, again, taken out of context—they cited a post where I talked about why I don't really believe sexual-assault statistics, because they're so flawed, and they don't tend to include trans and nonbinary people, and men report even less than women. And I explain all of that, and yet, I guess that post was kind of triggering. And to your point, you're doing a really great job of contextualizing and zooming out a little bit, whereas I think I forget to do that sometimes. I'm like, "Well, we're talking about this thing right now, and obviously I'm not saying I don't care about victims of sexual assault," but someone who comes across one post may not know that. I've been accused of really bizarre things. I think you have too, like being a rape apologist, a men's-rights activist, a trad wife, and very, very weird stuff.... [*Both laughing*]

Anyway, I don't believe in canceling people or exiling people. Personally, at this point, I refuse to participate in that. And yet, we have to let go of what we can't control. We don't know what people are going to say about us out in the world. We don't know how people are going to interpret what we say. But then there's often really serious, real-world consequences if someone is trying to get you fired, or make sure that people don't work with you anymore, or start reporting your account—which might be, at least for me, where I get the majority of my business. I don't have the answers to that. I can't control it, and it has real consequences; for example, my book [*Unsolicited Advice*] got canceled by my first publisher when my editor got an email from someone I believe was a former student of mine who'd had a bad experience. There are very real things that can happen. So, yeah, those questions of, What can I control, and what can I not? Where am I people-pleasing, and where am I no longer willing to do that? Does that put me at risk? These are all just unanswerable questions. I'd like to hear what you think, but I'm not asking for any...

Kai Cheng: Solutions... [*laughing*] yeah, I think about this all the time, too. It is really my commitment as well to not participate in cancel culture, or call-out culture. Maybe those are the same or different things, but I don't want to participate in either of them. And I think it's really just true that we can't control how people react or respond to what we put out in the world, but we don't have to condone it, either. And that's a practice, knowing that people are gonna do what they're gonna do, but also being like, "Well, I don't have to condone it; I don't have to help you." Right? Which is fundamental to this kind of consent practice we're hoping that other people will take on, too. Like, ideally, people would not try to control what we say on the internet, particularly when the things we say are in no way whatsoever advocating for violence.

Mia: Right.

Kai Cheng: You know... it would be great if people could just disagree...

Mia: I would love that. Bring back regular old disagreeing.

Kai Cheng: Yeah, please, that would be good, probably. People don't know how to regular old disagree. It feels like the internet makes it more intense.

I think that there's an edge between people-pleasing and being relationally caring. That's always an interesting spot. What I want to model and demonstrate, and what I want people to model and demonstrate for me, is that, if I'm gonna say something that's iconoclastic or whatever—it's funny how little things can become iconoclastic these days—then I think it's a nice move to acknowledge that, wow, this might be a big idea for somebody. And that's okay that it's a big idea for them, and they might disagree, and there might be some important reasons why they disagree. I wish other people, if they were gonna critique Kai Cheng Thom, or if they were gonna contradict me or whatever, would do it thoughtfully, acknowledging the reasons why they might feel and believe the way they do. That would be good.

Mia: That would be lovely. I do try to remember that sometimes the people online . . . it's easy to think, with the facelessness of online interaction, that the people critiquing us are as invested as we are . . .

Kai Cheng: Or they're totally not.

Mia: They're totally not, but not only are they not [as invested as we are], but sometimes they're twelve years old, you know? Sometimes they're staying up at night avoiding doing their homework, on their phone. Or they share a lot of political beliefs and values with people that we completely disagree with, you know?

Kai Cheng: Oh yeah, or they're trolling, or whatever. I used to be a counselor for teenage queers, right? And I cannot tell you the amount of absurdity, but also real, very important psychological harm and damage, that happened because of fandom wars. I don't mean anything that any kind of balanced adult would consider weird . . . just people being like, I did a fandom art, and it didn't match someone's expectations of what fandom art should be. I would see fourteen-year-olds or thirteen-year-olds get hundreds of death threats—from presumably other fourteen- or fifteen-year-olds—because of disagreements about fandom, which were then quickly politicized. It's in this same way that real-life political conversation can get turned into something else, but by removing it completely from context. Anyway, it's a pet peeve of mine—and also, those teenagers that I was working with were delightful, and also teenagers!

Mia: Right, right. I know, you really lose a lot of humanity in the facelessness of social media. I don't want to end this on a note of us, or me, complaining about the internet . . . .

Kai Cheng: I love to complain about the internet.

Mia: I know, we could probably vent for hours about the internet, but what I hope that conversations like these help other people do is to loosen this grip on making sure that you're saying the right thing, and to be less afraid to put yourself out there. I know so many people who are very afraid to say their thoughts aloud publicly, or to put them on social media. But social media can be an incredible tool, you know? And I am somewhat invested in helping at least artists feel like they can express themselves authentically and vulnerably, without needing a content warning on everything they say, without being afraid of blowback and critique. I hope that these kinds of conversations help people feel more comfortable and confident putting their own voices out in the world.

Kai Cheng: I love that. I think this is actually a really nice note to end it on. It kind of comes back to what consent is not. I think that so often, when people are lashing out in these really intense ways—harassment campaigns, death threats, trying to get people fired from their livelihood jobs, all that kind of stuff—in some way, what they're often saying is, "I don't consent to you hurting my feelings or making me feel uncomfortable by putting your thinking or your art on the internet." And it's like . . . this is an unhealthy and unhelpful way to be as a society, because it means that we all then lose the benefit of getting to think together and think out loud. Which is kind of the thing that we want consent to be: this empowered choice-and-voice thing, where people get to say how they're feeling about something and what they want, a tool for more freedom rather than less, so . . . it's funny, that did kind of cover a full circle.

I think what's really important, what I get passionate about, is understanding that the impact of the restrictive or negative kind of consent models is a recognizable pattern. It happens at many different levels, in many different ways, and in many different contexts, but the result is often very recognizable. So, let's take an example from progressive social-justice circles in North America. A lot of us agree that when people say, "I don't want you to protest against genocide in Gaza because that makes me feel uncomfortable or unsafe," we understand that this is censorship, and that the application of the consent model here, or the safety model, doesn't make sense. It's actually contrary to life. But what we often miss is that we do some version of the same thing when we say, "If this person is saying an idea about consent that I don't like, then they should be punished and driven off the internet." It may not always be as severe, but we are actually still saying, "I don't consent to being uncomfortable, and therefore someone should be punished, or maybe even killed, or have their livelihood removed." And that logic is almost always negative. It is always contrary to healthy human relating, and it's my really big hope that as people get into these ideas, they'll start to recognize these patterns from context to context.

Mia: Thank you for adding that. I just used that example for the first time yesterday. It just came to me in a class where I was like, yeah, we can't be saying, "I don't want to talk about what Israel's doing in Gaza and around the world, that's just my boundary." That is a misuse of the term "boundary," and it's a way to avoid accountability and self-reflection.

Kai Cheng: Yeah, it disappears this whole other [realm] of life! So, yeah. Something that consent is not.

Mia: Something that consent is not, yes.

PART III

WHERE ARE YOU IN THE PICTURE?

The Downside of Being a "Thank You for Telling Me" Person and That Time I Was Called a Greedy Bitch

I remember learning early on in my consent education that when someone shares a boundary or feedback, it's best to say, "Thank you for telling me."

Expressing gratitude when someone states a boundary or gives you feedback is an incredible, connecting mechanism. When someone tells me "no," saying "thank you" can stop my own shame spiral in its tracks ("I shouldn't have asked," "They're rejecting me," etc.), while communicating to the other person that I'm a safe person to say no to, that I want to know their boundaries, and that they can do it again. It's powerful for both the person saying "thank you" and the person hearing "thank you."

I teach this in my consent classes through practice exercises that, when I first learned them, changed my life. I first learned this practice at the Cuddle Sanctuary in Los Angeles from Jean Franzblau in the very first orientation before a cuddle social. There was an area of the room where people knew to leave you alone, and I spent ninety minutes of the three-hour social crying on pillows in that area. My body was so shocked by the unfamiliar experience of saying "no" and the newness of hearing gratitude for saying it.

While I still believe saying "thank you for telling me" is a good rule-of-thumb practice, I've also seen what could be called a shadow side of this practice, ways that it can go too far and damage one's sense of self. I've had a good number of people in my life take advantage of someone's or my own willingness to listen and respond with "thank you for telling me" as we get projected onto, as we get someone's past trauma taken out on us because we've demonstrated ourselves to be safe. For example, as an educator independent of any institution of higher learning, a lot of people who are invested in finding alternative modes of self-edification and growth sign up for my classes. Many of these people have a lot of trauma from ivory-tower academia. A lot of us didn't feel we could speak truth to power in those institutions because of the fear of being given grades that would permanently impact our transcripts or even being kicked out if we seemed disagreeable or ornery. Those who have had experiences like this sometimes take out those frustrations on people with less control, and I sometimes fill that role for them as an educator outside of an academic institution, a person they have direct access to. A similar way this phenomenon shows up is when people with awful bosses or clients, who feel they can't speak up for themselves at work, take out their frustrations on customer-service people who are often told they can't talk back and that "the customer is always right." (Which, by the way, is a gross misreading of the original text in which that sentiment was expressed. Originally, that statement meant that the customer's preferences and choices are always right, as in, if the customer wants ketchup on their pasta, they're right. This was not meant to mean that any and all feedback from a customer is correct.)

When projection is at play—and it so often is—I have to be able to discern what is about me and what is about the person giving me feedback. I have to have strong boundaries and a strong sense of self so that I can bring relative objectivity to the feedback I'm receiving. What is mine, and what is not?

Feedback is a gift . . . but is it?

As my Instagram following has grown (as of January 2026, I'm at about 44,000 followers), I've had to learn my own boundaries with taking feedback and commentary. About two years ago I turned off comments on all my posts. This garnered some criticism from followers and colleagues, whereas most of my friends and family and my therapist were proud of me and encouraged the choice. Some followers left without saying anything, and others told me if they couldn't publicly share that they disagreed with me, they wouldn't be sticking around. One colleague and friend even severed our relationship because of this (as well as because of my feelings on cancellation and how I expressed myself online). This colleague told me that as a white content creator, I had to be willing to take any and all feedback from any BIPOC follower who was willing to share with me. Ironically, this colleague was a therapist and burnout specialist.

The choice to turn off comments and limit my DMs to people who follow me has improved my mental health as well as my offline relationships tremendously. I sleep better, I experience less stress, and the quality of my friendships has increased. I've learned to trust myself and those close to me more deeply and trust my own energy and radiance. Those who can't or won't see me as I am, who bring their projections and cast me in a negative light, tell me about themselves, not about me.

With no way of knowing who most of my followers on Instagram are, with no way of discerning if we have anything in common in terms of our beliefs and values, and with no way of knowing if I trust their judgment or value their opinions, I've had to learn that:

1. Other people's opinions of me are quite literally none of my business.
2. What people say about me is not in my domain of control.
3. I only want the opinions of people whose opinions I would solicit.

Plenty of the most frequent commenters on Instagram are incels, are catfishing someone, or are twelve years old. We have no way of knowing. Think of going to the grocery store or being on the subway: How many of the people you walk past or sit next to would you ask for feedback about something you said, about what you're wearing, about how you move through the world? How many people do you come across daily whose opinions you value and trust?

Having a large presence online with open comments and open DMs is like if everyone you saw on a dating app—regardless of whether you swiped right or not—could message you directly and tell you what they think of you, your profile, your outfit, your face. There's a reason most apps now require you to match with someone so the interest is mutual before you can even speak to them. But on social media, anyone can contact you without your opting into the interaction.

You may have had a friend who constantly told you that what you did or said was wrong in some way. I used to think this was love. I thought, "They're telling me because they care about this friendship. If they didn't care, they wouldn't say anything." But as I have learned to appease less, I've learned that my needs and boundaries don't change because of someone else's needs and boundaries. There are things I can be flexible on and things I can't be. And if I'm frequently doing things that offend or trigger someone, we're probably just not compatible. Trying to fit a square peg into a round hole is not something I want to be doing in my relationships. We can go our separate ways without blaming each other.

In real-world (as opposed to parasocial) relationships, feedback can be a gift. I'd like to see more friends giving each other feedback, because often it's those instances of rupture and repair, of conflict, that bring us closer together. Secure attachment is formed from rupture and repair, not through the absence of conflict. We learn about each other and ourselves in those moments. We learn how to treat our loved ones the way *they* want to be treated, not the way *we* want to be treated (Empathy 2.0). But sometimes, in a friendship or relationship where feedback is constant, we can understand that perhaps we are simply incompatible. It's not personal; we just aren't a good fit. And that's okay.

That time I got called a greedy bitch

An experience that solidified these feelings for me and helped me move into this much more empowered place of not giving a shit what strangers say about me was when I got called a greedy bitch by someone who had signed up for a class of mine and wanted a refund after she missed the first class.

My refund policy clearly states that I offer refunds up to twenty-four hours before the class starts. This policy is stated several times before you can check out, and you even have to check off that you read the policy before you can register. I replied that I would not be offering a refund, that she had agreed to the policy and received the recording of the first class, so she could view it at any time. She replied that she thought I was trying to "protect women" but now she sees that I'm "actually just a greedy bitch."

I've previously shared about why I don't like this sentiment that consent-education work is about "protecting women" (see "Consent Is for Everyone"). But the part about me being a greedy bitch was such an egregious accusation, coming out of a totally standard practice of having a refund policy, that I laughed out loud. This person revealed herself to be mean and hostile in a way that told me that her opinion of me was not something to take seriously. If she'd told me my refund policy was unclear, or hidden, or missing, I'd have had to consider where I could have been more up-front about it. Calling me a greedy bitch meant nothing to me, as I know this is not true. I'm confident about how I make money and about my pricing, through years of working through my own money trauma and internalized capitalism. No one is a consent educator "for the money." Lol.

I began to think of many of the other pieces of criticism I'd received, much of which I had believed to be in good faith, from people with valid takes I should consider. But here's the rub: There will always be someone who will find something to get angry with you about. Countless others will tell you that their take is the "right" take and that others are wrong. It's hard, but I think it's a necessary stage in adult development to be able to go, "That's not how I would do it, but it's how they're doing it, and that's okay."

Know yourself.

"Thank you for telling me" is a beautiful tool for connection that can serve us well in conflicts of varying levels. But it can also begin to chip away at the edges of someone's sense of self. We simply can't receive and incorporate feedback from everyone around us—not even if it's only from the people we actually know. Inevitably there will be different takes and different advice that will conflict and not be possible to integrate all at once.

The only way I see to mitigate this potentially diminishing effect of being open to feedback is to get solid on your own beliefs. Have a clear personal philosophy and ethic, a lens through which to locate your boundaries, a voice with which to express them, and the self-discipline with which to hold them gently but firmly. My personal philosophy and ethic will always distill most things down to this: Know yourself. This is the place from which we can build healthy, long-lasting relationships with open communication.

How to Read a How-To Article

ORIGINALLY PUBLISHED BY KILLING KITTENS, 2022

Through my teens, at airports and grocery-store-checkout lines I was a total sucker for catchy headlines about "How to Give a Mind-Blowing Blowjob," "How to Know if He's Really Into You," and "How to Make Him Want You More." With what I now understand to be mild OCD and a propensity to look for "the right way" or "the truth," these articles held a promise of perfection if I could just "do it right."

Cosmo was my drug of choice. In my teens, their how-to articles suggested that there was only one way to suck a dick and that all dicks are the same, which was awesome—and so convenient, because it meant if I read this article I would be awesome at sucking all dicks forever, right? They suggested that you could tell if your partner was cheating on you with the coveted insight that they blessed you with. How? She hides the phone from you when she texts. But what if she's planning you a surprise party, or her friend is having a tough time and she's consoling them, trying to give them privacy?

What these articles often lack is nuance, context, and you and me. Now when I read a how-to article, I scan it for evidence of *me*.

1. Verify the author.

Who is this person? Why are they writing this article? What are their motives? What are their qualifications? I don't mean that in a certificates-and-degrees, academically elitist way; I mean, Who the fuck are they and do you trust their judgment? Where are they getting their information? What are their beliefs? Can you get a sense of what their politics or ethics are? This helps you understand the context in which the article was written.

Of course, this also requires you to know yourself. Your own belief system becomes the filter through which you sieve these articles. How coarse or fine the mesh is depends on you and your integrity.

2. Who is the intended audience?

Is this article for cis people? White people? Heterosexual people? Able-bodied people? Thin people? How-to articles are rarely intersectional, in terms of who their advice is for. I'm a genderfluid, queer millennial with invisible disabilities. When I read these articles, I ask myself, "Was this written for me?" If not—and that's often—I can take what I like and leave what I don't.

This brings up the universalist myth of cis, hetero, white men. Historically, this group has been heralded as the pinnacle of humanness that we all strive to emulate. They've been deemed relatable to all, as some kind of blank slate onto which all the rest of us can project our own realities. When we are shown stories of cis-hetero-white men, we are all expected to be able to see ourselves in them. This is (slowly) changing in the media. We have seen it in publications like *Them*, *Teen Vogue*, *Salty*, and all over social media, where journalism, for better or worse, has been democratized. Turns out—shocker—people can relate to more than just this one archetype.

3. Who's publishing it?

What is the overall vibe of the publication? Who do they *want* their audience to be? What is their mission—or do they even have one? Does that mission align with your values or personal mission?

4. Reject binary thinking.

Is the article dividing people into categories? How many? Whenever I see someone referring to only two categories of people I think, "There are two kinds of people in this world: People who think there are two kinds of people in this world, and people who reject binaries." Whenever someone has a binary standpoint (where something is either *this* or *that*), it means they don't have a more nuanced argument. There are always more than two choices. How-to articles typically suggest that there's one right way to do things, and that there is some Platonic, objective, universal method. This necessarily implies that there is a wrong way—or countless wrong ways—to do whatever they're writing about. There's shame built in there: If you don't do it the author's way, then you're doing it wrong. There is no relativity, there is no subjectivity, there is no nuance. But are they speaking from their own experience or projecting their experience onto the universal "you"? A major tenet of my own belief system is that there is no such thing as an objective reality. I believe that a common reality is a myth, and that there are as many realities as there are subjective experiences in this world. Any article I read is an invitation by its writer into their reality, but that doesn't mean it has to be mine as well. There's a certain amount of power we give to an author when we read their work. They invite us in, and if we choose to accept their invitation, our reality can meet theirs in the liminal space between us. It's important not to lose ourselves when we join them.

5. How do you feel while reading it?

Check in with your body. What is your face doing? Is your brow scrunching? Do you feel skeptical or relieved? Confused or validated?

This is a practice of checking in to *attune* to yourself and your emotional and embodied experience. It requires us to slow down so we can listen. Our bodies don't speak in language—they speak in feeling. We tend to prioritize thoughts over feelings, intellect and reason over emotion, mind over body. This is a vestige of Cartesian dualism, which is Descartes's idea that we have a mind and a body. He's the Enlightenment-era philosopher who famously said, "I think, therefore I am." He believed not only that the mind and body are separate entities but that the mind can control the body. "Mind over matter," essentially.

Culturally, we value things that can be quantifiable as evidence and proof over the more ephemeral sensations, hormones, chemicals, and intuition that we call emotions. I believe it's irrational to ignore feelings because they are part of our experience, so when people want me to be rational *instead of* emotional, I think they're being unreasonable. Our bodily sensations are a huge and often overlooked part of our lived experience, largely because of colonialist, patriarchal ideas that prioritize intellect, reason, and logic over feelings and emotions. These sensations help us gauge when we feel safe or in danger; when we reject them, we essentially gaslight our body, and it just screams louder, often in the form of illness. Reading an article that is giving advice on how to be in the world is yet another opportunity to engage with our mind-body.

6. Where are you in this equation?

Again, answering this question requires you to understand your own politics, ethics, core beliefs, moral compass, and the like. Does this article feel aligned *with you*? Does it resonate with your lived experience? Everything we read, see, consume, and want is filtered through our own experience, which is an amalgamation of our inherited and lived trauma, our upbringing, our DNA, our education, etc. Do you see yourself in this article? Where? Engaging in a process of checking in with your body while reading will help you connect to your intuition, so you can take what you like and leave what you don't.

7. Form an opinion.

Some of the best advice I've ever gotten was to have an opinion. When I was twenty-five or so, I wrote a play called *Making Strangers* about a breakup in real time. The two characters were played by five rotating actors, intended to let me and the audience examine shifting power dynamics as gender, race, sexuality, and other identities changed. Days later, I met with the founder of a theater company who had come to see the show. He told me that it sounded like I had something to say, but I was holding back. He was right. I had prioritized making the piece universally accessible at the expense of specificity, which I know as a consumer of art is where the deepest resonance can be. Somehow, I was struggling to apply that principle of specificity in my own work.

I grew up studying classical piano with Russian teachers, with a major emphasis on music theory. I aced my Certificate of Merit exams, but had no voice of my own. I could sight-read well, and I could play Chopin, Bach, Mozart, and the like. But where was I? I was not encouraged to make music at all, let alone make music I liked. Experimentation was not on the table. This approach to music either caused or affirmed (chicken or egg?) my search for "the right way." There's some room for expression in classical music, but you're really just supposed to play it as it's written. My feeling was that if I could play it perfectly, that would be success and would mean I was good enough.

For a couple of years now, I've been working with a music teacher who frequently has me play a chord progression backward and play the majors in minors and the minors in minor sevenths and the sevenths in a higher key, and then she asks me which I like best.

There's so much power in that question: "Which do you prefer?"

I have to check in; I have to ask myself how it feels; I have to form an opinion. That requires me to value my own subjective reality. I have to have a healthy relationship with my ego in order to believe that what I feel matters to anyone other than me. It's a deep attunement to myself that allows me to feel and follow the pleasure.

This is where I believe magic exists. The attunement with myself helps me attune to others and my surroundings. This deep listening lets us hear the messages from our body, which holds ancestral wisdom that we experience as intuition.

So having read *this* how-to article, how do you feel? Do you see yourself reflected in this piece? Note the sensations in your body as you're arriving at the end. Form an opinion. Do you feel like I'm talking to you? What of this article will you take with you, and what will you leave behind?

Commitment as a Relationship with Past Versions of Yourself

When I was twenty-one, I fell in love with acting. I had wanted to be an actor since I was nine, and I promised myself at sixteen that I was going to follow through on that dream. But it wasn't until I took my first theater acting class in New York with Sondra Lee that I really understood what acting meant. It's a process of deep listening (what I call "full-body listening," meaning more than just words), of being present, tuning in, attuning to self and the other, reacting honestly, not anticipating, and so much more.

The deeper I got into it, the more I began to understand myself to be a process-oriented person, more than a finished-product person. I wasn't so interested in performing as I was in rehearsing. My love of acting led me to directing, but no one will ask you to direct anything until you've directed something, so I began writing my first play with the goal of directing it so I'd have a credit. I let go of the acting dream in favor of directing and ultimately writing.

But I was torn. I felt tethered to my sixteen-year-old self. I wanted to uphold the promise I'd made to them, or that they'd made to me. I felt I was betraying that me. I wanted to go back to talk to them, to tell them that I know things now that I didn't know then—things that, if they'd known, would help them understand the choice I was making.

My art practice is perpetually folding in on itself, bringing versions of me closer together and further apart, layering like (in my case, gluten- and dairy-free) croissant dough. (Who am I kidding, gluten-free dough doesn't do that.) When I was twenty-eight, I started a practice of writing letters to my sixteen-year-old self every day, a habit I kept up for quite a few months. Four years later, as I was learning guitar and songwriting, I was struck with an idea for a concept album using those letters to generate lyrics. I remembered that in high school I had frequently made mix CDs for myself and friends. I found them at my parents' house and used them as source material. Now some of those songs have made their way into the musical I'm writing about the tapeworm I had a few years ago. In a way, this project started eighteen years ago, a true collab between the many versions of me and myself.

I remember a thought experiment from a philosophy class in college: A man told his wife when they got married that he would give all the land his father owned to the serfs when his father died. He told her, "If I don't, then I'm no longer the man you married." The logic unfolds in a few different ways. If he doesn't give the serfs the land, is the marriage nullified? If he doesn't give the serfs the land, is his wife married to a different person, and what are the implications of that? Does she have a right (in that time period) to leave him? Can she remarry him if she wants to? Has he died? Who has replaced him?

I see this experiment playing out in the movie *Poor Things*. Bella Baxter, played by Emma Stone, dies by suicide while pregnant. Her brain is removed and replaced with the brain of her unborn child, who survived. Her abusive husband—who drove her to suicide—returns and demands that his wife come back to him. She made a commitment. But now, with a new brain, who is she, and who made that commitment? And I think we can ask, even without a new brain, just how much do we change? And further, if we allow ourselves to change, what is left of the whole project of commitment?

I love commitment. I see it as flirting with nihilism and as an endurance sport of sorts. I love the "fuck it" of getting a new tattoo. I love the way getting a new pet holds me responsible for potentially decades. In partnership I find commitment incredibly romantic. I think a fear of commitment is something akin to perfectionism—a constant wondering if you've made the "right" choice, as though there's only one, and a lack of faith in your own ability to change your circumstances and make new choices when you realize you don't like a choice you made. It's some kind of #FOMO. (More on this in "FOMO as a Manifestation of the Pursuit of Perfection.")

I used to feel this fear deeply. I essentially exposure-therapied myself out of it by making massive commitments, as I mentioned, such as permanent art on my body and caring for numerous living beings (two cats, a husky, and dozens of plants). I want kids; I want a life partner. I want a house to call my own, where I can plant trees in a yard, have an herb garden, lay down roots—both figurative and literal—paint walls, and tile counters with tiles I make myself.

But I'm ambivalent about this paradox: allowing myself and others to change (including acknowledging when perhaps we've outgrown each other) while believing in the sanctity of commitment of all kinds and valuing follow-through as a positive trait in a person. *Do what you say you're gonna do*. How else do we cultivate trust with ourselves and others?

I don't have clearcut answers to this. Thinking about times I've let myself break promises past selves made to my current or future self, I usually have a sense of having learned something I didn't know when I made the promise. I'm allowing myself to outgrow perhaps an idealized sense of something I didn't yet have much experience with firsthand. But when other people are involved, things get more complicated.

I have questions about how much work is too much to uphold a commitment made. I have questions about burning out trying to uphold a commitment, about sacrificing authenticity or a sense of self or time now needed for other things. I have questions about allowing myself and others to change. I have questions about the experience of time as linear when I don't believe it is, about fate and free will, about freedom and autonomy. But I keep coming back to the very real experience of trust built and trust broken—both with others and ourselves—when it comes to doing what you say you're gonna do. I said I was gonna write a book. I don't always want to write it or edit it, but I made an agreement with myself, with my publisher, with my editor, with my agent, and with my audience that I was going to write this book. Sometimes it's uncomfortable; sometimes it's agonizing. I've made a commitment to all of my paid subscribers on Substack to put out content at such a pace and of such a quality that you all feel like it's worthwhile to pay me six dollars a month. It's important to me to be a person of my word. That doesn't mean I can't change my mind or change course, but it does mean I have to be in relationship with the me who made the commitment and sometimes gently push my current self to finish what I started. We have to have open, ongoing dialogue about my current capacity and limits, my resources, health, and mental state, and where I'm making my money as it relates to where I'm spending my time.

I see this as a spiritual practice of engaging with past selves, with ancestors, with future selves, and with descendants (biological or otherwise). There is a deep kind of listening, a required presence, and an attuning to our bodies, essential core selves, and the bodies and selves of others to hear the messages about what is true, right, meaningful, authentic. Acting skills come in handy. Sometimes I have to engage with a past self in a kind, compassionate way to break the news to them that I won't be following through on a promise they made to me, current Mia. Something they want is something I no longer want, or something I'm no longer willing to do. I try to be gentle and let go of my own fears of feeling like a hypocrite.

There can be a lot of grief in this process: The grief of letting go of a past desire or dream. The grief of ending a project before it's done because you've changed your mind. And even the grief of perhaps breaking up with a former self who can't understand.

Interview with Janice Griffith

Sex Work, Autonomy, and Knowing Yourself

Janice Griffith is an adult film performer, producer, and cultural commentator.

Mia: It's funny to be interviewing someone in a professional context when we have been friends for quite a while now, and we're so close, and I was sort of like, oh, there's probably a lot about Janice's career that I really have no idea about. And now I can ask you.

Janice: Yeah, and we speak so often, it's funny, the random things that we don't cover. But now it's happening.

Mia: Well, when I was thinking about talking to you for this book, and in particular for this section about knowing yourself—you're someone in my life who I think knows themself better than most. And I wonder how much of that has been conscious, or unconscious and then made conscious. How do you track that in your life? Getting to know yourself so that you're able to then have these conversations so fluidly about what you want, and what you don't like, and what you don't want, and things like that.

Janice: I think it's been unconscious for a while, and there have been many influences throughout my life at different stages that have helped me develop this skill, but—I don't know if I've told you this story, and I think that you would love it. It's about my first sleepover, and it wasn't my friend, it was a family friend, and I think my dad needed to work overnight and didn't have someone to watch me. So he brought me to my Uncle Roy's house, and they had a daughter a year or two older than I was. But it wasn't like, "Oh, slumber party," you know what I mean? It was kind of under a different context, and I remember my dad saying, "You can change your mind if you want to." I'm, like, four. He leaves, and apparently, the entire night, until I fell asleep, I just kept going, "My daddy said I could change my mind if I want to." Over and over, ad nauseam. I've heard this story told back to me, you know?

Mia: Yeah, that's so funny.

Janice: Falling asleep, being like, "My daddy said I could change my mind if I want to."

Mia: Wow, I mean, you have told me that, but it's funny because you told me that really recently, and I don't remember why it came up. But it's interesting that that's such a formative memory, too, right? Because that easily could have been kind of forgotten, but obviously it really left an impact.

Janice: Well, I don't know that I necessarily 100 percent remember it, but I've been told the story over and over. And just even unconsciously, I'm sure that helped build a foundation. Even if I don't remember it, just being taught that I can change my mind if I want to. And the fact that my dad cared to instill that kind of idea in me very young, to give me a sense of agency and a sense that it's good to advocate for yourself. That's sort of what I take away from the story, that my dad is an integral part of my knowing who I am, and that I can change my mind, and that changing your mind is human, and not to stick things out if it's not feeling right.

Mia: Yeah. I mean, I'm also thinking, clearly that is something that was important to your dad to teach his child. And so it was probably something that showed up in many other places.

Janice: Over and over and over.

Mia: Right, right. He instilled it very clearly, explicitly, at least this one time. But it was obviously something that was pervasive in how he was trying to raise his kid. And then when it came to consent . . . I remember when we first met, and when we were starting to get to know each other—and this was also deep COVID lockdown, we were taking COVID tests so that we could hang out on your couch.

Janice: And being extremely safe and reasonable, and actually communicating about what we were doing.

Mia: Right, right. And I do know, and have known it to be true, that people who work in sex and porn and people who engage in BDSM tend to be very good at these conversations. You have to be. Especially when you're having sex for work with, often, people you're friends with, or friendly with, or who are friends with your friends—the boundaries have to be really clear, the things that you're okay with and things that you're not okay with. And you have a lot of practice with that, but I sort of have a hunch that this was something that you were doing before . . . . [*laughs*] Yeah, that it's not just because of your job, and so I'm wondering how that came about in your life.

Janice: I think, honestly, I have my father to thank for so much of my personality. My parents are both cops, and he really wanted to protect me. So, to help protect a child, you have to instill confidence and the right to self-advocate, you know? It was important to him to give me all of the tools possible to protect myself the only way a person can protect themself in, say, a bad situation, you know what I mean? I have known for a very long time in my life that I just don't really take shit from people.

Mia: Yeah, you don't.

Janice: You know, elephant in the room, I just would rather not. I can smile and bullshit like everyone else here and there, but it's not my preferred system or mode or whatever.

Mia: Yeah, yeah. And you think you've always been that way?

Janice: Absolutely. I might have been a bit more of a people-pleaser, and I still have these people-pleasing tendencies of, maybe not wanting to upset people or rub people the wrong way, but I think that's also just because I've accepted that I *do* often rub people the wrong way. [*Both laughing*] It's not my intention, but kind of, also, not my problem, because it's not my intention. If I'm trying as hard as I can to communicate something clearly,

I would rather have you be rubbed the wrong way than for me to communicate less clearly what I'm trying to get across. Does that make sense?

Mia: Yeah, totally. I mean, it's interesting, because I'm just coming off the heels of this other interview that I did with Kai Cheng Thom, and she talks about caring if someone has an interaction with her, or reads something she wrote, or takes a class, and leaves that experience with hurt feelings or being upset. And we talked a little bit about what is in your domain of control and what's not.

Janice: Nothing is in your control. Because I learned a lesson a long time ago online—sorry to interject here.

Mia: No, please.

Janice: It's part of why I don't post as much generally. I will be misunderstood in the way that people choose to misunderstand all the time, no matter what, no matter how hard I try. So I kind of gave up on being understood, and really dumbed it down and simplified it, and stopped sharing bigger ideas, because it felt harmful to me to be leaving people with these crazy sort of ideas that I was like, wait a second, that's not what I was saying. And yeah, it was hard for me to realize what was in or out of my control.

I'm curious to hear . . . where did that interview lead?

Mia: Well, what I noticed was this feeling—and it's funny, because I'm feeling like I'm sort of between the two of you a little bit on this point—when I heard her say that, like, Oh man, that's so kind. But that was a reaction coming from the fact that I kind of . . .

Mia and Janice: [*At the same time, laughing*]: Don't care.

Mia: . . . don't care so much. And it is a facet of doing so much of what I do on social media specifically.

Janice: Yes. Yes, I completely agree.

Mia: Yeah, and it is very much related to what you're talking about. Obviously, I experience it wildly differently, given that the reasons why people know us and follow us are very different, and you also have a way larger following than I have.

Janice: People want to argue with you almost more.

Mia: Yeah. It's true. But . . . out of these experiences of having people either wildly misinterpret what I'm saying or read their own motives into what I'm saying . . . or, the contrary, these really bad-faith interpretations—you know, "I'm gonna hear what you say, and then I'm gonna tell you everything that's wrong with what you're saying in every way that it could possibly be misinterpreted, misconstrued, and used to justify violence and bad behavior." I'm like, man, I'm not here trying to change people who want to do bad. You know?

Janice: And I think this is a conversation we've had a lot, too. What we're doing is not at the 101 level—and there are people who *are* teaching at that level, or having conversations for absolute beginners, entryways into the conversation of consent and advocacy for the self, and harm and repair and accountability. There are levels to this shit. Sometimes I think people who are not equipped to handle the nuances of certain topics or conversations are just jumping the gun and ready to get in, and it's like, wait a second, it took us a while to get here, too. We didn't start here, you know? I've had a long, storied journey with how I feel about consent, and I've even changed my mind on certain topics here and there. I think it should be an ever-growing, changing process as you age and get to know yourself.

Mia: Right, right. You're really good at being like, "I'm having a feeling right now . . . and I'm probably not gonna have this feeling later. So I'm gonna give it time." You let things breathe, and I think you're able to do that because you know yourself so well. And, what, you disagree?

Janice: No . . . that was just, that's so kind [*laughs*]. You're like, "You disagree?"

Mia: Your face is so frozen, I was like . . . you don't feel like that's true? Well, you're someone in my life who frequently reminds me that you don't have to say everything as soon as you feel it or think it.

Janice: I'm a very reactive person. [*Both laughing*] Taking a beat is, like . . . I have to do it. I say I'm not allowed to be reactive about things, sometimes. I need to take a beat. Also, I don't like them. I don't like that person [that I become].

Mia: I was just gonna say, this is not at all where I thought we would go, but let's talk about Cheryl. I have shared with you that I have named my inner critic "Cheryl," and she's a real bitch, she's super mean. And one of the things that you've started doing that I appreciate is that I'll say something to you, and you'll be like, "Oh, hi, Cheryl! Here she is! What is she doing? What does she need right now? Can we put her away?"

Janice: "What is she doing here? What is Cheryl doing here?" It's one of my favorite bits, because we aren't our thoughts or our feelings, we are the decisions that we make, over and over. Thoughts and feelings happen to us, and they're influenced by who we are, but you can think a thousand things, and it doesn't make you . . . like, if I sit here and I think right now I should blow up the whole world—that's a thought exercise, I'm not gonna blow up the world.

Mia: Right, right, right. Or, like, thinking about murdering someone who doesn't use their turn signal when driving, you know?

Janice: Like, having OCD, having these obsessions and compulsions where it's like, "Oh no, I thought about hurting someone. That means I'm a bad person, and I want to hurt people," and it's like . . . no!

Mia: Yeah, yeah. Who's your Cheryl?

Janice: They don't have a name, because they're not prominent enough in [my head].

Mia: Has that always been the case?

Janice: Yeah, because the person who was being mean to me before was just me. It was totally me.

Mia: Oh, wow.

Janice: I really identified with them.

Mia: Well, how did you stop being so mean to yourself?

Janice: I was like, Why would I do this? Over and over, I was like, I'm suffering, and what can I do to suffer less? I need to stop contributing to my own suffering.

Mia: Yeah, yeah, that's really beautiful, and so sad in such a relatable way.

Janice: And it's hard. It's really hard. Being mindful helped me, because the thought would kind of creep up, and I'd be like, "We don't do that around here. I've told you about house rules, you're not allowed to be mean to yourself in my house." It's like, "You're not allowed to use my words to be mean to yourself." And that applies to everyone . . . it applies to me, it applies to you, if you were in my house.

Mia: Yeah, that's really sweet. That is something that you do provide as a friend that I think is so special. I literally hear your voice in my head now, when I'm mean to myself.

Janice: Aww!

Mia: Yeah, what was it recently? I heard you in my head saying, "You don't need to say everything else."

Janice: Sometimes I call them "inside thoughts" . . . is this an inside thought or an outside thought? Or I ask the question, "Is this helpful?"

Mia: Yeah, yeah, "Is this helpful?" is a big one.

Janice: Because I actually like to identify with the idea of being a helpful person. I like that idea, and so sometimes it's like, Does this actually fucking help? You know what I mean?

Mia: This wanting to be helpful, wanting people to feel like they can come to you—you know, we're both Cancers [*laughs*], and you're actually the first person in my life where you did something or said something, and I was like, oh my god, that person has to be a Cancer. And then it turned out you were.

Janice: What did I say?

Mia: We were at your apartment in LA, and it was something that you offered to me that was just so specifically helpful to me, you know? And I just was like, "The only other person I know who would think of this is me, when's your birthday?" [*Both laughing*] But also, you have a reputation as "mommy" to your friends, to people in your work life. How have you gotten the reputation of mommy?

Janice: By being mommy. I also have a reputation of being a daddy, because I am daddy. I'm both of your parents. I focus on the little things. It sounds kind of simple, but it's real, like, Maslow's-hierarchy-of-needs-type shit. Have you eaten? Did you sleep? Are you thirsty? Do you have a roof over your head? And then we can move on to the other stuff. But honestly, half of us aren't eating enough, we're not drinking enough water, we're not sleeping enough, we don't feel rested, we don't feel good in our bodies.

Mia: Or we forget about our prescriptions . . . .

Janice: We feel anxious, and we don't take medicine, even though we have it. I talk to people almost every single day about specifically the stigma around taking benzos for anxiety, and I am always just saying, "It's okay to take medicine when you're sick," and I understand that addiction is a real concern when taking medicine. However, if you're already this scared of taking it, you think you're gonna get addicted when you're too scared to take it once?

Mia: And you also have me thinking, is it perhaps the anxiety that you have the benzos for that is stopping you from taking the benzos?

Janice: And yes.

Mia: Yeah, that's funny, that has never occurred to me before, even as someone with a prescription.

Janice: I talk to people all the time about this, and I'm always like, "What do you notice?"

Mia: Like, you need a Band-Aid when you cut yourself; it's okay to take medicine when you're sick. This brings up a question for me, because you've said that you don't really take shit from people. I've seen that in action. You also, it sounds like, have gotten way better with people-pleasing, I would imagine . . . or is it accurate to say, you never really experienced it to a super-huge degree?

Janice: Yeah, I think I always had a not-taking-shit approach, even to my people-pleasing. I didn't like . . . make waves, but, if necessary, I would be resistant, or whatever it was that I needed.

Mia: Well, what this is making me curious about, this conversation about Janice Griffith's being mommy, is that in order to be able to give that way, and offer that kind of attention and care without people-pleasing and burning out and going past your own boundaries, you have to have a really strong center of gravity.

Janice: I think it also really comes naturally to me. And I've practiced so much that I'm good at it. It feels good to be good at it, and I don't give more than I can offer. You know what I mean? I actually know where it's like, "Okay, wait, this is what I have."

Mia: Right. I think that's what I'm sort of getting at. I'm wondering, how did you learn not to be taken advantage of? I feel like [taking advantage] would be typically so easy if someone didn't have that "no bullshit" [approach].

Janice: Well, I think that they're not always mutually exclusive. I do feel like sometimes I am taken advantage of, but it is okay, because of my intention.

Mia: And it's within a window of tolerance or something?

Janice: Yeah, and it's still within my desire, like, I still want to do the right thing. Even if you think you're taking advantage of me, are you? If I'm aware and still doing it? Like, you might benefit more from the situation, or whatever, but sometimes I just want to do stuff for people, and it brings me joy to do so. I think also, though, I do ask a lot of people, especially those close to me, but it's because I give a lot as well. And I think that I have an interesting dynamic with some of my very close friends where we anticipate each other's needs, and we go out of our way to prepare for them before they happen, and we sort of naturally take turns doing so. That is something that's really special to me, and it's not something that is in every relationship. But in some of my very close ones, it is just so nice to know that almost exactly what I'm giving is being returned to me without asking, without establishing a dynamic overtly, just because that's who we are and that's how we mesh. And you've gotten to see that really caring side of me, and obviously, I care about other people, but I am more reserved with, say, strangers.

Mia: No, of course. Yeah. Yes, I have seen so much . . . I'm really hung up on this . . . it's like the specificity of the care. You're not just . . .

Janice: That's just because I love . . . because it feels good. It's so satisfying . . . . It's like, I see you, and I want you to feel seen. It's selfish in that it's satisfying, but it's . . . I think it's just paying attention to people, and noticing what people do or don't do, and kind of filling in the gaps, because sometimes people don't realize [those gaps are] there. And being made aware of things is the first step into mindfulness and understanding [those traits or behaviors], and being intentional about everything you do.

Mia: Yeah, this ties into this question of being pretty well-versed in consent and it coming pretty intuitively, because what you're talking about is a way of observing and listening that's well beyond just what people say. And, yeah, it's caring in a much more holistic way than in this kind of tit-for-tat of, "Well, you said this." I'm seeing how those things all kind of tie together, but I don't quite have the words.

Janice: Yeah, it's interesting, because it's kind of hard for me to describe how I do it as well. Maybe initially, many years ago, the sort-of bud of this identity facet, let's say, was that I thought of myself as a really good gift giver. Because I am. But that was just the way that I could identify this. I notice what people like or want or need, whatever it is, and have a desire to give it to them.

I learned so much about consent from Tim Woodman, a.k.a. Pro Villain.

Mia: Oh, I love Tim Woodman.

Janice: I met him when I was eighteen years old. A girl I did a scene with invited me to hang out, and they were gonna go to a play party. He was the first person who ever tied me up. And he taught me so much about consent, and asked me so many questions, and when I was like, "I don't know, anything is okay with me," he was like, "Nope, wrong answer. So you're okay with this?" And I was like, "Well, no," and he's like, "Exactly. So you're only gonna say the things that you are absolutely okay with." And he also asked, "Is there anything you're curious about?" He was so unbelievably respectful, and I was overtly naive. I was the perfect person to test the boundaries of, because I didn't know what I was okay with yet. And he obviously didn't do any of that, and was the most respectful, kind person, as he is to this day, which I find really interesting because of the genre of content that he makes. But of course, if you're gonna make that kind of content, you do have to be . . . perfect at consent is a hard thing to say, but you have to be really fucking good.

Mia: Yeah, can you explain a little bit about the kind of content that he makes?

Janice: So, his porn name is Pro Villain, and he makes simulated rape fetish content, and kidnapping, and stabbings, chloroform—things like that. But again, it's strictly fetish content, and I think the biggest thing is he knows the difference between fantasy and real life. And I think a lot of people get that shit twisted.

Mia: Right, right.

Janice: You know? Because I'm sitting here saying, twelve years ago, that man was teaching me about consent, and laid a foundation for almost everything that I feel today. When people talk about consent and how I feel so comfortable, empowered, whatever you want to call it, I really always have to credit Tim Woodman for helping me cultivate this attitude and perspective and, honestly, experience as well. I was suspended at this play party, he hog-tied me, I tried a lot of new things, and I felt completely safe doing so. And it also established an amazing precedent for when other people wanted to do kink stuff, but they wouldn't match that level of care and consideration. I immediately was like, wait a second . . . So it just sort of informed itself over and over, and built upon itself as well.

Mia: Yeah. I mean, that's amazing, and that's such a fortunate experience to have. At such a foundational moment.

Janice: Yeah, and I was eighteen years old, you know? I'm literally, like, four months into being eighteen. I was a baby, like, six months prior, I had to ask to use the bathroom in high school, and here I was . . . .

Mia: Right. It's funny that you bring him up, because I've had a few conversations with him, and I just so appreciated what he said and how he talked about these things.

Janice: I love him. I love singing his praises, because I think people might see his content and just be like, "How could you do this?" But I also believe that there actually is a place for it, because it is so explicitly fantasy, and not real. And if you have urges, isn't it safer to satisfy yourself with fantasy, rather than hurt a person, and to learn that it is also actually a fantasy that maybe a real person would be open to roleplaying with you?

Mia: I want, and I crave, to see this type of conversation that you're talking about, because I think that so many people who try to replicate this fantasy in their own lives don't know what went into it. They don't know what they need to be talking about ahead of time.

Janice: Do you mean . . . I'm sorry, I'm being a stupid idiot, and I'm being a silly goose. I'm just imagining a *Jackass*-style disclaimer of . . .

Mia: "Don't try this at home?" [*Both laughing*] No, no, I mean, like . . .

Janice: I know, I know, I know that's not . . .

Mia: "These are professionals," yeah. No, I mean, with my work, my god, I'm trying desperately to help people have these conversations.

Janice: We don't have the conversation anymore. I do have to say, and I'm not saying that this is right, but I have some scene partners where, we know each other, we have a vibe, and we're just like, "Alright! Anything change? No? Cool."

Mia: Well, that's a beautiful place to get to get to with somebody.

Janice: Yeah. And I think it's something that is really special and kind of unique to the industry, where we're doing this performance together, and it is like a dance in that way. Like, flow.

Mia: Right. And we know each other, and there's trust that's been built. But this thing about . . . I can only imagine what people think of people who have consensual-nonconsent fantasies, or who make that kind of porn . . . It reminds me of a lot of misconceptions around punk musicians that they're all angry, and they're all violent, and they just scream all the time, when in reality, they're all straight-edge vegans, you know? Like, they're all into crafting, and they make zines, and volunteer at the animal shelter, or whatever . . . .

Janice: And they're punk.

Mia: Right. It's a similar thing with people who are like Tim Woodman . . . I think people have these misconceptions around people who are into pain with sex, different kinds of kink—like, oh, they must have these dark issues, or they've been really traumatized, or they're traumatizing other people. And part of that, I think, is because we're not seeing what goes on behind the scenes, and then the other side of that is then people try to replicate this in their real lives, not knowing the legwork that went into it. And I'm not saying that I think that porn has an obligation to educate people. I know we've talked about that, too.

Janice: I swear to god we would put it in there, but no one would watch it. No one watches that part, because Kink.com has been putting that part in their videos for at least a decade.

Mia: And people fast forward.

Janice: Yeah, or, that's not the part that they watch for free on the tube site, or the clip site, you know what I mean? People don't watch pornography in its entirety, from intended start to its intended finish. People really jump around, and so the sort of content warnings or consent discussions like that get lost, even when we do provide them.

Mia: Yeah, that totally makes sense. I don't even think it necessarily has to be shared alongside the porn that is made out of that conversation. And maybe this is the seed of some sort of future idea, but I'd love to see people having those conversations, and show people having those conversations. Even in my own partnership, we'll have conversations, and I'm not the one initiating them—I sometimes struggle with them—where he's like, "What kind of sex do you want to have tonight? What do you want to do?" And I'm like, oh man, I don't know, I thought we would just do it normal. [*Both laughing*]

"Do it normal!" I'm kidding, I mean, I'm sort of saying this in jest. I appreciate that he challenges me to get creative and think about it, because that's also hot, and that works up an appetite, you know? There's such a fear of consent being so dry. It just does not need to be. I think that's really funny and silly, just . . . "Let's just do it normal."

Janice: And also, sorry, but if you get turned off because of, like . . . Grow up.

Mia: Grow up!

Janice: You don't get to have sex, sorry.

Mia: The title of this book is *How to Do Consent Without Sounding Like a Robot*, but the conclusion of even that essay is like, if you sound like a robot, who cares? Who fucking cares?

Janice: That's exactly what I'm getting at right now . . . it's better to get it out there than to not say it at all. I don't care if you say it badly, because it is important.

Mia: You know, I have a really great, totally non-sexual, mundane example of this. Recently, we were gonna have burgers for burger night. And my friend is going through a rough time, and we were texting, and I thought about inviting her to come have burgers with us, because I knew we had enough food. And I thought, oh, you know, Andis loves cooking for people, and he loves this friend, I'm sure it's fine. And then I also had this thought that was unconscious, briefly, which was, "I'll just invite her, and if he's upset, I'll apologize later." And then I was like, *no, no, no, no, no*. That thought is exactly the thing that tells me that I need to ask. And then I was like, "Why wouldn't I just ask?"

Janice: Like, where does that resistance come from? You have to ask.

Mia: Yeah, and the resistance comes from the fact that I just want to be able to invite my friend over, and I don't want to have to ask permission. I just want it to be okay, so I'm just gonna do it instead of asking. And then, of course, I did ask, and he was like, "I'd rather not." He just wasn't feeling up for the socializing, and he was like, "You guys can hang out and do whatever, and I can go in the other room." And I was like, no, no, no, no, it's burger night, we're having burgers.

Janice: Good that you asked, because you kind of knew . . . somewhere. You knew that was a possibility. Yeah, he might not want to.

Mia: Right, and then when it comes to sex, the stakes go up, emotions are more likely to come up. Why would you not just ask if you're not sure? And then, what I think so many people find really surprising, is that by asking for and getting very explicit permission, they get to really go 100 percent.

Janice: I was gonna say, it's freedom. It gives you freedom.

Mia: Totally.

Janice: Because then you know exactly what is allowed, you don't have to wonder anymore. I love knowing the explicit boundaries and parameters of what I'm allowed to do, or say, or engage in.

Mia: Yeah. I know. It is really . . . you're right, it's freedom. Permission gives you freedom.

Janice: Also, when you bring up hard things, even though it's hard, or awkward, or whatever it may be, it gives the other person permission to do the same.

Mia: 100 percent.

Janice: You know what I mean? So even if it feels like really putting yourself out there, or going out on a limb, it's this gift that you also give this other person, so that they can feel brave enough to ask for the same things without sort of having to take the first step like you did.

Mia: Absolutely.

Janice: It's a beautiful way to open that conversation and welcome it.

PART IV

SEX, TRUST, AND MAKING MISTAKES

How to Do Consent Without Sounding Like a Robot

ORIGINALLY PUBLISHED BY KILLING KITTENS, 2022

I'd never been on a date with someone who was only in town briefly. I'm not one to forge connections that can't last, because I'm turned on by feeling safe and cared for. Recently, though, someone *pinged* me on Feeld. He said he was only in town for another week and that he was feeling "very giving sexually."

I was intrigued by his profile and this particular nugget he had dropped. I was curious how I'd feel in this kind of dead-end encounter, so I decided to see if there was potential for some immediate physical fun. I said, "Let's meet up and see if there's chemistry." (This was 2021, so then I asked him if he's vaccinated, because I'm not a monster. He was. Vaccinated, not a monster.)

I have a habit of dropping myself into strange and challenging situations, like I'm a lab rat in a maze, so that I can witness myself navigating my way out. It's a recurring practice in learning about myself. Often, I'm surprised and impressed with my emotional piloting skills, and I get to go, "Hey, look how you did that! Nice work."

This experience was no different.

We met for sushi. I was struck by unfamiliar thoughts and new feelings in my body. Instead of thinking, "Do I want to see this person again?" or even "Does this person seem like someone I could build something with?" I was asking myself, "What do I want right now?" and nothing more. It was a new kind of living in the moment. It was a pure sense of now, untainted by past or future. My desires could be exclusively of the present.

The first indication that there was a schism between us around consent arrived in the form of a request disguised as an offer. We were done eating, and he said, "What do you want to do? Want to get a drink? *Or you could introduce me to your cats?*" He wanted an invitation to my apartment and hid that desire in a cute package about my cats. It may seem innocuous enough, but it's a manipulation of the truth in order to get what you want without asking for it. I said, "You're trying to get invited to my apartment?" He smiled sheepishly. I told him I had never been on a date where a connection had no potential to go anywhere beyond one date. It was new for me, and I was finding it curious. He said he appreciated my candor.

We got a drink next door. Eventually, I asked if he wanted to sit next to me. He thanked me for the invitation and sat down. He moved his hand over my thigh haphazardly.

"What do you want? You can ask to hold my hand. I like being asked."

"Can I hold your hand?"

"Yes."

He was sweet. I liked how he touched my hands like he was exploring them. He played with my nails like they felt good against his fingers. Then he asked if he could kiss me. We made out for a bit. I liked how he kissed and I liked how he smelled. I suggested we go back to mine "for more of this but possibly nothing more than this."

We started making out on my couch and immediately his hands were on my chest over my shirt, then quickly under my shirt, then his hand started going down my back under my pants.

"Whoa, you gotta ask, man!" He froze. "Just ask. Check in." I kissed him and he didn't move his hands at all.

"Did I frighten you?"

"A little, yeah."

"Just ask before you do something new."

We started making out again. He approached with caution due to what I imagine was new self-consciousness.

"Can I lick your nipples?"

"No," I said with as much patience as I could muster. I had just pulled his hands away from my boobs and now he wanted to use his mouth?

Kiss, kiss, kiss. I was paying very close attention to my desires. I was struck by my ability to know that I was definitely not ready to have my nipples licked, but could back up and work my way toward having my chest touched over my shirt. After a little while, I felt a movement forward in my body and a craving for something more. I invited him to touch me when I was ready, and my body very clearly told me when it was ready. But then he used his mouth over my shirt. I was a little exasperated. "I guess I didn't specify that he could touch me only with his hands," I told myself. After some time there, my body told me it was ready for him to go under my shirt. There, he used his hands, and this time he did wait for the word that he could use his mouth. He asked what I liked. Nibbles? Yes. Licking? Yes.

I told him I like my neck to be kissed, but not with too much tongue. I asked if he liked his ears nibbled and checked in on pressure.

"Is this good, or harder? Do you like this spot?" He was able to tell me what he liked.

I liked how he was touching me, alternating firm and soft. I liked the sounds he made. I liked that he kissed me on the cheek very tenderly from time to time. I thought he was starting to get it. He touched my foot very gently, thoughtfully. He was giving. It felt really nice. He worked his way up my leg, massaging. I liked that, too. I was wearing very wide leg pants and he was able to make it to my underwear, at which point he pulled away and stared.

"What do you want to do?" I asked.

Blank stare. Deer in headlights.

"See, *you* have to know first, so you can ask for it."

"Can I touch your vagina?"

"No. But you can squeeze my butt over my underwear."

I still had my pants on. He had been leaps ahead of me the whole time. I couldn't help but think, "He's been having sex like this? Not waiting for invitations, just doing things and thinking that not getting a 'no' means it's okay?"

We both got tired, and I knew I wasn't going any further than that. We put our shirts back on. He stared vacantly into the distance in what looked like shock.

"What's on your mind?"

"I've never communicated like that before."

"It's cool, right?"

"Yeah, I like it. I think I need that."

"Welcome," I said.

So . . . where was this guy in 2017? Did he hear the stories and think, "That's not me, though"? He had obviously never been exposed to communication like this, and he had likely been violating people's boundaries left and right. People hadn't been telling him to slow down, hadn't been telling him "no," hadn't been modeling this kind of talk during sex or any kind of physical intimacy. Clearly, he was interested and liked it, but he wasn't seeking this information out, nor was he dating people who were already doing it.

So, how *do* you practice consent without sounding like a robot?

1. Practice asking before you do anything new and practice doing it confidently. This can take many tries. You can record yourself and watch it to see how it comes across. Do it in the mirror. I used to think it would be weird if someone asked me, "Do you want to have sex with me?" but then someone asked me, "Do you want to have sex with me?" and it was so fucking hot I was floored. Have you ever tried it?

2. Pay attention to your *prosody* (*how* you say what you say: intonation, volume, pitch, vocal quality) as well as your body language and eye contact.

3. Get in touch with what your desires feel like and then practice asking for them. This takes time. It takes mindfulness and patience. We can't feel our desires if someone is going for what they want without checking with us. Notice if you *want* something or if you're *letting it happen.* Start with, "Can I ____ you?" "Will you ____ me?" and "Would you like to ____ me?"

4. Be clear about whether you are making an offer or a request. Are you asking to do something to someone for them or for you? Are you asking someone to do something to you for you or for them? All are great! Having clarity on which is happening in each moment can help you relax into the action. I love being felt up because I love seeing someone else take pleasure in my body and touching me the way they want to touch me. That's someone doing something to me, for them. I also love giving face massages. That's me doing something to someone, for them.[1]

5. Take your time. Check in with your body and ask it what it wants. Our bodies know, and they tell us; they just don't speak in words, and most

1 For more on this, watch Betty Martin's video on the Wheel of Consent, posted January 8, 2014, YouTube, www.youtube.com/watch?v=auokDp_EA80.

of us have spent our lives telling our bodies that we (read: our brains and thoughts) are in charge.

Remember, not getting a "no" is not the same as getting a "yes." Wouldn't you rather know not to do something that someone doesn't want you to do? Equally, it's so hot to know that what you are doing is eagerly wanted and truly welcome. When I ask if someone likes something and they go, "Yes, I *love* that," I'm so much more confident doing it. And when I know that someone can tell me "no," I know I can trust them.

And if you sound like a robot, so what?

We Both Got Too High and Had Sex Anyway, and We're Fine

My partner and I have an ongoing joke that I can't get high anymore. We only say it when I'm gloriously, obviously, incredibly stoned.

A few months ago, we ate some edibles, as we often do. I then smoked some of a joint, and then . . . I can't remember, but I think I might have even eaten half of another gummy. We started fooling around in the shower and things started to get weird for me. I was repeating myself and couldn't really find the words to say what was in my head. I continued to get more and more high, as did he, as the edibles reached their full potential. We moved to the bed and I almost could no longer speak, unable to translate my thoughts into words. My body was feeling hypersensitive, so things that normally feel good felt kinda like . . . nothing, or they became overstimulating really quickly. Because I couldn't speak, I gave up and decided to just wait until it was over, somewhat crushed under his weight.

This sucks. It sucks for both of us. If I knew anyone was "waiting for sex to be over" with me, I'd be mortified and upset, and I knew he felt the same. I had told him previously that he could trust that I would say so if I ever didn't like something or didn't want something, and I hadn't been able to do that. I felt I had betrayed that promise. I hated that I had put us both in that situation.

I think a common reaction to this story thus far is, "He should've been able to tell and stopped." But he was also high out of his mind. When I asked about it later, having regained my speech, he said, "I had déjà vu the whole time and I felt like I had extra limbs." We laughed about it.

There's a way that consent knowledge can be really appealing to those who love rules, who want to know how to make sure no one ever gets upset with them, who have any kind of perfectionist tendencies, who crave structure, who struggle with people-pleasing, who have a brain with any kind of OCD. The list goes on. We might learn about consent and go, "Aha! I've found it. I've found the way to *get it right* and *never fuck up*. No one will ever be mad at me again!" But we are flawed, and we live within the variable of time. We change. Those we're in relationships with change. Sometimes changes happen over many months or years, sometimes within a day. I have boundaries that change based on whether it's light or dark out: I'll walk through Morningside Park when the sun is out, but not after dark. I like having my boobs grabbed, but not right before my period. My partner can squeeze my butt anytime, anywhere, unless we're hanging out with my parents. We change, our boundaries change, and how we like to practice consent changes, sometimes without our awareness. Sometimes you don't know you have a boundary until it's crossed. When consent seems like the panacea, falling flat on your face feels much worse than if you expect to fall and have a plan for how to get back up. Secure attachment isn't formed through a lack of conflict but rather through rupture and repair.

The next day I felt awful. I hated that I had told him he could trust me to speak up and then I couldn't. I thought of situations I've heard of like this, where one person decides retroactively that because they'd been too high or drunk to consent, that they'd been raped, even though both or all parties were inebriated. I felt I'd put us both in a risky situation and I was afraid that trust was broken. But I felt that I had particularly put *him* in a risky situation, as a man having sex with me, where inevitably any blame would fall on him if anyone else were to hear this story, despite the fact that we were both way too high.

I think a lot about how memory changes. We had been dating for almost two months at that point. We had established trust and really good communication. I knew my feelings were growing deeper and would likely continue to do so. But this experience got me thinking about how the memory might have changed if this had been only our first sexual encounter, or third or fifth. Or if shortly after, he decided he didn't want to keep seeing me. I might have been left feeling really shitty. I might look for a reason for my shitty feeling. I might try to find something or someone to blame for my shitty feeling instead of moving through my feelings of rejection and taking responsibility for them. I might decide that had I known he wouldn't want to see me anymore, I wouldn't have slept with him. I might twist consent vocabulary, looking for a black-and-white answer, for a binary of right/wrong, good/bad, consensual/nonconsensual, and retroactively determine that because I was "too high to consent," this was assault or even rape, because so much messaging about consent will tell you that if you're high or drunk, you can't consent.

I say this as someone who's experienced sexual assault: This behavior is in fact a slap in the face to people who've actually experienced sexual assault and rape. We have to be able to discern between our feelings of rejection or regret and the experience of being violated. I'm not suggesting rejection can't be traumatizing; it sure can. But feeling bad after a sexual encounter is different from being raped. When we collapse all sexual encounters into binaries (any encounter must be either consensual/nonconsensual or even either consensual/rape), we do away with the humanity behind our actions, and we sever connections with others and with ourselves. Memory is fallible. We have to contend with this reality in order to properly support survivors.

If things had been different, I might have lost touch with what really happened, with the choices I made knowingly, and with the reality that we were both too high and ended up having what can be explained simply as *a weird sexual encounter*. I might obsess about *what happened* instead of directing my attention to *how to prevent it from happening again in the future*.

I spoke to a few friends and colleagues who do similar work to me about this experience. We had very nuanced and complex conversations about trust, intimacy, consent, and sex. We discussed what it meant to care for each other in a situation like what had occurred. They felt I was being especially hard on myself *because* of my work, that I was unnecessarily holding myself to a very high standard.

As a consent educator, my standards for consent are high, but my compassion for consent mistakes is also high. My expectations for good communication are high, but my expectations for good repair, check-ins, and apologies—from my partner and friends, and from myself—are also high. I've violated consent and crossed boundaries. So have you. And we will again. Striving for perfection impedes the very kind of listening required to connect in the way necessary to practice consent with ourselves and others.

Something I really appreciate about my partner is that he doesn't take things personally very often. When I make a request, state a boundary, or give any kind of feedback, he doesn't look backward in time for all the instances where he may have already "gone wrong"; instead, he looks forward at the ways he can incorporate the new information in the future. "It's just information," he says.

One time he cooked me dinner and my sensitive tummy found it too acidic. I was hesitant to say anything, a little embarrassed by how sensitive my body is. This was also very early in our relationship, and I knew it was important to him that I like his cooking, as it's one of the ways he shows care and love. I wasn't eating much and it was apparent, so I told him, "I'm afraid this is a little too acidic for me." His face is etched in my brain. He was trying so hard not to seem devastated. I could see it in his eyes and in the way his lips curled inward. It was adorable. I reached out and touched his knee. He said, "I'm glad you told me. It doesn't mean you think I'm a bad cook. It's just information for next time." I think he was saying this for himself as much as for me.

We talked a day or two after our weird sex about what happened. He said he'd help make sure I didn't take too many edibles if we were gonna have sex. I shared some information about my body that he didn't know at the time, mostly about how I'm really sensitive and I think his level-three intensity is like a seven for me; that I typically need a "less is more" approach; and that pleasurable touch can cross a threshold into being overstimulating pretty easily. I said I'd try to communicate better about when I'm approaching that line, when I'm aware of it. He heard me, and while I think it made him feel a little insecure and nervous, he didn't make it about himself or ask for reassurance, even though I would have been happy to provide some.

I think there's a lot of messaging that suggests that you shouldn't have to comfort someone who has hurt you. While I think it's true that this shouldn't be a requirement, I don't think there's anything wrong with—after addressing the hurt you felt—checking on how the other person is doing and comforting them, because we all know it can be terrifying and upsetting to find out that you've hurt someone. In this situation, even though we were both too high to engage in consent, I was the one in distress after the fact, and I was the one delivering that information. I think it would have been totally appropriate and caring for me to check if he was okay after the conversation and even to ask if there was anything he'd like me to do differently in the future when I share something like this with him. After all, consent and boundaries are a mutual effort.

Even through all this, he was able to say, "It's such a shame you can't get high anymore." It still makes me smile.

I Can't Trust Someone Who Can't Say No to Me

The other day I was talking to my friend, business baddie Hannah Said of Saffron Cowboy Coffee, about struggling to ask for support. She told me she finds it hard to make requests for help from people in her life. She asked me how I learned to ask for help.

I told her that I used to really struggle with it—I think I'd fallen for various myths around hyper-independence and self-sufficiency, like asking for help made me weak. But once I worked through a lot of that, I realized that I felt nervous asking for help from someone if I was afraid they wouldn't say no to me. If I trusted them to say no, then it felt way easier to ask.

I could see lightbulbs go off. I've learned that it's really hard to trust someone who can't say no to me, so if I don't think they will, I won't even make a request of them. In more intimate situations like sex, if I don't think someone can say no to me, I'm going to be terrified the whole time that I'm going to do something they don't like or want and I'll never know, or I'll find out later and be horrified. It's an awful feeling, finding out that you've done something that someone else wasn't okay with. It can be very disorienting, like there's a schism between your two realities—you thought you shared one experience, only to find out they had a totally different one, be it a conversation, an activity, sex, or anything else.

Unfortunately, the tough pill to swallow here is that conversely, if I push myself past my capacity or boundaries without telling the other person, so that I can give them what they want (or what I think they want), and then I blame *them* for my burnout or my regret, *I* am not a safe person for *them* to be in relationship with. If I don't tell them when they do or say something I don't like, or I let them do things to me that I'm not okay with, and *I don't say anything,* I am not trustworthy.

I teach a class on people-pleasing and I wrote a workbook for people-pleasers—that is, people who perpetually give more than they are able, who struggle to say no, and, often, who've lost their sense of self by nearly *living* for the sake of other people at their own expense. When I bring up this point, it can really rub people the wrong way if they're not ready to let go of their identity as a people-pleaser. If people-pleasing is inextricably wound up with your sense of self, you get to be perpetually in the right because you're the one always getting taken advantage of, taken for granted, and used, and everyone else is the culprit. You get to stay indignant and blame other people for your burnout, your resentment, your lack of time. The world has wronged and continues to wrong you, and so you don't really have to change anything about yourself because it's the world that's wrong. You get to be a martyr, which means that when you decide it's your turn to get what you want, you'll likely take it without much consideration for other people—and without consent—because you feel it's owed to you. Perhaps ironically, this identity gives you a certain amount of power, but you may not be willing to recognize it because that would be antithetical to how you see yourself in the world.

Most people experience people-pleasing at different times in their lives. But when it comes to chronic people-pleasers or people who identify as such, there's often a perception that they are *always* in a position of less power. This of course isn't true, but the perception is so powerful that it clouds an ability to even notice when they're in a position of more power. They won't notice when other people are people-pleasing with them, or they find them intimidating.

But so much people-pleasing is just plain lying! Saying I'll be there in twenty minutes when really it's twenty-three plus parking; saying, "I'd *love* to read your writing" when I totally wouldn't; saying I definitely want to hang out or go out with someone when I don't at all, but I'm too afraid to say it. And I do believe very strongly that we are responsible for the lies we tell, even if we don't know we're telling them. We mislead, we omit, we obscure, and we refuse to remove the veil between our unconscious and conscious minds, remaining opaque to ourselves and therefore others. It's absolutely possible to people-please your way into staying in a relationship that you don't want to be in, and it's absolutely possible to do so without knowing you're doing it. You can lie to yourself so successfully that you don't even know that you're lying to other people.

So when it comes to my close relationships (I include in this category romantic relationships, friendships, and even certain working relationships where I work closely with someone and require a significant amount of trust), if I can't trust someone to say no to me, I'm not safe because their truth is obscured. They can't be known to me, and therefore I risk finding out later that I've done something terrible that has rotted into resentment and even hatred when it could have been addressed immediately.

If someone can't say no to me, they will likely avoid difficult conversations and conflict, as well as feedback, and they certainly will not give *me* feedback. This does not make for a solid foundation on which to build any kind of lasting relationship. As I mentioned to Hannah, I will be too afraid to make requests of someone I don't trust to say no to me.

From my journal:

> Saturday August 16, 2025, 8:42 a.m.
>
> I wrote a piece for the book yesterday about how if I can't trust someone to say no to me, I can't trust them and I won't make requests. Then a couple hours later, Andis asked if I would take his friend M to the Burbank airport Thursday night [after I'm already taking Andis that morning at 6 a.m.]. I was appalled. Absolutely not. How could you even ask me that? I would never in a million years, it wouldn't even occur to me to ask you . . . etc. But then I thought . . . he trusts me to say no, and perhaps this is permission to ask things of him that I wouldn't have thought to. A more expansive definition of friends and community. "Your bffs are my bffs." Kindness beyond social etiquette. And then, he said that Monday and Tuesday when he's done editing the sizzle reel [for my musical], he can send emails on my behalf per our marketing meeting from the other day. What?! How? So sweet!

There's something of an antidote to this. I've noticed that as I've worked on my own ability to say no, I trust others more to say no to me. When I struggled more frequently with people-pleasing (never fully done, never fully over it), I didn't trust others to say no to me because I couldn't say no myself. Practicing my own "no" has not only helped me trust others' "no," but it's also helped me cultivate a sort of radar for other people's ability to say no.

In moments where I feel the people-pleasing impulse, it helps me to remember that if I people-please and say yes to something I actually want to say no to, I'm making myself less trustworthy. In moments where my people-pleasing would just be lying, I can compel myself to be the friend or coworker or partner that I want to have by being more honest. This leads to more authentic self-expression, less resentment, and more energy and time to do the things I really want with the people I really love.

I want to carefully note here that I'm in no way against doing things for other people even if I don't want to. After all, we live in community and we are relational beings. But I've gotten better at discerning when I'm *choosing* to do that and when I'm on people-pleaser autopilot. If I end up feeling regretful or resentful, I take responsibility for the *choice I made* to do something that I didn't want to do.

Here are some questions for reflection:

1. How do you know when you're people-pleasing? What do your eyes do? Your voice? Your body language? Your face?
2. In what situations do you most frequently people-please? At work? With friends? New friends or old friends? On dates? With family?
3. Who do you think is people-pleasing with you? Who might find you intimidating or defer to your judgment over their own?

Utterly Unenthusiastic but Totally Consensual Sex

This essay is intended for people who find that required enthusiasm in sex is not working for them, who have found that perhaps it leads to people-pleasing or fake enthusiasm. It is for those who are getting back into sex after a period without it or after trauma; those who have chronic pain or live with disabilities that make sex challenging, but who want sex in their lives. This essay is *not* for those who have just encountered the concept of required enthusiasm for the first time and perhaps are reckoning with many instances of having sex they didn't want to have. This essay will challenge binaries and demonstrate how a lack of enthusiasm is not the same as rape, assault, violation, lack of agency, or lack of consent.

"Enthusiastic" consent has been the most repeated tenet of consent education for years now. It comes from Planned Parenthood's suggestion for defining consent, the acronym FRIES:

Freely given

Reversible

Informed

Enthusiastic

Specific

But a growing number of consent educators have critiqued this so-called requirement. We've seen that requiring enthusiasm leads to a lot of fake enthusiasm, that enthusiasm looks different for everyone, and that you can, in fact, have perfectly consensual sex that isn't a "hell yes."

Some of the reasons someone may engage in sex that isn't a "hell yes" include:

- trying to get pregnant
- connecting with your partner, even when it may be physically strenuous for those with chronic pain or disability
- being a sex worker
- trying to bring sex back into your life after sexual trauma

Simply put, the requirement of enthusiasm excludes a lot of people, including survivors of sexual assault, and is neither trauma- nor disability-informed. As you might imagine, this point of view ruffles some feathers. Some people will insist that no one should be having sex that isn't a "hell yes." I find myself wondering if those people have ever had sex after a long day's work, while tired, or in a long-term relationship, for that matter.

Here's why I harp on this point about enthusiasm: This kind of bumper-sticker education ("no means no," "anything other than an enthusiastic 'yes' is a 'no'") reinforces false binaries and eschews critical thinking. There are false binaries of wanting/not wanting and consensual/nonconsensual that can be very appealing to a lot of people who want clear rules that will help them *never do anything wrong* or *never experience anything bad*. So when you say, "Anything other than an enthusiastic yes is a no," it can easily become, "If the yes wasn't enthusiastic, then the sex wasn't consensual," which then becomes, "If consent wasn't enthusiastically given, then the sex was assault or rape." But plenty of consensual sex is less of a "hell yes" and more of a "sure, why not?"

An example:

Person A: I'm so tired.

Person B: Do you wanna have sex?

A: I dunno. Start touching me, let's see what happens.

Person A may just be tired, but they also may have what's called "responsive desire," where they need to be aroused before they desire sex.

Another example:

Me: Can I go down on you?

My partner: Sure, if you want to.

Me: I do.

So . . . I do.

Consent educator Betty Martin[1] teaches a difference between *wanting* and *willing*. Within this framework, *wanting* is when something is my own, innate desire (e.g., "I want to have sex"). *Willing* is when I'm open to something because it's someone else's desire (e.g., "You want to have sex. I know I like sex with you. It wasn't on my mind and I'm not horny, but, sure"). Related to this, I think there's multiple kinds of *not-wanting*:

1. "I don't want to" = I don't actively have that desire
2. "I don't want to" = I actively do **not** want that

Those are very different! Sometimes I want to have sex and my partner says, "Sure." This isn't particularly enthusiastic, but because I trust him not to have #2 sex, I'm happy to accept #1 sex. Our roles have also been reversed. Part of building trust with him comes from building trust with myself *not* to have #2 sex.

Call me cuckoo for Cocoa Puffs, but I think having sex with a partner because they want to, even when you're not "a hell yes," is an incredibly intimate and special thing. I think this is a gift only given when immense trust is present, and everyone feels safe saying no. This is a choice only you can make.

The absence of enthusiasm does not mean it's nonconsensual. Nonconsensual does not necessarily mean it's assault/rape.

I think it's worth mentioning that lately, when I've brought this up on social media, I've been accused of being a trad wife. Some people equate my stance with that of straight cis women who think it's their responsibility and obligation to have sex with their cis male partners.

First of all, I think trad-wifery falls apart in queer relationships. I'm queer, and my gender doesn't fall within the man-woman binary. Second of all, if someone enjoys feeling useful, helpful, obligated to someone, and generous, and sex is one of the ways that helps them feel those feelings, they can have sex for whatever reason they want. They can't make anyone else act that way,

1 Learn more about her work at www.schoolofconsent.org.

but they have every right to have whatever kind of sex they want to have with another consenting adult. Third of all, it's just really silly.

I recently listened to a podcast interview with a professor who was talking about why people struggle to say no. Her research had led her to a lot of really fascinating conclusions as well as ways to help people say no. She described a quote she had prominently displayed in her office, something to the effect of, "If it's not a hell yes, it's a no." She swore that she lives by this statement. Then she went into depth about her own process of deciding whether or not to do something when asked. She had a nearly mathematical formula for decision-making. How much effort does it take? What is the cost (energy expended by her) and what is the benefit (for the other person)? She gauged her capacity at the time and various resources—time, energy, money, etc. This process is utterly devoid of "hell yes." The contradiction was never acknowledged.

I don't like this "anything other than a 'hell yes' is a no" approach. It doesn't work for me personally. If someone *only* wants to have "hell yes" sex, that's their prerogative. But I really enjoy my "sure, why not" sex—and I believe in my right to have it.

Against Pleasure

Why on earth would a consent educator argue against pleasure? You might see that title and go, "Is she crazy?" To answer that question, 1. It's they, but 2. Maybe, and 3. Let me explain, jeez!

In the course of my reading and research as a consent educator, I've found a lot of emphasis on enthusiasm and pleasure, on saying no, on finding your "hell yes," and on not doing things you don't want to do. To be clear, I don't think there's anything wrong with any of that. However . . .

What seems to have been lost is curiosity. It can be scary to try new things, expand your horizons, learn by doing, and explore and play, even if it results in a not-so-great experience through which you learn, "Hey, that's not for me." Consent is a tool that allows us to do all of this with care, with risk management, and *as safely as possible.*

Think of the first time you had sex. Were you 100 percent sure you wanted to do it? Were you 100 percent sure you would like it? Were you 100 percent excited? Did you have any idea what you liked and what you wanted? I know I was not and did not.

There's a lot of value in following pleasure and following your desires. I'm not arguing against doing so. What I am suggesting is an openness to trying things even when they make you nervous. I am suggesting that we often can't know what we like, what brings us pleasure, until we try, and that in that process we will encounter things we really *don't* like or even regret and that this is no one's fault. No one is to blame.

I say this so clearly and emphatically because ever since enthusiastic consent became the dominant model or vocabulary in consent education, I have frequently seen people who had a totally consensual sexual encounter, with totally consensual dynamics, retroactively label the experience as assault or even rape because they were not enthusiastic. I've written extensively on this topic many times, but I'll say here that enthusiasm looks, feels, and sounds different to everyone; it's an emotion often mixed with many other feelings (trepidation, nerves, hesitation, fear); and you can be absolutely curious, interested, and willing to do something without being enthusiastic, and everything is copacetic. I want to be very clear: You can *choose* to do something even if *desire* is not present. And we *have* to take responsibility for our choices.

We've also lost sight of the beauty and joy in doing things for other people because *they* like it. In so many conversations about people-pleasing, the conclusion is, "Don't do it." Doing things for other people that you may not enjoy or want yourself gets collapsed under the people-pleasing umbrella and thrown out entirely. But we are communal beings; we have relationships, we make commitments, and we support each other. We offer service, care, and labor to others, some of which we may enjoy but much of which we don't, and a lack of pleasure does not equal nonconsent. We do things we don't have a genuine desire to do all the time—this is part of the maintenance of life. We do the dishes, we weed the yard, we change the bedsheets. If we learn that consent should protect us from doing things we don't want to do, there's a consistent, irreconcilable dissonance in our daily lives.

Furthermore, many difficult things—worthwhile things, important things—feel incredibly painful and challenging. Having tough conversations with people who disagree with you politically, religiously, or fundamentally about human rights, justice, the law, whose needs are valid, whether Israel has a right to exist, trans issues, marriage equality, or pronouns can be painful and challenging. It can feel like pulling teeth! If we prioritize pleasure at the expense of this kind of hard work and only associate with people who think like us, how can we expect any change to occur? If we refuse to even try to understand where people are coming from and why they think the way they do, what can possibly change? How do we think we can change hearts and minds if we are not at the table with the people whose hearts and minds we need to change? I don't believe we can.

Dr. Jens Foell said in a viral tweet, "As we say in Germany, if there's a Nazi at the table and ten other people sitting there talking to him, you got a table with eleven Nazis." I think it's important to note that Dr. Foell grew up in Germany. The guilt around the Holocaust still permeates German culture today, so thickly that the government silences pro-Palestinian voices and reduces any critique of Israel to antisemitism. I was recently at a Yoko Ono exhibit in Berlin. In one of the rooms where viewers were encouraged to take markers and write on the walls, someone had written, "Trump is the new Hitler." Someone—and I have reason to believe it was the museum staff—blacked out the word "Hitler." The shame runs so deep that it's built into their laws and rhetoric in the form of speech policing and suppressing protest. So it tracks that Dr. Foell would have this very black-and-white, very binary thinking about associating with Nazis. Now, I'm not suggesting that anyone should knowingly dine with an out and proud Nazi; I certainly wouldn't, as a Jew. But this quote has been co-opted primarily by the left to suggest that if you associate with a Republican, someone who voted for Trump, someone with racist beliefs, someone who believes trans people aren't real, a Zionist, etc., that you are as bad as they are or that you condone their beliefs.

I strongly disagree with this. This mentality breaks my heart, quite honestly.

I deeply hold the belief that people learn by osmosis and exposure. I've seen this with consent. You can't force people to learn about consent; they have to come to it on their own. And the best way I've seen for people to learn about consent is by being exposed to it through people they know and care for. Seeing it demonstrated in real life opens up new avenues, new ideas of how to engage with other people and with yourself. When you practice saying no, you give others permission to do the same. When you ask someone if they like how you're touching them, they may ask themselves for the first time if they do, instead of assuming that *you* do and so they should let you. When you state a boundary and hold it, others learn to do the same.

So many people who hold racist beliefs, think gay people shouldn't be able to get married, think drag queens and trans people are pedophiles and want to convert kids, think sex workers are all trafficked or destroying the fabric of society or all traumatized or have daddy issues because that's the only reason why someone might "resort" to that line of work, or actually think Jews have horns, don't know people of color, queer people, trans people, sex workers, or Jews.

I think of stories of people who used to be in white supremacist groups but left once they saw the errors of their thinking. I think of trans people who struggled to come out because of their own transphobic pasts. These people's eyes were not opened by being isolated amongst their fellow white supremacists or transphobes. They changed slowly by being exposed to people and ideas different from what they knew.

When we decide that *all those people are bad and therefore I will not associate with them,* we remove the opportunity for people to learn in this way. It's a super sinister route to avoid difficult conversations by disguising the refusal to engage as "living in alignment with your values." But this doesn't help us achieve our goals, and it allows many of us to totally bypass the hard work of not just progress but relationships.

Not everyone is cut out for that role of being the point of exposure. Honestly, I'm not always that person. I get impatient; I get heated; I get activated. This is where our work is cut out for us: We need to build our tolerance for activation with self-regulation tools and practices, stretch our patience, and strengthen our stamina for the marathon ahead of us. It's not necessarily going to feel good, but we must choose to do it anyway.

Interview with Andis Solomon

Polyamory, Communication, and Making Consent Hot Through Dirty Talk

Andis Solomon is a film director from Portland, OR, currently residing in Los Angeles, CA, with me and several animals. He's a giant sweetie pie and the best partner in the whole world, and he makes me laugh so hard we had to instate a rule that I'm never allowed to have to pee so badly that I might pee my pants. He's a caretaker and a nurturer, and he emanates good vibes. Anyone who gets to date Andis is forever positively changed. Getting to know Andis makes anyone lucky enough to do so a better, more open person, and as a result, the world becomes a better place for me to live in. Andis is considering starting a movie-review Substack and I think we should all encourage him to do so.

Mia: One of the reasons why I wanted to interview you was this thing that you said a while ago, when I was telling you about this person whose mother was afraid that the parents at the school that she worked at would find out that she and her husband had opened up their relationship. And that she'd get fired and it would ruin her life. So when I told you about that story, I don't remember exactly what you said, but it was like, you know, if people wanna get upset about that, like . . . whatever, because you've put so much work in. It takes so much work to be able to be polyamorous, in an open relationship, whatever, and to be able to communicate that way. And I was really struck by that, and I was wondering what the work is that you have put in.

Andis: Yeah. You have to have a sense of resiliency that comes from confidence, because there's this perspective that polyamory in some senses is an easy out: Like, if you want to do something, you can go ahead and act on that desire. But once you start looking past the very initial layer of just acting on desire, it starts to get really complicated really fast. The thing that most people say when they talk to me is, "That's crazy. Why would you do that? Why would you want to do that?" But it's a journey with your partner. It's something where you have to put time and work into figuring out what feels good for everybody involved. A lot of it revolves around the unique boundaries that each person needs to feel safe, and respected, and in integrity with themselves and with the relationship. I feel like there's this concept of infidelity, or this concept of cheating that's very heteronormative and in line with compulsory monogamy. Because I don't honestly think that the carnal act of sex, or the physical act of sleeping with another person is really what pisses your partner off or makes them feel hurt or disrespected. I think it's a unique set of needs that are not being met in this moment, and maybe that unique set of needs for an individual includes something like, "I can't share your body with anybody else." But I think it's often something much more than that. There's like a secondary and tertiary pain that comes with infidelity, right? The physical act may be something that leaves a bitter taste in your mouth, but I think it's because it's a reminder of what you're really feeling.

Mia: Yeah, that a promise was made and then broken. And if different promises have been made, then it's not a broken promise if you sleep with someone else. But I also think that a lot of people have a view of polyamory that it's about sex, that people just want to be able to have sex with whoever they want, and I don't know anybody who is polyamorous for the sex. [*Both laugh*] Really, I don't. Everyone in my life who's poly is trying to have long-lasting relationships, and let their relationships change, and they're trying to have more connection and more love and not have to get all their needs met by one person, to not put that pressure on somebody. They're looking for various kinds of autonomy. I mean, for me, I'm not willing to lie to a partner or to myself about whether or not I have feelings for somebody or I'm attracted to somebody or have a crush. I know that a lot of people in monogamous relationships can agree with their partner that they can talk about crushing on people or being attracted to other people, but . . . I've been in a relationship where that was absolutely not allowed.

Andis: Or even if it's allowed, they won't do it. You know, they're like, "I don't want to start that fight." And I think it's that deceit that really sets up the fall, because it's like . . . "You slept with that person? I didn't even know you had feelings for them, or you told me you didn't."

Mia: Right, right. Yeah, I've seen so much betrayal come out of a partner being like, "It seems like you kind of have a crush on that friend," and they're like, "No, no, I don't, I don't think of them that way," and then they want to act on it, and there's this sense of betrayal.

Andis: Yeah.

Mia: Can you talk a little bit about what kind of work you've put in?

Andis: Totally. I had a partner who, we were starting to get more serious in our relationship, and I was pretty young—I was, like, nineteen—and we had this conversation where she said, "If you want to be in a monogamous relationship, I would do that for you." And I just had pretty instant clarity, like, "That's not what I want at all." And I think I just knew, on a level, that's not the kind of relationship I want, that's not the kind of life I want to live. And so moving forward, in my own life, I found out how to deal with the challenges of being able to see other people, how to find compersion[1] for my partner, and how to find people who have compersion for me in other relationships. These are all different sorts of learning experiences that I've worked through.

You can't make a monogamous person polyamorous. I do feel like it's a spectrum. There are people who just feel a certain way. Monogamy works for them, and that's awesome. It's just like any other spectrum that we have

1 Compersion is a term used to describe the feelings of joy or happiness about a partner's other romantic partnerships. While it's certainly in contrast with jealousy, it sometimes gets described as the opposite of jealousy, though I don't think that's necessarily quite right. I also think compersion and jealousy can coexist.

in this budding world of increased sexual boundaries and orientations. But I think the work that I've done starts with that feeling of jealousy, that feeling of this raw kind of anger and sensation of shame and guilt that's all tied around thinking of your partner being with somebody else. For example, if you're dating a bisexual person, saying something like, "Well, you can date other girls, but I don't want to see you dating other guys"—and I feel like that's a binary thing, but it's pretty common, right? And it's like, okay, well, where's that coming from? What's going on? So I think you gotta peel it back and be like, What am I feeling? Why do I feel that territorial, what's been instilled in me by culture? What's been taught to me? What do I actually feel? I think it's a little bit of unlearning, and it's a little bit of finding where your comfort level is, because maybe that is your boundary. I would challenge it, but maybe that's what you feel, and that's fine. That's great, whatever makes you happy, ultimately, in a relationship.

But the work for me was the unlearning and the challenging of my own feelings of, "Why do I feel this way?" I think the biggest thing for me was realizing that the unknown is so much worse than the known fact. When you don't know who this other person is, or you've never talked to them, or you don't know what the dynamic is between your partner and this newcomer, there's a lot of fear and anxiety that things could be better with them, things could be deeper. Maybe you're worried about your partner experiencing NRE [new relationship energy] and getting taken away with that. Totally real fear. But ultimately when you meet the person, you're like, oh, this is a flawed individual who is just as human as I am, and there's a moment of understanding. Maybe you're like, I can see why my partner thinks this person's hot, or, I can see why my partner wants to go out with this person or have sex with this person. Then I think that makes working through your own emotions and your own ickiness so much easier. I've known relationships that have worked for a while with the sort of "don't ask, don't tell" policy. But for me, personally, I've always wanted to be in the closest circle, I want to know before anybody else—as soon as you know you have feelings for somebody, or you know you want to sleep with somebody, I want to know, I want to talk to you about it. It's not just a reporting-for-duty thing, though, right? It's like, I want to gab, I want to gossip.

Mia: [*Laughs*]

Andis: I want the tea. That's how I feel about it, and other people might feel differently. But, yeah, I think that was the majority of the legwork that I did to sort of get off the ground of being like, okay, how can I be an ethically nonmonogamous slut, you know? How can I get there? And working through jealousy, working through, "Why don't I want *this*? But I want *this*, I'm okay with *that*," to try and find a true sense of compersion.

Mia: You're really good at asking questions that might be scary to get the answer to, and I'm not always very good at that. I think I'm afraid to jump off a cliff or something. Jealousy, to me, has always been a feeling . . . I call it a flag feeling, where it's like, "Look under here." It's not a feeling in and of itself. There's usually something else going on, whether it's insecurity or a fear or anxiety, so I don't really think of it as its own feeling.

Andis: Is any feeling its own feeling? Interesting question.

Mia: I don't think that many other feelings are removed from the *actual* feeling like that. Jealousy is kind of a protective layer over something that maybe you don't want to know or don't want to look at. And I also think there's this myth that people who are polyamorous just don't experience jealousy, and it just couldn't be farther from the truth. [*Both laugh*] But something that I've really come to with jealousy is, like, jealousy isn't a problem. It's a problem if you try to let it justify controlling somebody else, like if I decide that it's a feeling that I need to stop immediately, and the only way for it to stop immediately is for your behavior to change.

Andis: Ostrich behavior. I think it's true of anything. It's true of anger, right? You can't just be like, "I'm just gonna walk away from this because it makes me angry." Okay, well . . . I might walk that back [*laughs*].

Mia: Because I did that last night? [*Laughs*]

Andis: No [*laughs*] because sometimes I'm like, yeah, you're angry, you should go for a walk . . .

Mia: . . . sometimes with distance . . .

Andis: I guess I don't mean literally walking away, but more like, you can't just decide that it doesn't matter because it made you angry, because it made you jealous, right? You have to unpack it, and I think that that's the "flag" thing of what you're saying. It's difficult to see or feel your emotions peaking and then realize it's not the end of the road, it's not a turnaround moment. It's like, I thought I was going this direction, and now I have to peel off and really see what's going on here. Why am I feeling this way? And honestly, a lot of the time, the answers are really not satisfying.

Mia: Yeah. Or there's nothing you can do about it, you know? And part of it, I think, is learning the arc of your own emotions too, being like, "I know that I'm upset about this right now, and I likely won't be in an hour, or I won't be in the morning." Or, "In the past, I've felt this way, and then we had a couple days of feeling distant, and then we were fine." That builds confidence, too.

Andis: And I think also—and this goes hand-in-hand with polyamory—it's a level of emotional intelligence that everybody has to work on at some point in their life, or should. I think most people do. You're going to have to feel bad about things, right? That's just life. And then, can you remove your emotional reaction from the result you want? Can those be two separate things? Are you able to say, "Okay, this is how I want to feel, and this is what I want to do. This is what's currently happening, and this is how it's making me feel." Are those two things reconcilable?

Mia: I think a lot of the time, it's like I'm split into parts, and I'm deeply ambivalent, and there are many different parts of me that are experiencing different things at different times. Or at the same time.

Andis: You gotta call each emotion into the room. Be like, "What are you doing? Alright, you got 100 percent of my attention right now, what's going on?" And then you can send it away, and pull in the next one, right?

Mia: Yeah, or have them talk to each other, because often, I'm having very conflicting feelings. One of the things that I have been very surprised by is that I don't really get jealous about sex. I think I'm coming to learn that I'm sort of living in a different paradigm than most people are around sex. I have friends who have sex for their job.

Andis: It's not about sex.

Mia: Well, it's not about sex, but I think also, jealousy around sex is learned, and I work with so many people, and I'm close friends with so many people who are having sex for their job, with people who they then are friends with, and don't date—or maybe they do date, or whatever. And it's not really the sex that bothers me. One of the things that has surprised me a lot recently is that a lot of my jealousy is not even about the people that you're hanging out with. It's that you have a much easier time dating than I do, in large part because of illness stuff. I don't have the social bandwidth that you have, I don't have the energy that you have, and I can't really just date . . . I have specific things that are nonnegotiable for me around my health and stuff, and it makes dating very complicated.

Andis: Yeah, I can date Republicans. [*Laughs*]

Mia: I mean . . .

Andis: That's a joke.

Mia: You know, I can't date people who don't care about dietary restrictions, or who don't understand that I am experiencing really serious upheaval in my body on a particular day, or can't use my pronouns . . . I have special needs, you know? [*Both laugh*] I do! I do, and it comes up a lot around dating, it makes me feel like a burden, and I don't know when to disclose these things to people, and I often don't want to go out and do things that a lot of other people want to do, and I don't really drink, and it's just challenging.

Andis: Well, sure, your dating pool is restricted, but I don't think that it's small by any means, especially in LA.

Mia: I don't either.

Andis: This is kind of tangential to what you're saying about how you're feeling jealousy, but a bigger part of it is you have such a strong community of friends, and I think that's what takes up most of your time outside of our relationship and outside of your work life, you know? You pour a lot of time and energy into that. I think you have, like, fifteen close friends.

Mia: I know, I do.

Andis: I have, like, four.

Mia: Yeah, over a decade long.

No, I mean, I agree with you, and I think that a lot of times the way that polyamory manifests in my life is that I have a lot of friendships that a very strictly monogamous partner might be uncomfortable with.

Andis: Totally. Oh my god, yeah, I hate that.

Mia: Yeah, like sharing a bed with certain friends, or being physically affectionate with certain friends, or that I've kissed certain friends, or had sex with certain friends.

Andis: Yeah, yeah, I mean, I know how people feel like it's a slippery slope and it scales up, but I'd challenge you if you're like, "I don't care if you hold hands with that person, but making out with them is where I draw the line." That's fine if you feel that way, but I would just ask you to understand why. Because I think more often than not, the more you peel that back, it might be because there's this deeply territorial and sort of conquest-related narrative that's been attached to relationships, and that's because of where marriage comes from, like buying a piece of property, right? And I don't think that means it doesn't have a place in our culture, or that it hasn't become so prominent that it's now something other than what it was originally.

Mia: What do you mean?

Andis: I mean, my grandparents have a lovely monogamous relationship, and they are totally Mr. and Mrs. David Solomon, you know? Love, love my grandparents, and they're very Catholic, and they have such a deep relationship that's so loving and really works for them. And same thing with my parents: I don't think either of them could ever be in a polyamorous relationship. I think that's who they are, and I think that that's removed from the question of the functionality of polyamory, like, "Could a polycule work in any given situation?"

Mia: Well . . . where my mind is going is that so many people we know in monogamous relationships are all basically in polycules without the sex or romance.

Andis: Tell me more.

Mia: They have godparents for their kids, or they have aunts and uncles, or they have their ex who's very, very close. And it's this web, this network of intimate relationships with varying degrees of closeness, where maybe they don't have an active romantic or sexual relationship with more than one person, but, aside from that, it's very much this similar web.

Andis: Yeah, I mean, what makes a relationship polyamorous? It's an interesting question. You know, is it just the label you put on it? Like, what is a polyamorous relationship between a web of adults?

Mia: Right, and also, how do you differentiate between different kinds of love?

Andis: I mean, I think it's clear and distinct to every individual person, but putting it into theory is a little hard to nail down, right? But I can imagine if I were to go into the headspaces of people that I know well and be like, "Okay, how do they see these relationships?" They definitely don't see it as polyamorous.

Mia: Totally, no, they don't. But then a lot of monogamous people will have threesomes, or go to sex parties. Or . . .

Andis: It's not really monogamous [*laughs*].

Mia: I know [*laughs*].

Andis: That's kind of like when you get head from that guy in high school, and then you're like, "But I'm not gay." It's the same energy, because I didn't suck a dick. It's like, "No, you're a little gay, man," and that's cool, too. And I think it's sort of stigmatizing poly. I think swinger culture has unfortunately done some damage . . . I don't know, I think about the episode of *High Maintenance* where there's all these couples having sex, and then one of them slept with someone outside of the sex party, and they got gonorrhea, and so it's sort of like, that's the joke. Like it doesn't seem to get that deep, and it's, like, "Sex is a lot of fun, and doing sex with other people is a lot of fun." I think it's created this perception that you can sort of dip in, dip out, and I mean, I think you can, but that doesn't change who you are, right? Like, there's very much the sensation of being like, "No, I'm not gay,

I do not want to touch that person's lips, I do not want any of that, that does not feel good for me, that does not feel right," and like . . . wow, I can't understand that perspective. I can see it, but I can't understand it. And I think that's the same thing of being, like, "I could not go to a sex party. I do not want to share my partner with anybody else. I do not want to sleep with anybody else. This is not something that functions for me at all." I'm kind of rambling here.

Mia: When someone thinks that poly is a way that you can just cheat [*laughs*], one of the things that immediately comes to mind is this is way too hard and complicated to just be about the sex. If I just wanted to have sex with other people, I don't think I would be willing to put in the work to learn how to communicate the way that's necessary in order to do this. When I first opened up my long-term relationship with my ex over ten years ago, one of the most surprising things about it to me was that all of a sudden, when someone was interested in me, and there was an opportunity, I couldn't just say, or it wasn't honest for me to say, "I can't, I have a boyfriend." I had to actually ask myself, Do I want to do this? And that was huge, because sometimes the answer was no. And then I had to be honest, instead of using this relationship as kind of an easy eject button.

Andis: That's so funny, because I feel like the flip side of it is, you know, guys being like, "Yeah, she says she's got a boyfriend, but I don't know if I believe her or not," and it's like . . . Well, it doesn't really matter, right? If she's using another excuse, she doesn't want to be with you . . . .

Mia: Right. But that was really eye-opening for me, just the whole idea of having this kind of relationship structure that allows me and kind of forces me to actually be in touch with what I want and don't want, and then to speak up about it, ask for what I want. Or say that I don't want something. And that became really important to me. It became a way to learn a lot about myself, and, you know, I learn a lot about myself through relationships, and with different people. So polyamory was like choosing to keep picking up a mirror, not wanting to stop that kind of exploration. And also, no one person is gonna have sex with you in all the ways that you're curious about.

Andis: I mean, just beyond sex, walking it back to what you said about relationships as a way to learn—there's no better way to learn about yourself in a relationship that you've been a part of for five or six years than to go date somebody else and see the things that you do, and you're like, Oh, that is a really shitty thing that I do, you know?

Mia: You see your own patterns.

Andis: Yeah, your habits and the things that you're comfortable with, all of a sudden, you have to explain to a brand-new person.

Mia: Right, right. And if you start getting the same feedback again and again, you have to be like, oh, okay . . .

Andis: Or you start to occupy a role that your partner normally does. It's like if you're with somebody else, and all of a sudden, you're doing something new, you reach a greater appreciation for the other people in your life that you're dating. I think relationships are a tool to better understand yourself, to better understand your relationships with other people. I think part of the reason why I feel strongly about polyamory is that one of the best ways you can better yourself and learn about yourself is to continue loving and receiving love from other people. You know?

Mia: Yeah, totally. I have a hard pivot. How did you learn to make consent hot?

Andis: How did I learn to make consent hot?

Mia: Yeah.

Andis: It *is* hot. There's all of these taboo things, these things that you don't want to talk about, these questions you're afraid to ask, and then when someone broaches it for you . . . I mean, it's kind of like getting pushed through a dark alley. It's not something that you necessarily . . .

Mia: Is that what you want?

Andis: I mean, for some people . . . I guess it depends on the dark alley. But coming back to the taboo thing, like, you're asking things that normally you're not allowed to talk about, so if someone's like, "Can I do this to you? Can I move you this way?" It opens up this possibility that you didn't think was possible, or maybe you've never considered it, and then also, it also prepares you for what's gonna happen, and that creates anticipation, and I think anticipation is . . .

Mia: Also, hearing what you want is really cool.

Andis: Yeah, I think that gets into sub and dom dynamics that people miss in very vanilla relationships—love them—part of it is about desire, and sharing desire, and who's leading that conversation, and who's setting the boundaries of it, right? So if you can say, "Hey, here's something I want to do," and then someone's like, "No," well, the person *doing* is the person being controlled in a sense, right? I think that's kind of where dom and sub dynamics get misunderstood, because people think you just get to do whatever you want. Yeah, no, you can *ask* whatever you want.

Mia: Right. But you also have to trust the other person to tell you no.

Andis: Yeah, and then the sub side of it's like, do you want to ask? But . . . Well, you could say no, right? Like, I want to be asked, I want to be propositioned. You know, I think that's part of a sub dynamic. "I want you to ask me that question."

Mia: Right. There's a lot of creativity in it. Sometimes you ask if I want to do something, or if I want you to do something, or if you can do something, and I'm like, whoa, I never would have thought of that, that's really cool. Then I learn something new that I like, and I learn something new that I can offer you that you like.

Andis: I'm just imagining we're having sex, and you're like, "That's fucking cool, dude." [*Laughs*]

Mia: All the time! Really! [*Both laughing*] I'm battling . . . I think my parents are gonna read this book, you know?

But no, it's not just that you ask, "Can I do this?" You make me say things to you that, unless I were willing to lie, I have to know whether I want or not? I have to ask myself if I want that, and then sometimes you make me say it three times, and then I'm like, I have to *really* want this, or I'm lying. A lot of my work is breaking this stuff down so that it's teachable and digestible, and I don't expect you to be able to reverse engineer how you got there.

Andis: No, no, no, not at all. The thing is, I got kind of distracted by how people fake orgasms. I started going down a bit of a rabbit hole with that. I think it's a very immature and young thing to do in sex, because it's this . . .

Mia: Well, certainly with a long-term partner.

Andis: Well, even the first time you have sex with somebody. You're gonna fake an orgasm because you think that that's what . . . ? I'm talking about the very first time you've ever had sex. I'm talking about when you're [in] high school, college, whatever . . . the first time you're having sex with somebody, it's really difficult to be authentic to yourself, and if you're nervous, or you're not able to reach climax, that doesn't invalidate the sexual experience . . .

Mia: Yeah, it doesn't even mean that you didn't like it.

Andis: Yeah, exactly, so . . . Not saying that orgasms are overrated, because they're not, but I just think it's . . . coming back to authentically really wanting something. It's sad that there's a disconnect in sex. I think asking the question brings somebody more into authenticity with themselves. Because if you're doing something to somebody, and then you're asking, Can I take this to another level? and they're like, "No, I actually don't like what you're doing right now," that's great information for both people. And it's hard to bring up when you're the receiver.

Mia: Well, and I think a lot of people then are afraid to hear the answer to that question, and they don't ask. They're afraid to find out that what they've been doing has not been enjoyed.

Andis: And I think that's where I would challenge you, if you're doing something with somebody, to be prepared for a no. And that's a difficult line to walk; it's really tough to know, and it's difficult to always be asking, especially when you start to get caught up in what you're feeling, because sex feels amazing. And that's tough. It can be intoxicating.

Mia: Yeah. How did you find that way of talking? Did you learn it somewhere?

Andis: Did I learn . . . during sex . . . to talk to people?

Mia: I mean, the way that you say . . . you know, "Tell me this," or "Can I do this?" or "I want to do it . . . " Did someone model that for you, and that's how you learned it, or did you see it somewhere?

Andis: No, I think if anything, you have this feeling of, "Oh, I want to ask if I can do this, but I'm not sure if I can or not," and then you have one of two options. You can either do it without asking, or you can not do it, if you're not going to ask the question, right? Then the third option would be to ask the question and be prepared for either answer. With those first two options, I feel like I've learned enough, both of not asking the question and doing it, and then not asking the question and not doing it, that I realize that's not where I want to exist, that's not what makes me comfortable, that's not what ultimately leads to a positive sexual experience. For me or the other person . . . persons.

Mia: Right, but you must know that most people aren't talking . . . .

Andis: During sex . . . No, and you're a very special person to have sex with.

Mia: I know . . . But, you know, I'm saying you must know that because I can't imagine that everyone you've ever slept with is doing it as much as you are.

Andis: Well, one person needs to be asking the question.

Mia: That's not true.

Andis: One person needs to be answering questions.

Mia: I just wrote a piece in this book this morning about how it's a shared responsibility, and if you decide that consent is someone else's responsibility, you're giving up a lot of autonomy.

Andis: I think that's true.

Mia: Ultimately, it's dangerous for the other person.

Andis: I think that's getting into an arena of theory and practice, though. Theoretically, I think that's how everybody should act. In practice, not everybody does. And there's still a lot of really good sex that happens, and there's still a lot of consent, but unfortunately in practice, a lot of the time it's put on one person to monitor all of consent.

Mia: A lot of people are relying a lot more on nonverbal . . .

Andis: Yeah, or they freeze, right? Yeah. And that's a tough truth, and that's a reality. But, in practice, yeah, everybody should have a shared responsibility for consent and for making sure that they're feeling safe. I think it's tough, though. How do you know if you're feeling safe when you're getting fucking pounded, right? You're like, what do I do? That's a tough spot to be in. So I do think there is an onus on whoever is doing the action in the sexual experience to just really confirm that consent, you know, and to be asking the questions. I think that's, again, where you sort of get into the dom and sub dynamics.

Mia: Yeah.

Andis: It's a responsibility you're taking on, and that's why people enjoy or don't enjoy that position.

Mia: I'm just thinking a lot of what I've learned from illness is how to listen to my body, and I know that many people really struggle with that, but one of the most beautiful things that I've seen . . . I'm often surprised by new things that my body is able to do because of trust and safety. I don't know if this is too personal, but I feel like novelty and surprises in general are something that take a second for your physical and mental homeostasis to react to and recover from. I wonder how much of that is tied to nature and nurture for you. Of just being burned so fucking badly by new things.

Andis: Yeah. You have any other questions for me? Any other things you want to talk about? Anything that you want to come back to? Look at that, see? Questions.

Mia: Great questions. I mean, I think we've covered everything that I wanted to cover. I think if we were to keep going, I would go into real specifics about sex, and . . . you know, I'm like . . .

Andis: That's for the erotica Substack?

Mia: Right, I'm like, am I ready to do that?

Andis: You wanna talk about rocks?

Mia: Rocks?

Andis: Yeah. One time when we were in Portland, Mia was really excited about this rock that they had in their pocket, and we were in a room of, I don't know, nine people.

Mia: Well, it was more than one rock.

Andis: Yeah, okay. And so Mia pulled out a bunch of rocks that they'd picked up, and I was like, look at all these rocks, and out of the nine people in the room . . .

Mia: Wait, I asked a question. I said, "Do you guys want to see the rocks I found?" And people said, "Yep!"

Andis: And then out of the nine people in the room, like, six of them all pulled out rocks.

Mia: They all had rocks in their pockets!

Andis: And one of them . . . had a meteorite.

Mia: Oh, yeah!

Andis: And I was like, that's a cool rock. So all of you people who were rolling your eyes as we started talking about rocks, I bet you perked up when you heard "meteorite."

Mia: Yeah, but you know that someone listening to this is drawing the connection between being anxious and stressed out by change and surprises and collecting rocks.

. . . I'm literally holding a rock right now that you gave me from . . . where were you?

Andis: I was in the Inyo National Forest on the Rae Lakes Loop.

Mia: It's a very pretty rock.

Andis: It was by Charlotte Lake.

Mia: It looks like it might have had . . . I don't know what makes rocks green, I guess.

Andis: It's nine or ten thousand feet up, it's an area with a lot of granite. . . .

Mia: Yeah, it looks like granite.

Andis: And there were . . . these big green veins that ran through parts of it, and this is a rock that's entirely green.

Mia: And it glitters. Okay. Do you want to share that? [*Referencing the joint Andis has been rolling during the interview and finally lights*]

Andis: I don't know, do you have work to do today?

Mia: Mmm-hmmm. [*Both laughing*] Okay, well, thanks, Andis.

Andis: Thank you, Mia.

Mia: I love you.

Andis: I love you, too.

PART V

GENDER + SEXUALITY

Gatekeeping Queerness Doesn't Make You More Queer

I've never understood the impulse to gatekeep queerness. As queer people, don't we want more people to feel free to explore their sexuality? Doesn't it benefit us for there to be more of us and for more of us to feel confident being vocally out? If we consistently tell people they're not queer enough and police their behavior, aren't we doing ourselves a disservice?

Gatekeeping queerness in my life recently has shown up in the form of comments like, "That's a straight couple that wishes they were queer," or a coworker cross-examining another coworker by asking, "How many women have you slept with?"—as though someone can't know they're queer (or straight, for that matter) without ever having had any sex at all. Discussions around "queer-baiting," loosely defined as when straight people co-opt a queer aesthetic, forcibly out queer people more often than they get a straight person to consider their privilege.

After all, wtf is a queer aesthetic? A weird haircut? Dyed hair? Earrings or nail polish on men? Sequins? Women who skateboard? I don't get it. Don't we want people to feel free to express themselves however feels authentic to them? Doesn't it help queer people if the cishets discriminating against us with policy changes can't tell who we are just by looking? I feel like if more straight people help obscure who's straight and who's queer, that's a good thing.

Harry Styles has been the focus of the queer-baiting conversation. So was Billie Eilish for a while, until she felt bullied into coming out as queer. This is exactly the issue with accusing people of queer-baiting. We don't know their sexuality, and if we say they're queer-baiting, that they are "co-opting" queer culture instead of genuinely participating in it, we have effectively pressured them into coming out before they might be ready. In accusing them, we are assuming that we know better than they do what their sexuality is. But so many queer people discover they're queer because they find themselves in and amongst queer community, look around, and go, "Most of my friends are queer; I feel at home here . . . perhaps that might mean . . . that I'm . . . queer?" It can be a chicken-and-egg situation.

Before I was ready to call myself queer or trans, one of the things that kept me from doing so was a fear that other queer people would tell me I wasn't queer enough or trans enough. What a tragic reason to suppress your sexuality and gender. Is this really what we want? We want more people to feel afraid to come out? We want people to feel like they have to have x, y, and z kinds of sex before they can say they're queer? What a pity. What a weird way to police people.

One particular instance of this in my life happened in 2019, with a friend who was vocal about her decision to no longer date cis men. She consciously pivoted her social life, and she began replicating toxic male behavior toward women, seemingly to prove her queerness. "Where are all the hot girls?" she asked at a picnic in Elysian Park. When our friend was on the phone with someone on their way, she said, "Ask her if she's bringing any hotties." I heard her objectify women in new ways, parroting what she'd seen others say and do. She called me her "honorary straight friend," which felt so dissonant to me, because I had told her months prior that I had a crush on a female friend of mine and was struggling with it because I knew this friend wasn't queer and was married to a man. I had had conversations with her about my experience of my gender well outside of the binary. I reminded her of this the first time she called me her honorary straight friend, but then she did it again at a BBQ she had invited me to, in front of everyone else. Once again, I corrected her. "I'm not straight," I said. An hour or so later, back in her apartment, she did it a third time. I said something like, "What do I have to say to make it clear that I'm not straight other than, 'I'm not straight?'" It was ignored again. I left. Another friend texted me afterward, saying that the host had brought it up when I left, asking everyone why I seemed peeved at being called straight. We are no longer friends.

I don't ever want to be responsible for preventing someone from feeling like they can come out. I've committed to being as welcoming and open of a queer person as I can be. I've committed to encouraging anyone and everyone to explore their curiosities and their desires. I don't want anyone to miss out on the full expanse of their sexuality and their gender because I've made them afraid or feel unwelcome in my community. Not me, no way.

If You Want to Make Someone Feel Good, You'll Figure Out How to Make Them Feel Good

As I sat writing at my favorite coffee shop in Silver Lake, I couldn't help but overhear the woman at the table next to me telling her friends that she had a crush on a woman (gasp!), but because she'd never been with a woman sexually, she was afraid to make a move. She wanted to reach out but didn't want to bother her crush. Frozen by insecurities about her lack of experience, she felt she couldn't go for it.

I had to stop myself from leaning over and saying, "If you want to make someone feel good, you'll figure out how to make them feel good."

I'm queer—I date people of many genders, and my own gender doesn't fit into one of two categories. I think I've more or less always known this on some level, but I've also deliberately chosen to focus on and expand this part of my life as I've gotten older. However, the majority of my sexual history is with cis men, or at least with people who were identifying that way at the time we dated.

In my early twenties, I dated a woman we can call L. Though she wasn't the first girl I'd had feelings for or been attracted to, she was the first one I entered into a relationship with. To put it bluntly, L wasn't very nice. She made fun of my lack of experience, and she invited me to meet her at a bar knowing that her ex-girlfriend would be there, to try to make her jealous, without telling me that was the goal. The relationship was short-lived and left me feeling fearful of continuing to explore my sexuality.

After that, I only dated cis men for many years. Though I had crushes on people of other genders, I didn't pursue them. I didn't want a repeat of what had happened with L. I would occasionally open my dating profile preferences to include genders other than men, only to find explicit requests that "baby queers" (newly out people) or "tourists" (straight women looking to explore their sexuality temporarily) stay away. I heard friends of mine gatekeep queerness by criticizing boys who say they're bi but "have only ever gotten a blow job once from a guy in high school," or asking another friend, "How many women have you eaten out?" as though numbers or particular sex acts could determine someone's sexuality. These friends seemed to think they could determine who was "queer enough."

Like the woman next to me at the coffee shop, I didn't want to bother anyone with my inexperience. I'd put the settings back to "just men" and labeled myself as straight. Unsurprisingly, this led to continued inexperience.

But let's look a little closer: Plenty of straight women don't like to be penetrated, or don't like giving blow jobs. Plenty of gay men don't like anal sex, while many straight men like to be fucked by their girlfriends with strap-ons. Some lesbians like to get fucked by cis men even though they don't want to date them. Furthermore—and this may be controversial—it has often confused me why, say, a blow job is straight if the person performing it has a vagina, but it's gay if they have a penis. Not only does this not take into account trans bodies (a trans man can go down on a cis man, or a trans man can go down on a trans woman—are we saying this is heterosexual?!), but let's get really granular here: Is it gay if a straight woman has a double-sided dildo inside her while she sucks her cis boyfriend's dick? What if it were flesh-toned and had those funny anatomically correct veins in it? Is it straight if a cis woman is giving a blow job to a trans woman? No, because straight women don't date trans women, by definition. The walls between straight and gay come crumbling down if you look with even mildly critical eyes.

Funny story: A few years ago, a friend of my mom told us that her husband had to have his prostate removed. I said, "That's a shame." My dad said, "Why?" I said, "Because prostates feel good." They're often described as the "male G-spot," pleasure centers for those who have them. My dad said, "Yeah, if you're gay." I said, "Gay men have anal sex because it feels good, not because it's all they've got," or something like that. Anyway, my dad might read this, so I'll stop there. But I'll say it again: What a shame!

Anyway, my dream life became the main source of a lot of my exploration. I had countless dreams of doing or receiving the sexual acts I hadn't done in real life. I figured it would all happen for me some day down the line.

Eventually I got fed up. I figured, "Loads of people know they're queer with zero sexual experience at all, some from a really early age. We take no issue with people knowing they're straight without having had any sexual experience. Why is this any different? Maybe I have to start being open about my sexuality in order to pursue queer relationships." So I did.

And I started dating people who weren't cis men. This was all wrapped up in discoveries around my gender, too. I'd always been open about my feelings on gender: I'd described myself in high school as a gay boy; in college philosophy and feminism classes, conversations about nonbinary gender identity resonated with me; while volunteering at the Bluestockings bookstore in my early twenties, I was constantly having conversations with fellow volunteers about gender and trans identity, and I found myself primarily drawn to trans authors. But it wasn't until my early thirties that I let myself adopt affirming language for my own gender identity—language that is still moving and changing, and which I think always will be.

Gender and sexuality are not the same, though they are related. If gender is how you see yourself or how you feel about yourself, and sexuality is who you're attracted to, they are distinct and yet have bearing on each other. As a nonbinary person, any relationship I'm in is a queer relationship because I'm queer. I can't, by definition, be "straight." Yet this doesn't solve the dilemma of being afraid to date someone because of a lack of sexual experience with their particular type of body. And to be clear, the dilemma is not the lack of experience but rather the *fear* associated with it.

At some point along this journey, I looked back at my sexual experiences with other people and recognized that all of their bodies were wildly varied—in shape, size, how they liked to be touched, what aroused them, what didn't, and what they liked and didn't like. I learned, through communication, trial, exploration, play, and curiosity, how to make them feel good. They learned how to make me feel good, and they often found new ways to do so that I hadn't been aware of. I also noticed that any time I did anything for the first time, or even the second and third time, or with a new person, I had been nervous.

I took this awareness with me into the dating world. I changed my dating profile settings to be open to everyone. I started going on dates with the intention of finding a connection, someone I felt comfortable with, someone who made me laugh. If I was nervous about any one particular sex act, I put it to the back of my mind and reminded myself that the strength of my consent practice, with both myself and others, was going to guide me through figuring out how to make that particular person in their particular body feel good.

And so it went.

There are still some things I haven't done. I suspect that will always be true. You know your interests, your desires, your curiosities. There's no single activity that will prove your queerness. So I tell myself, as I tell my younger self, "If you want to make someone feel good, you'll figure out how to make them feel good."

My Sexuality Has Changed over Time

Most people seem to agree that we are all shaped and sculpted by the world around us. It shapes our beliefs, our hopes and dreams for the future, and our interests. We are a product of our experiences, histories, and surroundings, molded by our relationships and particular contexts. But if you suggest that our sexuality and sexual preferences are subject to the same kind of sculpting, you'll get a whole lot of pushback.

A lot of people believe that their sexual orientation consists of an innate set of preferences and desires. Those same people often agree that beauty norms and standards are socially constructed, as we have seen them change throughout history. They'll acknowledge that fashion magazines and Hollywood movies dictate a lot of what our society deems attractive (who's pictured) and unattractive (who's not, or who's the butt of the joke). But bring the conversation around to sexuality and suddenly it's a no-no, taboo, forbidden.

A colleague of mine once told me he thinks that more than sexuality being innate, we might be born with an innate proclivity toward fluidity or rigidity. This really resonated with me. I see myself as someone with a fluid gender and a fluid sexuality, and I've experienced both of them changing over time. They have not been fixed or rigid.

I knew sometime in high school that I was attracted to more than just boys, even as I would refer to myself as "a gay boy," not realizing what that meant for my gender identity. I never experienced a sexuality that was based in someone's physical body. My attraction was a lot more in the head. I needed an intellectual and emotional connection first and foremost. And yet, because of compulsory heterosexuality (also known as *comphet*), I remember almost training myself to be attracted to boys. I'd look at their bodies and try to figure out what I liked. Once sex entered the picture in college, I learned through *having* sex to feel turned on by boners because of what they meant was coming (so to speak). Knowing that my attraction went beyond cis boys, I eventually made a conscious choice to go through the same process with other kinds of bodies, bodies more like mine. Not much of a challenge, if I'm being totally honest. What's not to like?

But I did this not only with gender. I worked on changing my inner monologue around beauty and attraction, trying to find new and different things attractive. This was particularly easy for me because, as I said, my sexuality is primarily mental. I'm way more into a vibe than a look. So the more I focused on gauging a vibe, the more qualities I found physically attractive. I found it really easy to open up to new physical experiences and expressions if there was a connection first, or at least a curiosity.

So far I've described a process by which I actively and consciously participate in sculpting my desires, but I've also felt waves that have a mind of their own, where I'm not present in the process but rather feel it happening on its own. For a while, a few years ago, I wasn't dating cis men. As part of the process of eliminating them from my dating pool, I remember deciding that I would look less at cis men and more at everyone else when at a restaurant or a music show or the farmers' market. I gave cis men fewer opportunities to engage with me, which meant not making lingering eye contact or smiling at strangers. Instead, I'd direct that attention and energy toward everyone else. (Of course, I can't know if I eliminated some trans men from my own pool without knowing it.) This caused a shift in who I was attracted to. Eventually I stopped really noticing cis men I didn't know and felt much more drawn to other genders. But when I met my current partner—a cis-ish man (we say)—I started to find myself looking at cis men again, all of sudden. We met during this period in which I wasn't dating cis men, which meant that I had absolutely no idea he was interested in me. In fact, we only met at a party because one of the girls I was seeing was going to come, but I was told I couldn't bring a plus-one, which I later found out wasn't even true. The idea of dating him was so far from my mind that it wasn't until he was leaving the party and asked to connect that I realized what was going on. And I still thought, "I'd be down for some casual sex, but that's it," only to fall totally in love. I've wondered if meeting this sweet, gentle, nurturing caregiver of a man opened me back up to dating cis men, or if it was just part of these waves I experience.

If you want to, you can choose to actively participate in sculpting your own desires and, as a result, sexuality. This could easily be misconstrued as a suggestion to have sex with people you aren't attracted to, but that would be a misread that misses my invitation to *choose to actively participate*. This is, after all, about choice. I don't think everyone has the same window of potential for stretching or exploring sexuality, so finding your window would be a good place to start.

At this point in any conversation around sexuality, someone involved usually feels it's important to say, "I can't help it if I'm not attracted to [trans/fat/any race] people." I'm never going to push someone who's not interested in opening their mind because I feel it's a waste of my energy and time, but I think it's necessary to call out *disguising prejudices as preferences or even boundaries* and *weaponizing consent to justify prejudices* when I see it. As I mention in "Consent Won't Save Us" in part II of this book, this is a misuse of consent to bypass questioning your norms, to maintain your comfort, to get out of difficult conversations, and basically to avoid any destabilization of your world view. This can look like:

- "I don't date trans people. That's my boundary."
- "I don't want to talk about race. That's my boundary."
- "I can't help that I'm not attracted to fat people. If I pushed myself to have sex with someone I wasn't attracted to, then it wouldn't be consensual."

I had a friend in high school who would often comment on how beautiful or attractive someone was, and I would feel my own surprise. These people weren't usually conventionally attractive according to mainstream media's standards. I took it as a challenge. I'd try to find what I found beautiful or intriguing about those same people. I felt my attraction change. But you have to be open to your sexuality and your desires changing in order to change them in more than a superficial way. This isn't going to happen authentically (nor, for that matter, in a way that's respectful of others) if you're not genuinely open to the shift. For that reason, I will never tell anyone that they should consider sleeping with people they don't want to sleep with. What I'm saying couldn't be further from that idea. In fact, I'll say quite the opposite: If you don't want to have sex with trans people (or anyone else), please do *not* have sex with us/them. But if you're interested in cultivating or nurturing a budding attraction to people you haven't previously been attracted to, you can do so. After all, just as our desires are sculpted by the world around us, we can participate in sculpting them, moving forward.

One way to do this is to seek out porn with different kinds of bodies in it. Another is via my strategy of shifting attention by literally shifting your gaze toward different kinds of people than those you usually notice. You can actively reach beyond your typical media-exposure pool of books, magazines, movies, TV shows, podcasts, porn, and music to expand your areas of interest and attraction. In the same way that we are unconsciously indoctrinated into conventional beauty standards and therefore desires based on those norms, we can deliberately inundate ourselves with media outside the mainstream. We can give ourselves more options when mainstream media won't by changing the channel or altering our feeds, literally and metaphorically.

Another vantage point from which to look at this phenomenon is through the eyes of someone who frequently experiences unrequited love. I had a friend some years ago who often shared with me experiences in dating that made them feel ugly, discarded, and shut down. I thought this friend was really hot and really confident, with unmatched style and swagger and an abundance of talent. This friend was also—and I say this with so much respect—a total freak. It was one of the reasons why I felt so drawn to them. They made such cool and bizarre performance art; they wore tiny pastel silk-chiffon tops over their nipple-less flat chest and top surgery scars; they taught sex ed, BDSM and kink. They seemed like such a self-possessed person who knew themself better than almost anyone I knew, and they seemed to enjoy being utterly confusing to straight cis people. They had lots of equally hot, smart, confusing friends and colleagues (myself included, I like to think). I couldn't quite understand what was going on when it came to dating. Eventually I put the puzzle pieces together and understood that they kept being attracted to straight, cis, exceptionally conventionally attractive white men. For better or for worse, this is not typically the demographic that falls in love with trans, disabled, Black sex-educator artists. Not unheard of! But not the most common.

I often thought about this friend when the conversation about learning attraction would come up amongst my friends or colleagues and me. I'd remember my own history of learning to be attracted to the same kinds of people who were attracted to me. (In my case, it's vegetarian boys who wear women's clothes and want to date lesbians, women who like to think they're the first woman I ever dated, and the in-betweeners, or what I like to call the boygirls and the girlboys—and I'm using "boy" and "girl" to encompass both trans and cis people.) I wondered if my friend would be open to trying to actively expand their own pool of those they were attracted to in order to find a partner who saw them for the beautiful weirdo they are.

I've found this process of participating in sculpting my own desires and attraction to be enormously rewarding. Excavating my own desires and mining them for their origins, looking at pop culture with a keen eye, and cultivating discernment around how I consciously and unconsciously absorb information is a never-ending and highly fulfilling form of self-inquiry that helps me not only understand where I come from but deliberately craft where I'm going.

I'm less of a "born this way" person and more of a "became this way" person.

I have felt like an active participant in the building of my life and self, simultaneously creating and uncovering a self and a purpose. These two experiences—one being the making of the self and the other being the discovery of an essential self that was always there—may seem incompatible, and perhaps they are from a logical standpoint, and yet they coexist.

But when it comes to sexuality and gender, and even before Lady Gaga, we repeatedly hear, "I was born this way." That's a totally legitimate experience and a totally legitimate narrative—I'm certainly not interested in trying to argue with anyone who feels aligned with it. It simply has not been my experience.

Perhaps I was born with a proclivity toward fluidity or a certain nebulousness, like my edges aren't quite firm or fixed and are easily mutable. That feels true to some degree. What also feels true is that I found and followed a particular line of questioning, and allowed myself to explore freely in the realm of sexuality and gender. I picked apart my behavior, preferences, and desires and interrogated the media and experiences that shaped them. I sought out the nuggets of self that were inherent, and I examined the ones that were learned. Some I kept, and some I tried to unlearn, to varying degrees of success. I found play at the bounds of gender roles and sexual orientation, reclaiming the now nearly forbidden term "preference" because I do in fact experience many of my sexual choices as preferences and, in fact, as *choices*. I *prefer* and I *choose* queer sex with other queer people. I *prefer* and I *choose* to embrace and indulge the parts of me that don't feel like a woman, and play with gender like a set of paints or musical notes that change from moment to moment, day to day, and over months or years, or even relative to who I'm with at any given time.

My dear friend Risdon is somehow both a statuesque blond bombshell and only 5'3" or so. I call her Gender Barbie. There's something queer and subversive about just how much Risdon paints on femininity, and I don't mean makeup. I mean in the way you might try a new way of walking like trying on an item of clothing or wearing a particular smile like an accessory; it's simultaneously performance and completely authentic self-expression. Risdon dates boys—boys like me. Well, Risdon doesn't just *date* boys like me; she actually manages to bring out the boy in me. Once we went on a walk in her neighborhood, and she got lost—and I feel I have to reiterate that it was *in Risdon's neighborhood*, and she was the one who got lost. I, on the other hand, who can't remember where I parked in the mall garage without a photograph, knew exactly where we were and how to get back to her house. This is not normal for me. But something about Risdon brought this out of me. I was in charge. I had it under control. I got us home. Whether or not being good with directions is a "boy" thing or not is totally debatable, but the point is that there was a change when I was with her, one that felt gendered to us. This showed me clearly that I sometimes experience my gender shift depending on who I'm with.

Perhaps others are born more rigid, appreciate the given structure, and enjoy having a clear role to play. I like to play with gender like I play with fashion or like I make music, at the whim of some combination of my mood, the weather, and the stars.

For a long time as I was grasping to define and name my gender, largely so I could explain it to other people or make a selection on dating apps, I thought I'd eventually find the right term. I'd *figure it out*, and then I'd be done with the search. But I found myself changing my settings pretty frequently: nonbinary, genderfluid, genderqueer, gender nonconforming, androgynous, trans, trans masc, and back again. My favorite option is "other" or "prefer not to say." ("My gender is prefer not to say" doesn't quite roll off the tongue, but who is this all for, anyway?) At some point a couple years ago, I was looking in the mirror post-shower and thought, "Whatever this is is my gender." Maybe part of my experience of gender is that I can't pin it down. It's not about figuring out what I *am*, as though it were fixed, as though I were born a particular way and just have to find the truffle under the soil so I can hold it, look at it, and know for sure that *this* is what I am. I am eternally trying to solve problems and puzzles, even when they don't exist, and the habit of trying to locate the cause or the solution is deeply ingrained. (I see this in how I approach my chronic health problems, and I have to fight the urge to *figure it out* because often there's just no way to know what caused my latest bout of bloating.) Gender felt like another puzzle to solve. But over the years, I've found comfort in never being quite able to catch that Pokémon. The fun is in the sport, not the finish line.

I recognize that the "born this way" narrative has been crucial and relied upon to secure rights for queer people. But I think it's also completely legitimate and valid to *become* queer or *become* trans. I'm not knocking anyone else's experience of knowing who they are with certainty and feeling like they've always known, or that they were born a certain way, with certain desires. That just isn't how it's gone for me. I feel more like I pulled on a loose thread on a sweater and that the more I pulled, the more threads came loose. I kept pulling, and I found I liked the sweater more and more as I unraveled it, patched it, darned it, and made it my own.

Virginia Woolf

Who Is She Writing for? (Or, for Whom Is She Writing?)

This morning, with tears in my eyes, I finished reading Virginia Woolf's *A Room of One's Own*. The piece is a combination of two lectures she gave in 1928 at two women's colleges within the University of Cambridge. In what she calls her *peroration*, she compels, begs, galvanizes the audience of exclusively women to write—to write for themselves, for her, and for the future.

I felt her words so clearly, not just as a reader or as a woman-type-person (my gender identity only made possible and known through the work of feminists before me, my mother included), but as a writer.

She spoke fictionally of Shakespeare's sister, who died young—a poet who "never wrote a word."[1] As tears welled and my lower lip quivered, I wondered if Virginia had any sense that I, her reader, nearly a hundred years later, would be doing the work I do, writing what I write, in no small part *because* of her and these lectures. In this sense, her words ring with atemporal truth: "For masterpieces are not single and solitary births; they are the outcome of many years of thinking in common, of thinking by the body of the people, so that the experience of the mass is behind every single voice."[2]

And yet, I was struck with a pang of sadness and confusion that even in an address specifically and only for women, Virginia uses the universal "he." She

---

1 Virginia Woolf, *A Room of One's Own* (Broadview Press, 2001), 133.

2 Woolf, A Room of One's Own, 79.

tells these women emphatically, "Write!" and then says, "The whole of the mind must lie wide open if we are to get the sense that the writer is communicating his experience with perfect fullness."[3] I flinched. *Who is she talking about?* And then I remember: This use of the universal "he" was—and often still is—considered grammatically correct.

I remember having a similar feeling sometime in 2020, after I'd begun using she/they pronouns. Eventually, when I heard "she" used for me, I'd have this out-of-body moment with a flash of the thought, "Who are they talking about? Oh . . . me." That's when I dropped the "she" and began using only "they/them."

Virginia attempts to "amateurishly . . . sketch a plan of the soul so that in each of us two powers preside, one male, one female; and in the man's brain, the man predominates over the woman, and in the woman's brain, the woman predominates over the man. The normal and comfortable state of being is that when the two live in harmony together, spiritually co-operating."[4] She suggests, "It is when this fusion takes place that the mind is fully fertilized and uses all its faculties. Perhaps a mind that is purely masculine cannot create, any more than a mind that is purely feminine."[5] Essentially, she's saying that *this* is the optimal state of a writer.

She goes on: "Shakespeare was androgynous . . . . Proust was wholly androgynous, if not perhaps a little too much of a woman."[6] And finally, "It is fatal for any one who writes to think of their sex. It is fatal to be a man or woman pure and simple; one must be woman-manly or man-womanly."[7] *A Room of One's Own* was written before "transgender" and "nonbinary" were part of our language, but it no doubt informed many great thinkers who created the vocabulary we use today.

The most common reaction from those resistant to using "they" as a singular pronoun for nonbinary and trans people is to say, "It's grammatically incorrect." Meanwhile, many of those same people can't use "whom" correctly in a sentence. My father has a graduate degree in journalism, and my mother was

---

3 Woolf, A Room of One's Own, 122.

4 Woolf, A Room of One's Own, 115.

5 Woolf, A Room of One's Own, 115.

6 Woolf, A Room of One's Own, 121–122.

7 Woolf, A Room of One's Own, 122.

a magazine editor for much of her career; I know grammar. But if one were to use what many people think of as perfect grammar always, one would sound like a veritable piece of shit in one's day-to-day life.

Meanwhile, the "grammar police" character on TV shows and in movies is typically portrayed as a pretentious asshole. Think about Ross Geller from *Friends*, who becomes the butt of jokes whenever he corrects the group's grammar.

We've already touched on Shakespeare. It feels important to note that we no longer speak like people did in Shakespeare's time. We've dropped the second-person singular pronouns *thou* and *thee*, for one. Language—including vocabulary and grammar—is a human invention, alive and organic. Born out of a need to communicate, explain, and understand, language rises up to meet the changing needs of humanity. We change it as necessary. How would Virginia have felt about a universal "she?" A singular "they?" The option of speaking to women *as* women? The option to reject womanhood altogether? Could it have saved her life?

In college when I read feminist classics, I began to notice that it took a strange kind of effort from me in order to feel included when writers used the universal "he." I didn't feel like the author was speaking to or about me, even when they clearly were. Then I found some writers who changed the universal "he" to "she." That helped. More modern texts began using "he or she," so I began to do so in my own essays. But in college, papers have a word limit. As a verbose writer with a buttload of opinions and a love of run-on sentences, I allowed myself to use "they" as a universal pronoun initially just to cut length. The world did not end.

Everyone is using "they" as a singular pronoun. "Someone left their keys." "How was the doctor? What did they say?" Or even, hilariously (because of both the content and the pronoun, clearly referring only to women), "Every girl wants a boyfriend who will peel an orange for them."[8]

As a writer, a child of writers, a grandchild of writers, I find policing grammar to be elitist, obnoxious, and perhaps even classist. (Who has access to

---

8 Mackenzie Filson, "TikTok's 'Orange Peel Theory' Will Test Your Relationship," *Delish,* January 23, 2024. www.delish.com/food-news/a46503270/orange-peel-theory-tiktok.

quality education? Who has parents with graduate degrees?) It's even a smidge ableist. (I almost never use the term because of how rampant it is on social media as a way to dismiss nearly anything, but here I feel it applies to those with reading- and writing-related learning disabilities.) Bluntly, I think it's just antisocial behavior.

But somehow, a lot of the same people who would react poorly to Ross forcefully saying "whom!!" at them are the first to say, "'They' as a singular pronoun is grammatically incorrect."

While I used to try to get everyone around me to use my correct pronouns, to educate themselves (and if they didn't, gosh darn it, I was gonna do it by force!), and to *do more* for trans people, I no longer concern myself with things I can't control. I no longer think that trying to control other people is the most productive way to make positive change. I try—even when my anxiety grips me—to let go of what I can't control and focus on what I can. It's a struggle, but a worthwhile one. I see this shift as part of my recovery from being a Cancel Kid Lite™[9] as well as my physical and spiritual recovery from debilitating illnesses, during the worst of which I felt no one was ever doing enough to keep me safe. My reaction was to attempt to control those around me.

As I write this, I feel Virginia close by. I'm thinking of that moment when I wondered if she knew that my and others' writing would be made possible by what she was writing. (Mom, is that right? "My and others'"? It feels clunky . . .) And not just because I do have a room of my own and make a decent living, but because of her willingness and courage to write, and write, and write so I could do the same. She says, "Good books are desirable and good writers, even if they show every variety of human depravity, are still good human beings. Thus when I ask you to write more books I urge you to do what will be for your good and for the good of the world at large."[10]

My copy of *A Room of One's Own*, which my partner gave me for my thirty-fifth birthday this past July, has highlighted parts from the reader who owned it before me, someone I will never know but who was also changed by this

---

9 Mia Schachter, "I'm a Cancel Kid in Recovery, You Could Say," Consent Wizadry, October 3, 2024. https://consentwizardry.substack.com/p/im-a-cancel-kid-in-recovery-you-could?r=1texa0.

10 Woolf, A Room of One's Own, 129.

text. In a sense, we read it together, their highlights drawing my attention more directly to certain parts. I wonder what became possible for them because of Virginia, where they are now, and, if our paths ever cross or have crossed, whether we would even know.

As Virginia says, every great writer is "an inheritor as well as an originator."[11] I find myself wondering who's inheriting this text right now, what you're already doing because of what my writing has made possible, and what you will originate in part because of it. *A Room of One's Own* influenced my work and its potential before I even read it. I wonder who may be touched by my writing without ever knowing it, or who will read this piece and refract it through their own lens to create something I can't imagine. Maybe that's you. Hi. :)

11 Woolf, A Room of One's Own, 128.

PART VI

BLAME, REGRET, PUNISHMENT, AND BUILDING COMMUNITY

Repentance Rituals and Cancel Culture

On Yom Kippur last year, as I struck my chest with every sin I read out loud, I thought about how hard it often is to say, "I've hurt people. I've acted selfishly. I've lied. I've been manipulative. I've said dumb shit that I wish I hadn't said and thunk dumb shit I wish I hadn't thunk." But through this practice of saying, "I've done some shitty things," I recognize and come to peace with myself and my flaws.

Within militant secularism, we don't often have rituals, nor the structures to contain them, that allow us to reflect on how we've hurt others, how to repair, and how to move forward, forgiving ourselves. We need these cycles, like a breath, inhale and exhale, so we can reset. We learn and get to let go. As a result, there is no beginning, middle, and end to our interpersonal conflicts, no expansion and contraction, only mounting harm and resentment, grudges held sometimes forever. Without these structures and without community in which to reflect together, this mounting harm eventually spills over into blame and punishment, often as extreme as what we call cancel culture. All too often, those pointing the finger of blame are unwilling to reflect on the ways they, too, cause harm. "*Those people* who violate consent. *Those people* who cause harm. *Those people* who are racist, transphobic, sexist. *They're* the worst! I'm not like them."

Whenever I hear people talk about "those people," my spidey senses tingle. I wonder if the person saying it is willing to consider the ways they, too, cause harm. Every time you leave your house you step on an unsuspecting bug. When you scratch an itch, you kill a microscopic organism or several. To be human is to cause harm. We hurt people, we apologize, and we repair. These are the cycles of rupture and repair that earn us secure attachment with ourselves and others. Trying to avoid it is futile; I believe that learning to repair, forgive, and put systems in place to prevent it from happening again is where our energy is most valuable. If you won't look at how you've caused harm, you are much more likely to repeat it than if you are willing to look right at it.

Without these practices, I see a lot of people looking online to creators, myself included, to fill in as prophets of their own privately curated religion. When these prophets reveal themselves to be merely human, to have moments of hypocrisy, to contradict themselves, to put their foot in their mouths, or to stumble out of integrity, it can be experienced as a betrayal so massive you'd think we actually knew each other. Instead of knocking that person off the pedestal, I wonder if it would be possible to see another side: a possibility that we can all be prophets, tuning into ancient wisdom contained within ourselves, creating our own philosophies of what it means to be a good person, and recognizing our own power. Lifting ourselves up to the level we thought someone was above us, rather than pulling them down to crush them.

I am very wary when I see online "conversations" that say, "If you do this or say that or follow this person or go to this place, you are _____ist/phobic and I don't want to know you," with no room for gray, for the in-between, for nuance. I can't help but wonder how these people engage in conflict and disagreement with their loved ones, with people they actually know. So often, these are the same people who are demanding more nuance from creators online, the ones who creep into my DMs telling me about this one time this one thing happened to them (and only them), and how I'm not including that perspective. They're not demanding nuance but demanding to be centered. To those people, I suggest that they journal, talk to their friends and therapist, and keep those critical-thinking caps on, because they know themselves better than anyone.

Are you willing to look at the ways you've hurt people and accept the ways you will continue to hurt people? Are you willing to look inward as much or more than you look outward, pointing a finger of blame? I firmly believe that if we spent less of our resources on trying to figure out who to blame and then punish and more of our resources on supporting people when they've been hurt or wronged, on healing support (such as quality mental health services), and on education to help prevent the same kind of harm from occurring again (such as comprehensive consent and sex education and media literacy), we'd be doing individuals, our communities, and ourselves a much bigger service than we do by removing people via incarceration or ostracization.

Having a healthier relationship with my own flaws has reduced my anxiety and stress. I've been able to loosen my grip and monitor myself less, which allows me to listen to other people better. I'm working on it and expect to be working on it forever.

The People Who Will Cancel You Agree with 99 Out of 100 Things You Say

Social media is a place where blue-haired pansexuals named Soap hate nobody more than other blue-haired pansexuals named Soap. They will make a PDF manual to distribute to friends about what they're allowed to say, where they're allowed to go, and who they're allowed to talk to in order to "be in community" (lol) with them. They'll tell you "dumb is an ableist slur" and have #ACAB #BLM in their Instagram bio lines.

I have a lot of compassion for the Soaps. I used to be a Soap. I policed my friends' language and behavior, believing that it was my responsibility to educate and advocate on behalf of others with less privilege than me no matter what. I followed in the footsteps of hypervigilant, dogmatic friends (whose friendship was entirely conditional and contingent upon what I said, where I went, and who I talked to) who promoted this behavior. These were people who had rigid beliefs about what was right and wrong, whether it was about trans issues, race, accountability, or anything else. I will be un-Soaping myself for a while.

It's my opinion that this kind of policing on the left creates an incredibly high bar to clear for working-class people, formerly incarcerated people, neurodivergent people, and people who don't have access to higher education—that is, the same people the left claims to be trying to help. To use some of the Soaps' language, this kind of policing behavior is *actually* ableist and classist. (*Guttural sigh.*)

What I've found is that all too often, people who say they're committed to change and abolition will fight with their proverbial neighbors before they'd consider having conversations with people who don't know what pronouns even are, even if those people have the power to install accessibility measures or influence policy decisions. They'd rather police the people closest to them with whom they should be fighting alongside. The people who will cancel you agree with 99 out of 100 things you say.[1]

⁂

I've found that in my work in particular, people come to me for consent education because they're looking for help in healing. They want to have better relationships and to heal from different kinds of violations. And so, many of them have immense unresolved trauma—myself included, at the time that I arrived to this work. I see a lot of people drawn to the field of intimacy coordination who have their own severe trauma history. They come into the work because they "don't want anyone to go through what they went through." This often means that they have a savior complex with a vengeance. The result is presumed guilt and cop-like behavior on a set, leading to the very negative reputation that the intimacy coordination field still has to this day.

Trauma warps memory. It doesn't just warp *a* memory or a series of memories, but it warps *our ability to remember*. The result is that often, two people leave a conversation with wildly different ideas of what was said. For some of these people, when I can't "fix them" (a fictional promise that no one made), they experience it as a huge betrayal, and I fall off the pedestal they put me on. I know this is common in helping professions.

I've noticed a few patterns here. One is that very often, the people who feel the most betrayed are the same ones who I can sense are fawning—a people-pleasing or appeasement stress response. In the past, this has sounded like someone telling me I'm "one of the good ones." It has sounded like someone telling me they "revere" me or are "in awe of me." It has sounded like a prospective client telling me, "I realized I actually just want to be your friend." It's sad

---

1 For more on this, listen to my podcast with Risdon Roberts, *You're Doing It Wrong*, especially this episode: https://podcasts.apple.com/us/podcast/youre-doing-it-wrong/id1708436950?i=1000650933341

to me that these theoretically nice sentiments have become red flags for me in professional relationships.

Another pattern is a lack of a sense of shared reality. I know this is happening when I feel that we've had one conversation and left on a particular note, only to hear weeks or months later that what the other person interpreted was wildly different from what I meant, or that they've been sitting on upset feelings about something I said for a long time, letting anger fester and rot without expressing what was bothering them.

I'd like to share a few micro-examples to demonstrate how this works:

1. A friend of mine was a consent moderator at a sex party. She noticed someone was so drunk that she was slurring her words and stumbling. My friend went to the person who'd been making out with her and said, "I think [sex/kink] play shouldn't be on the table tonight within this party," and then was told by another moderator that the two women who had been making out felt my friend had "slut-shamed" them.

2. I was planning to co-teach a professional development class with a mentee. They wanted to set the base of our sliding scale at $10. I said I didn't want to charge less than $25. I didn't want to suggest that this class was only worth $10, and I had found in the past that when I charge less than $25, people don't show up even when they've paid. I felt this was a class best fitting people at a point in their careers where $25 should be doable, but I said that of course, if anyone wrote to me offering $10, I would make them a discount code (as is always my policy). In our exit interview when the mentorship ended, my mentee said they were surprised to hear that I "don't want to work with poor people." We are on very good terms and continue to work together. We discussed this misunderstanding when it came up. But I can imagine there are countless other instances of misinterpretations like this one that people carry with them, without speaking to me, that can spread widely.

3. I had a student who told me she was concerned about money and asked what opportunities there were to work for me. There weren't any. I asked, "Have you considered trying to find a job, while you build your business, where you clock in and clock out and that doesn't take up your mental space beyond a shift, with the priority of building

> community with your fellow employees, customers, and even your employers such that any of them could become future collaborators or clients?" The next day, I received an email from her saying she felt it was ableist that I'd said she should "get a job." She gave me reading assignments to "learn how to treat trans femmes better." We had a follow-up call where she told me I was a fraud, that "true abolition would be living off the grid and not paying taxes," and that she thought it was fucked up that I told my students to raise their rates for the services they offer. Meanwhile, she was living with her family rent free.

This is how cancellation happens. This is how people on the left—in organizing and social-justice circles, art spaces, and organizations that work to make change—fight amongst ourselves. We fight with the people actually doing the work instead of the people who are actively working against us. We clog up the gears within our own projects with this infighting muck. We do this to ourselves.

And yet, I also have the awareness that my recollection of these conversations is warped by my own context and history. Actual reality exists somewhere between two people's perceptions of an experience. But I've learned that when I feel like I'm living in a completely different reality than someone, I need to keep my distance. This might look like simply not contacting them or pursuing any kind of relationship with them, backing away from a friendship or deescalating a romantic relationship, or even exiting the relationship. What this *doesn't* mean is telling all my friends and anyone who will listen how awful this person is, that they're bad, evil, a nightmare, and a monster, or that if you hang out with them, you're enabling an abuser and we can't be friends anymore.

* * *

I have dealt with mysterious, undiagnosed chronic illness all my life. It got to its worst as I approached thirty. During that period, I thought about dying a lot. I didn't want to die, but I figured my body would give out or I'd have to end things myself because I was suffering so much. I frequently wished for a bus to hit me or to slip in the shower to take the decision out of my hands.

Once I got my diagnoses and began treatment, I improved a lot. But then I went to Mexico and got very sick, and my health declined over the next two and a half years. During that time, I also went from she/they pronouns to they/

them pronouns and became more outspoken about my experience of being nonbinary. Regarding my health, I never felt anyone was doing enough to help me, to keep me safe, especially from the foods I couldn't eat. Regarding gender, I never felt anyone was doing enough to educate themselves or to practice to be able to speak respectfully about me or use my correct pronouns. I know this is common, and I'm not alone. I see it amongst other trans and disabled friends, especially when they first come out or first become radicalized (as in, recognizing the systems that keep them sick, generally rooted in capitalism and the medical industry). It's a kind of puberty. The truth is that no one *is* ever doing all they can, but what is "enough" and who determines it? All of this was a lesson in self-advocacy, but I also recognize that my own hypervigilance was a trauma response.

After two and a half years of my health's decline (again), I had a week of violent illness. On the sixth day, I looked down in the toilet to find a two-foot-long tapeworm. This had been the cause of my new illness. Now, almost two years later, I'm healthier than ever. This newfound health has come alongside finding equilibrium with gender stuff. I now feel that when someone can't get my pronouns right or can't talk to me about gender issues, it's a great filter: It tells me about where they're at and therefore how close I can be with them. I've prioritized connection in my life, which has led me to see that I have to expand my patience and my tolerance for activation. It also has shown me that I can advocate for myself and I can educate (these are professional as well as personal skills for me), but I can also *choose not to*. I see that choosing *not* to do so is not a failure but rather a choice I'm making to preserve my energy and time and, sometimes, to keep connection intact.

Prioritizing connection has led me to be better at having difficult conversations and navigating conflict. It has even pushed me to choose kindness over pure "honesty," at times. It has helped me be able to hear something I disagree with and think, "That's where that person is at," or, "That's Shannon Shannoning. I would do it differently, but I am not Shannon." It helps me recognize that we don't see eye to eye, but that person is not a monster, evil, invalid, toxic, a narcissist, transphobic, racist, ableist, etc. At worst, we can simply be incompatible.

But this mentality has come from an enormous amount of healing: healing of my body, of my mind, and of attachment wounds. I'm grateful to my amazing therapist for the healing I've been able to do and to my parents for covering the cost of a lot of my medical expenses. I've felt a return to myself in the last year. I've felt my warmth and my magnetism return. I see it in how people respond to me, how strangers smile and say hi to me at a coffee shop, how the vendors at the farmers' market light up when I come to buy my salmon or berries. The worm made my light so dim. I felt constantly under threat, constantly unsafe. Now that I feel safer, I've been able to let go of many rigid rules and break down the walls I've built to protect myself.

I cringe at a lot of my behavior from that hypervigilant time. I've lost some friends from that period after I tried to talk with them about how I was feeling policed and how I found some of their behavior controlling, how I was prioritizing connection and didn't want to live with that death grip around my throat anymore. I wanted more vulnerability, and that meant sharing freely without worrying so much about being politically correct or failing to give a content warning. Some were unwilling to have these conversations or kept putting them off, and I had to let the relationships go. Sometimes this sounds like, "If you continue to be friends with that person who hurt me, I can't be your friend." (I'm not talking about instances of abuse; I'm talking about messy breakups, business conflicts, or roommate fights.) I can see how this behavior comes from not feeling safe. It seems safer to attempt to control everything around you. It seems safer to be able to determine who is "to blame" and who is "bad," so we create binaries: guilty/innocent, abuser/victim, good/bad. It seems safer to isolate yourself from anyone and everything that you feel threatens you. But happy, healthy people have more important things to do than stand in the way of someone else's wellbeing, career, or sense of community and belonging.

Ultimately what this tells me is that we need better, more affordable mental health care. The more people can heal and have access to healing support, the more they'll be able to focus on what they can control rather than trying to control others. We could stop replicating carceral systems inside our own so-called activist circles, where we police each other and fail to see the irony of saying "all cops are bastards" while turning into the cops ourselves. I think if we stopped spending all our resources on trying to determine who's bad and who's to blame for our feelings of unsafety or even for our trauma, we'd direct more of our resources toward things that can actually help us heal. To me, *this* is abolition. Because identifying the cause of trauma doesn't make it go away. That healing work lies ahead.

Personal Responsibility in a Post-#MeToo Feminism

In the wake of the #MeToo movement, we have seen a lot of improvements to the discourse around consent and consent education, but there have also been some unintended consequences that we are just beginning to undo with better strategies.

When #MeToo went viral in 2017, misandry (or the hatred of men) became a kind of currency for connection amongst many feminists. As I touched on in "Consent Is for Everyone" in part II, the problem with this is that (1) hating men does not help them change, nor promote societal growth, nor the education or rehabilitation of men, and (2) misandry actually takes away women's agency by leaving the safety of women solely in the hands of men.

It's also important to note that the #MeToo movement primarily focused on the experiences of cis, heterosexual women. While I think it was and is important, it largely failed to serve queer, trans, and nonbinary people. As I've mentioned already in this book, I'm nonbinary and I date people of all genders, including cis men, but you should know that in 2017 I identified as a woman (lacking the proper language to describe my experience at the time).

An unequivocal mandate appeared on T-shirts, bumper stickers, and embroidered pillows: "believe women." Now, I'm not suggesting we shouldn't believe women; that would be a wildly bad-faith read of my point. What I think "believe women" initially meant was that when a group of women tell you they've been assaulted by a man in a position of power, believe them. When an individual woman tells you she's been sexually assaulted, believe her. But we can't ignore any and all other contexts. This may be hard for some to hear, but women are no less prone to lying, manipulating, forgetting, altering memories in hindsight, or blaming other people for their icky feelings than any other gender. Unfortunately, while they are in the minority, some women do make up sexual assaults. And although I have to imagine these women are experiencing a lot of pain and suffering from perhaps a lifetime of not being heard, what they're doing is, quite frankly, a huge "fuck you" to people who've actually experienced sexual assault (myself included).

I think what happens in many of these cases is that someone had sex she may have felt conflicted or ambivalent about, and in hindsight, the sex feels less than consensual. For example, she liked him and wanted to have sex but didn't like the sex; or she was really tired but agreed to have sex anyway, and now that he hasn't called her back she feels resentful and regrets the sex. She may then tell her friend that she had sex she didn't feel great about, or wasn't "enthusiastic" about, and due to black-and-white thinking on matters related to sex (which stems from bumper-sticker education like "Anything other than an enthusiastic yes is a no"), her friend may label her experience as rape or assault and pressure her to report it or, god forbid, make a TikTok video about it. Her friends might say, "We need to hold men accountable!"

But, to my first point, the cry, "Hold men accountable!" so often stems from misandry. It's not about holding an individual man accountable for *his* actions; it's usually more about holding one man disproportionately accountable for the entire history of patriarchy on this planet. We want to make an example out of him, burn him at the stake for the sins of all men who came before. Meanwhile, many of these women (including the bisexual ones) continue to date men, which creates a horrible environment in which their male partner is supposed to learn and grow while being constantly shat on by the woman he loves.

And I have to ask if the misandry and the blanket statements have actually helped make sex and relationships better or improved the quality of life of women and survivors of sexual assault and rape. Has blaming men, attempting to "hold men accountable," and taking people at their word without considering any factors other than what they said helped survivors get the support they need to heal? Has it brought consent education to the masses? Has it reduced rape? Has it improved people's sex lives and relationships? I dream of a world in which shame, guilt, and fear of exile and punishment aren't the motivating factors to being a half-decent human being.

Out of the deserved and appropriate public indignation following the fall of truly despicable people like Harvey Weinstein, Matt Lauer, and others came a stratification of responsibility. Men had to get better at consent because consent was 100 percent a man's responsibility in a heterosexual dynamic. This excludes queer couples and trans people. As soon as you consider those groups, you can't clearly determine whose shoulders consent falls on. This is not because queerness is confusing or something, it's because *consent is a shared responsibility regardless of gender*. We all need to practice consent for each other. I've said it so many times: Consent is not something men do for women; consent is something we all do for each other, including ourselves.

What's missing here? Personal responsibility. You can choose to have sex even when you're conflicted. You can choose to have sex you're not sure about. You can choose to have sex you know you'll regret (like sleeping with a good friend's ex, perhaps). You can even—and this may shock some people—choose to have sex you don't want to have. This is the case for sex workers plenty of the time, and it's sometimes true for couples trying to get pregnant (see more on this in the essay "Utterly Enthusiastic but Totally Consensual Sex"). We each have to understand ourselves well enough to know the difference between "I don't *want* to have sex, but I'm willing" and "I *don't* want to have sex." Another linguistic distinction like this came up for me recently when I told a friend, "I wouldn't say I'm a person who *doesn't* want to get married, but I would say that I'm not a person who *wants* to get married," by which I mean I'm not opposed to getting married if someone else really wants to or if it makes practical sense for me some day, but I'm not a person who desires marriage or fantasizes about being married.

Out of this black-and-white thinking also came a definition of consent that includes someone being able to retroactively withdraw consent. They said yes at the time, and can later say that the encounter was nonconsensual, assault, or rape. Again, I think in extreme cases this is valid. You may have felt coerced or pressured into saying yes, or you may have said yes to "the sex" but not to something that happened during it that you didn't agree to (choking or slapping comes to mind), and so your "yes" either was forced or fake, or it kept you safer than saying no in the moment. You may have been in a situation with egregious power dynamics, like your boss came onto you and you felt you needed to oblige in order to keep your job. However, the dangers of this line of thinking have become clear and rampant. We now have people saying yes to sexual encounters that are in fact totally consensual, devoid of extreme power dynamics, and devoid of coercion, pressure, and force, but which leave someone feeling *a li'l bit weird* about it—and because the human impulse to blame and punish has such force, they decide that the other person is responsible for their icky feelings. The idea that you can retroactively retract your consent takes the very real notion that "a yes is not a yes if no is not an option" so far as to allow us to shirk all responsibility for our choices if we can agree, as a whole adult person in the world engaging with other adults, to do something and then simply . . . decide we didn't mean it.

In the wake of the Harvey Weinstein articles and the #MeToo movement, many people, myself included, received unsolicited and sometimes very awkward apologies from men we'd slept with or been propositioned by, stripping us of our agency during the encounter. Many of us felt pressured by the societal discourse or real people in our inner circles to examine and recategorize consensual experiences as nonconsensual or worse. Some of us did so and later regretted ruining someone's life, robbing them of their community, their job, and their support systems.

Eventually we saw Aziz Ansari get called out for what I would diagnose as being a bit of a socially awkward doof (working on getting this into the DSM) and failing to acclimate to his newfound fame and the female attention that came with it quickly enough for the public. We don't immediately understand the power we have as soon as we get it, and fame is a real doozy. This story split the court of public opinion into more than two camps, but primarily it was divided between those who thought that misinterpreting social cues and acting according to culturally dominant norms for heterosexual men (as promoted by mass media in movies and TV shows) were criminal offenses and those who felt that "#MeToo had gone too far."

A particularly sad outcome of the movement was the total paralysis of sweet, kind, feminist men looking for love. The same number of straight women who'd wanted to find committed partners still wanted that, but a growing number of men suddenly felt afraid to flirt, to make their interest known, to ask women out, or to even look at them in a way that could be misconstrued as creepy. And these fears were valid, because even those of us looking for partnership with (anybody, but including) men were often quick to pounce on a man for anything we deemed unwanted. Behavior from someone we thought was unattractive would be called creepy and inappropriate while the same exact behavior would be welcomed from someone we thought was cute. The kinds of men we wanted to date were working on themselves and often painfully afraid to ask us out, while the men we really didn't want to date had no problem being creeps. We had backed our potential partners into a hole where they remained, scared to come out and play with us. We wanted relationships with good men, but we frequently took their nervous and timid advances in bad faith, coloring them in a sexist and unflattering light. Many women then got frustrated that they couldn't find any men to date.

I see us coming out of this trench we've dug. I see it in my work as a consent educator, in my classes where a growing number of students emphatically champion a paradigm of consent that includes personal responsibility from all genders. I see it in the press, in the media, and online. I see it in shows like *Adults* that parody cancel culture and social media. I see more accounts appearing on Instagram and TikTok that draw attention to the ways that we sabotage our own goals in social-justice spaces with binary thinking and by replicating the very carceral systems we claim to want to weed out. I see it in the growing number of people who are no longer willing to participate in cancel culture after seeing their friends, colleagues, and family members get canceled or experiencing it themselves. We're tiptoeing into the gray area, the in-between, the space where nuance and complexity live and thrive. In the face of rising fascism, a recession, genocide, and the potential end of marriage equality and reproductive rights, we have to learn to work together. Our lives are made up of a series of actions and choices we make, so the way we are in our intimate relationships ripples out into the world around us. I don't think it's a far reach to suggest that learning to practice consent together, for each other and for ourselves, can help us fight these bigger fights.

We Have to Stop Canceling Each Other so We Can Start Saving Each Other's Lives

Once upon a time, cancellation was about removing people from positions of systemic and institutional power, where they had been bolstered and protected so that they could continue to perpetuate abuses of power, typically sexual in nature, while those institutions protecting them actively tried to silence their accusers. And then, something changed. We saw it go from serial abusers like Harvey Weinstein and Matt Lauer, and then Louis C. K. and others, to people like Aziz Ansari, which was where many people started to draw a line, thinking we'd gone too far.

But at some point, we (by which I mean activists, leftists, organizers, millennials, and blue-haired pansexuals named Soap) stopped giving people the benefit of the doubt and started assuming the absolute worst. We stopped believing people could grow and learn and started reducing them to the worst thing they've ever said or done—but we never wanted to be held to that standard ourselves, because of course we are capable of change but those people are evil. We stopped being able to distinguish malice from ignorance, and we decided we could only handle conflict by publicly stoning people and denying their humanity instead of learning how to navigate interpersonal conflict amongst ourselves.

In 2024, I lost my book deal because someone from within my own community wrote to my editor with second- or third-hand information, twisted wildly by ignorance and a sense of saviorism, to get my deal canceled. They were successful. A few weeks later, I released a piece on Substack called "The

People Who Will Cancel You Agree with 99 Out of 100 Things You Say." (Also in this book.) That essay functioned as observational, naming patterns I had witnessed. This essay, I hope, sheds some light on how I've moved on from the pain of my book's cancellation, and how I hope we can work together for a better world. Since I published that essay in 2024, I've seen a shift away from cancel culture on and offline, one I hope is here to stay, as I encounter more and more people sick of the death grip they feel around their throat lest they use the wrong word or don't show up superhumanly perfect in leftist activist spaces or on social media, or even just with their friends. Thank goodness.

As I've prioritized connection, joy, and vulnerability, I've had to learn to be more patient and more tolerant of my own activation as I seek to build bridges with people who are different from me. I hope more of us will prioritize building these bridges and deprioritize finding the one, single "right" way to speak, act, and be. I think these bridges are the seeds of real change, as I reach beyond my immediate community and see perspectives that are different from my own. I learn to hold those perspectives and respect them, even when I disagree with them.

I wasn't always able to do this. As I've mentioned earlier, I went through something of a mental, emotional, and intellectual puberty when I first realized that they/them pronouns felt more fitting for me. I found myself letting go of a lot of relationships or not wanting to be around people who couldn't use these pronouns for me with deftness and ease. I was amongst friends who did the same, labeling anyone who argued about grammar or who talked about their own confusion or struggle with the new language to be transphobic. Surrounded by people who were quick to cut out friends and family (sounds a little cult-y, eh?) and quick to talk shit about people they knew because of a linguistic slip, I held hard lines with my own friends, family, and people I dated, determining quickly who was allowed in and who had to stay out. This resulted in isolation, lost connections, and an echo chamber that became echo-ier every day.

What shook me out of it? Well, it's not so clear. I began to see how the policing of what you say, where you go, and who you're friends with is antithetical to the mission of inclusivity. I have seen a lot of care and energy going into activist content and events that are insular and exclusionary to those who don't have the "right" lingo. I've gone to events that beat you over the head with a land acknowledgment without any tangible support for Indigenous peoples or the Land Back movement; I've seen events use terminology like "safe space" but kick out anyone who isn't familiar with the proper terminology around trans identity—which, by the way, includes a lot of not-yet-out or newly out trans people! Perfectionism is valued over vulnerability; the rules are valued over learning and sharing. In other words, there is little to no grace.

I started to see patterns amongst the behaviors of people in my life that no longer seemed like they were rooted in a fight for justice, or anything akin to solidarity, but rather seemed like control tactics. These methods of control positioned those who knew the rules as the top dog, and anyone else who didn't know those rules had to get in line lest they be ostracized. We were taught that the winners of the oppression Olympics in any dynamic were to be uncritically trusted and receive all our faith, and we were told that we should aspire to be more like them. The more radical someone was, the better. The more inclusive a space was, the better—unless it was an affinity group. (That's an acceptable reason for exclusion, but you have to be able to discern the difference and be the gatekeeper—but without "gatekeeping," because that would be an abuse of power.) I found myself kowtowing, a perpetual yes-guy, to those who I saw as more radical or more oppressed than I was.

But one of the biggest foundation-shifting events in my life was expelling a tapeworm. As I've mentioned, before I knew I had this parasite, I had spent years dealing with both acute and chronic illness and decades living with undiagnosed or misdiagnosed chronic illness (which I believe set the stage for a very welcoming environment to a worm in my gut). I grappled with my identity as a disabled person. I found labels that suited me and spoke to my experience—dynamically disabled; invisibly disabled; chronically ill. But I also saw so much infighting in the disability justice community, so much argument over language, and so much disagreement that I wanted to stay far away. I also saw clearly how no one person knows The Truth or The Way.

I, too, had been failed by a for-profit medical industry. I, too, felt uncared for and underserved by society at large as well as my immediate community. I felt no one was ever doing enough to support me. I often had unreasonably high standards for those around me. Of course, I can see that I had good reason to feel this way; no one was doing "enough" for me because no one could. How could they? I had extreme restrictions on my diet and my life. I had multiple conditions that created circumstances unlike any I've ever heard about. How could anyone know exactly how I needed to be taken care of? Even if I told people (and I frequently did), how could I expect them to remember everything all the time?

After the worm came out and I began healing my body, my trauma, and my mind (and my heart), I began to see how much power I had wielded by identifying as a victim so much of the time. When I was at my sickest, I was at my most controlling. When I was at the height of my trauma, I was at my most unreasonable.

I've been able to open up to others' needs and feelings about my illness. Because while I don't have to support them through their own frustration and feelings of helplessness around my condition, their feelings are part of our relationship.

I've learned to be more patient and compassionate with those in my life who don't understand what it's like. Even if their inability to understand is a facet of privilege, I can still recognize that this is their experience and, because I care about them, I care to know and understand their experience.

I'm more able to see where I do have power and where I wasn't willing to see or acknowledge where I had power all along. I'm more able to see the power I wielded by identifying as a victim so much of the time because it kept me firmly in "the right" and others in "the wrong." I can see more clearly what is within my control and what is not. I have more space for others to not understand. I have more patience while others learn how to care for me. The foundation has truly shifted, thanks in large part to this alien worm.

I made a decision to start prioritizing connection, joy, and awe. I saw that when I felt least in control of my own life, I was at my most controlling of others. I had hard-and-fast rules about who could be in my life. A lot of those rules revolved around other people's own choices in language, behavior, where they went, and who they talked to. I held the bar they had to clear, and I would raise or lower it at my own discretion.

I have always thought cancellation within communities was bullshit—I remember a conversation with an ex in 2013 or so about the way that the punk community ostracizes people without so much as a conversation, so that they become a *different* community's problem, because they'll never learn why they got kicked out by people they thought were friends or have a path to rehabilitation or reentrance into their community, and anyone who associates with them also gets ostracized. But now, I noticed the patterns in my own thoughts that fell into that kind of thinking. I'd say, "Before we watch that movie, you should know that that director said some really problematic shit last year." Or, "I don't go to that venue because my friend's girlfriend had a few bad experiences there a few years ago as an employee." I'd quietly distance myself from people who shopped at Amazon, because I was convinced this meant we had incompatibly different values. (As I type this, there is an Amazon box ready to be recycled by my front door.) This leaves no room for anyone to grow, to learn via exposure and osmosis, and it positions me as the beacon of goodness and truth. It also leaves me really fucking lonely.

The shift I'm seeing is exciting. It gives me hope. I have to imagine that many people are seeing their friends get canceled over some nonsense, or getting canceled themselves, and they want to express themselves freely and vulnerably, want to be allowed to make mistakes and learn, and are ready to give others the grace they want given to them when they fumble. They want to give others the benefit of the doubt the way they want it to be given to them. Perhaps they see that we have bigger problems and bigger fights to fight. That we need to stick together because the billionaires and politicians we are fighting won't cancel each other, and yet they're the ones with the money, the power, and the guns.

We absolutely need methods to exorcise serial abusers of power from their positions in institutions that preserve their ability to abuse said power, and we absolutely need to figure how to do this swiftly and outside of the prison system. But we also have to see that perhaps what works on a large scale doesn't work on a small scale, and vice versa. What works at a company might not work with my ex or my coworker. We have to be able to work through conflict, to expand our tolerance for activation, to be able to discern between malicious intent and an oopsie. We have to be willing to let other people grow and learn in the same way that we want to grow and learn. We have our work cut out for us. This is a long road, and we have to be willing and able to protect each other from our common enemy—literal fascism—instead of having to protect ourselves from each other. We have to remember that it's okay to simply *not like someone* without needing everyone around us to agree and then remove that person from our and their community. We can't simply chuck the bad apples when the water itself is poisoned; there will only be more. We need strategies for navigating complex conversations and increasing our patience for disagreement, and we need to be able to go, "That's not how I would do it, but your way isn't wrong." We have to grow up, get our heads out of the clouds, humble ourselves to the reality that no one, no organization, and no movement is perfect, and save lives. That's the direness of the situation right now: We have to stop canceling each other so we can save each other's lives.

Interview with Risdon Roberts

Cancellation, Transformative Justice, and Sex Work

Risdon Roberts is an intimacy professional specializing in divergent sexualities, sexual dysfunction, and relational repair. In addition to working with clients privately, she also works in film and TV as a consultant, sex expert, and intimacy coordinator. You can find her featured on Slate.com, AskMen.com, and the BBC discussing issues related to sex work, contemporary dating culture, and the masculinity crisis. Risdon lives in Los Angeles. We co-host the podcast, "You're Doing It Wrong."

Risdon: You wanna do it wrong? I've been doing it wrong this whole time.

Mia: Let's do everything wrong. Honestly, it's more fun.

Risdon: I've never done anything right in my life.

Mia: Less pressure, yeah. If you just go into it knowing that you're doing it wrong, there's no way to fail.

Risdon: That's right.

Mia: Okay, well, I'd like to start by asking you what your definition of cancel culture is.

Risdon: Boy. Well, I want to start by saying that I think people get confused about what cancel culture is a lot. One thing is that I think there is a strong distinction between consequences and cancellation. So for example, setting a boundary with somebody that I don't want to hang out with isn't canceling.

Mia: It isn't canceling *them*, but you might be canceling plans.

Risdon: Yes, yes. I would argue just blocking somebody isn't canceling them. Canceling goes beyond the personal relationship, and I think specifically, to me, cancellation has a lot to do with trying to remove someone from your reality. So, being like, "I don't ever want this person to come to my coffee shop again." "You're not allowed to come to my coffee shop because we had a bad breakup." Or, "You're not allowed to have your job anymore because I don't think you should be able to earn a living." And I also want to say, that is different from being like, "You can't have that specific job because it gives you access to people who are vulnerable, and you've proven you can't be responsible with that power dynamic." So to me, cancellation has to do with consequences that are not about your relationship with that person. A lot of times, they're more extreme, having to do with, essentially, an attempt to ruin someone's life as a consequence of something they've done. Instead of just being like, "I can't really be around you anymore, dog." You know?

Mia: Yeah, once upon a time, cancellation was about removing people from positions of power where they had been institutionally and systemically protected such that they could continue to abuse their power and take advantage of people who had less power than them. Like, we saw some twenty-odd women come forward about Harvey Weinstein. There was Matt Lauer, Louis C.K.—and it was about patterns. It was about stopping patterns of abuse and giving voice to people who'd previously been powerless to stop this abuse. And then . . . it splintered into these tinier and tinier conflicts where, you know, someone felt slighted, or someone said something that was ignorant but not with malicious intent, even. Or yeah, someone broke up with somebody and somebody else felt that that person, as you said, shouldn't have the right to make a living, to have community, to have support. And what I've seen is . . . I really don't believe that people can grow and learn and heal and change in isolation, and these attempts to essentially remove somebody from their community and strip them of their ability to make a living creates conditions in which they will never learn, and never change, and have zero support, which I think ultimately damages us all.

Risdon: Yeah, you're pushing those people into more marginalized communities. If the original community that somebody is in when they're canceled has enough power to kick them out and to create a public outcry that people listen to, that's a community with some level of privilege, right? So, if you're pushing them out of that space, where are they going? You know what I'm saying?

Mia: Hmm. Yeah, that's really interesting. I think it creates a situation where that person not only doesn't really have the ability to learn from their mistakes and actions, in part because there's no communication or conflict resolution with the person or people who feel they were harmed. But also, if all of that context and history is removed because they no longer are connected to any of those people, then they can't get any feedback or guidance. They just become someone else's problem, like a new community's problem, and then those people don't know about them. Because, you know, there are certainly people that you and I have both known where we're like, "Oh man, if that person just up and leaves Los Angeles because a lot of people are upset with them, nobody in New York City knows what's up with this person." That person can't change, but also now they just sort of perpetuate the same kinds of harm.

Risdon: Yeah, and I think what's interesting, too, is when we have these conversations, we need to ask: Is this person interested in change? Is this person capable of reflecting on their behavior and seeing that maybe they have a part in what's transpiring? And also, do the people who are calling them out or in or canceling them have any interest in that person changing? Because a lot of times, they don't. There's a fantasy that the people who've hurt me can go away forever, which is part of what prison is about, right? We're enacting that fantasy.

Mia: I think it's a sticky conversation to have, because I think there are a lot of people who feel incredibly disenfranchised and not supported by various systems we have in place that are, you know, at least theoretically intended to achieve some kind of justice, and when people don't feel like those are serving them, or care about them, then this mode of—giant air quotes—"achieving justice" can feel like the only option. Which I think just speaks to so many problems within our prison system, and police system, and law enforcement, and legal system, and so on and so forth. But I think you and I have both also seen such a range of reasons why this happens, anywhere from, someone has done something very objectively wrong that everyone would agree is wrong, all the way to, like, someone broke up with somebody because they didn't want to date anymore, and now that person is being smeared on social media, and someone is telling all their friends, "It's a betrayal to me if you hang out with that person," or writing to their employers, past employers, anyone who works with them, saying, "You're complicit." Anyway . . . you work directly with people who have experienced this, and who have been on the receiving end of being canceled. You've developed your own coaching container for that, and you're also trained in restorative-justice circles, or circle facilitation?

Risdon: Restorative-practice circles, yeah.

Mia: Can you talk a little bit about that training, what it's like, and what it has equipped you to do, and then how you have developed your own practice of supporting people who've experienced this?

Risdon: Yeah, talking about restorative practices is interesting, because being sort of in this work—and I say "sort of" because I'm in grad school now, so I can barely do much else—but people still reach out to me a lot to be like, "Hey, like, can you facilitate?" And I don't think people understand how formal and specific restorative circles are. So, people will come to me and be like, "Oh, we're facilitating a peace circle," and they've just made up a protocol. They're like, "Oh, it's a restorative practice," and it's the person who's in trouble, and thirty-five people who hate them. There's a very specific way that this stuff works, including that the facilitator is supposed to call and talk to all the people involved. Both the person who's caused harm and the person who's experienced harm are supposed to have a support person with them. There's really not a ton of room for creative license, and so . . . .

Mia: It's very codified.

Risdon: Yes, yes, there's a specific way of doing it. And so, it's interesting—people kind of love to throw around these terms, like transformative justice, restorative practice, and they're just making shit up, and I'm like, "That's not . . . you don't get to use . . . " But we have a lot of that culturally now. I feel like people use the word "predator" a lot when it's not predation. I don't know, these big words, like "justice" . . . .

Mia: Well, you and I did a whole episode on violence and harm, and I made a post about that recently and got some flack for it, but, you know, I think words mean things. And when you just decide that they mean other things, or you collapse it all into one extreme or the other, into a binary, you remove all nuance. So when we call it violence when someone punches someone in the nose, and then we also call it violence when someone bumps into you at the grocery store . . . and those are sort of fake examples, but those are extremely different, and if you define them both as "violence," you remove a lot of the truth of what's going on.

Risdon: Yeah, not to get us totally off-topic, but it reminds me a lot of how people use the word "trauma." Trauma is a medically defined thing. Capital-T Trauma. Like, there's five things that count as actual trauma, when we're talking about the DSM. There are people who can actually be diagnosed, who can say, "This was a traumatic event." But then, for some reason, people want to use being traumatized to justify their behavior, and so things are being called trauma that aren't trauma. And that wouldn't be a problem, except that, yeah, you're grouping the experience of, you know, somebody forgetting your birthday with somebody surviving war, and those just aren't the same thing. I'm sorry, they're not.

Anyway, getting back to what you originally asked me, yeah, I would say the first thing that I do with clients when they come to me after a cancellation is I make them do nothing. Usually people who are calling somebody out or canceling somebody really want them to perform a choreographed dance for them as quickly as possible: behave in a certain way, post something, say something, do something. And my strong feeling is that pretty much anything done out of urgency is inauthentic. So usually, I actually have clients do an accountability statement as the *last* thing that we do together, once they've really worked through a process of accountability, rather than just saying it from a place of, frankly, people-pleasing, trying to avoid consequences, you know what I mean? They're sort of throwing things to the mob in an attempt to not be executed, essentially, and what we need to do instead is to stabilize the person, because—I don't know if it's real trauma or what we call lowercase-t trauma, but the experience of exile is extremely . . .

Mia: Well, very activating, at the least.

Risdon: Yes, yes, it's in our nervous systems to experience it as a fear of death, even though it is not death. Historically, when we were living in communities and tribes and interdependent, it would have been death to be exiled, so there's this thing in us that's so terrified and so upset when that happens. So stabilizing the person is a big part of what I do, making sure they have support. Do they need to be in 12-step? You know, what's going on with drugs and alcohol? A lot of people come to me, and that's a thing that's causing some of their behavior, or is in some way at play. I've definitely sent people to inpatient and to the psych ward . . . so I'm laughing because I'm just, like, I know it's not a great place to go, but it's better than people killing themselves. So if you ever need to know trans-informed psych wards, I'm your guy for that in LA.

And then, before we start reaching out to people to see about processes, we really go through the accusations. And one of my favorite exercises is to make a T-chart of what's mine and what's not, because a lot of what happens in these experiences is, like we've said, there's an oversimplified picture being painted of, I'm a bad guy. A lot of people I work with are of masculine experience . . . Take that as you will. And so, yeah, the accusations can include everything from "you were a terrible roommate" to "you dated people and leveraged power dynamics in ways that were really inappropriate and caused a lot of harm." That all gets kind of grouped in together to paint a picture of this person's character as bad. So it's really helpful to go through and separate the accusations, because it'll snowball into this thing of, "you're a pedophile, you're an abuser, you're a sociopath," and it's like, okay, did you actually abuse anybody? Did you actually experience minor attraction, or did you act on any minor attraction? You know, let's really go through this and parse it out.

And generally, what we find is that people are acting from either, again, uppercase-T or lowercase-t trauma, and they've fucked up big time. One of my favorite things to say to my clients, usually, toward the end, when

I've really built trust with them: You fucked up big time, homie, you know? And once we identify, really, what is theirs to own, we stabilize them, their nervous systems, emotionally. Then we can eventually move into taking responsibility, ownership, restorative practices, asking: What do those people need? What can we give them that's going to move us forward, and how do we change our behavior? What does changing behavior look like? And then, most people don't need a public-facing statement, I don't think. Sometimes they have people write what I call an internal statement—like, they just write it for themselves. But yeah, that's an overview of what it looks like.

Mia: Amazing. I love what you're talking about, and I can't help but go to this place of, like . . . what you just outlined is what you do, and what can happen, when someone has, in fact, fucked up big time, and in so many instances, someone just doesn't like somebody else, right? Someone has a bad experience with somebody. Someone is triggered by somebody in a way that has nothing to do with that person in that moment, but has everything to do with their capital-T Trauma from before coming up. And what concerns me so much about that is that it tears communities apart. It pits people against each other in ways that are not helping us fight larger injustices, are not helping us fight systems of oppression, and ultimately are not bringing healing to the individual or the community. It's this wild overreaction instead of being able to just say, "I just don't really like that person." You're allowed to just not like people, find someone annoying, or not get along. You're even allowed to wanna avoid somebody in your life, you know, at a party, at an event, at a venue, without deciding that they don't deserve love, don't deserve friends, or connection, or to be able to afford to live. You can do that without deciding that they're a monster, or a nightmare, or a horrible person, or evil. And I'm so often so confused and heartbroken by what I see. So I'm just wondering how you see those as different: someone has actually seriously fucked up and harmed someone versus hurt somebody's feelings. Or, they just don't like you, and that's somehow not enough.

Risdon: Yeah, so my general rule for what we call accountability coaching—even though I fucking hate that word, "accountability," but whatever. It's just been so co-opted, do you know what I mean?

Mia: Yeah.

Risdon: The person who's caused harm has to be the one who reaches out to me. So, people who have been harmed, or let's say, accusers—I don't want to use that language, I don't know. I've been open to some phone calls from those people, [but] it's never moved forward into work because it [has to] start with the person who's caused harm being willing to change. Regardless, like you said, if it was just a bad breakup or if they did something terrible, if they're not the one initiating it—because they're the one who's going to be paying me, first of all, and they're the one going to be doing the work—then it's just not going to happen. I've worked with people where there were very different extremes of real harm. Like, damn, you really fucked up here, you know what I mean? Like . . . this person was really triggered by your behavior, and we could have done something differently, and some of this isn't yours, and I can still facilitate a conversation for you guys. And maybe there's still something for you to learn here, because you're probably gonna encounter other people with trauma. But this person isn't gonna lose their job. Do you know what I mean?

Mia: Yeah.

Risdon: But I would agree, I just don't really have people come to me who are saying, "I'm being falsely accused of something." A lot of times, it's something that has snowballed and become more grand than it actually is, exaggerated. But it's very rare, for people who come to me, for there not to be some truth, because I think people are wanting to do the work, and there's something to do the work on, if they're coming to me. Does that make sense?

Mia: Totally. To tie this in with consent as a larger theme, I have seen . . . you know, obviously, I love consent. It's so important to me. It's sacred to me, you know? And there's a way that I have seen consent used as a tool for punishment. We've talked about this. And also, I've had so many people come to me who want to do better, who want to learn, who want to be good people, who love and value their community and their friendships. And what they tell me is, "I violated someone's consent. I'm so upset, I think I really fucked up. I violated this person's consent." And then they tell me the story, and I'm like, "No, you didn't. That person just doesn't like what you did."

Risdon: It's like, retroactive.

Mia: Yeah, it's retroactive, for sure. Like, they feel bad at the end of an interaction, and so they look back at what happened to find the moment that they can put a dart in and be like, here's where you fucked up. And then calling something a consent violation is sort of like a conversation-ender, because now you are on the defensive, and all you can do is apologize and promise to do better, when what I'm hearing is that this person just doesn't like a decision that you made, doesn't like something that you said.

Anyway, the reason why I find myself thinking about this so often is that ultimately, I'm so invested in building community, building connection, you know, building long-lasting relationships. And to me, that's what consent is really for. That's what it is a tool for. And so to see it get weaponized in this way is so disheartening. It really makes me really sad, and honestly makes me wonder what I can possibly do . . . . Sometimes I just want to kind of give up and quit what I do, because I'm like, how do I get it across that this is a beautiful way for us to stay connected, when I see it get used so often to tear us apart? I feel like relationships are kind of my life's work. It's almost like an art, you know? It's something that I practice and practice and practice and practice, and it's something that is so important to me. And so, when I'm teaching consent, and I'm talking about consent, and even this book, it's with the goal of helping build more and deeper connection, you know?

Risdon: Yeah, and, you know, something that's coming up for me a lot recently is that I've been faced with a lot of fragility in my life lately. And, when you talk about consent, a word that comes up for me is resiliency. When you, Mia, talk about and teach consent, it's not about yes means yes, no means no, this is a contract—you know, the way we think of a sort of overly simplified version of consent. But it's actually about the space between people, and asking, Where's my no in my body? Do I feel safe to say no to someone? Am I regulated enough to hear no from somebody else and still walk forward with them? That shit is really important, and that is the opposite of fucking fragility, and I think a lot of times when people use consent, yeah, they throw it down like a red card. Consent violation. You know what I mean? The game stops, everyone's like, wrap it up, put them in the box. I can't believe I'm using a fucking sports metaphor right now.

Mia: Who are you?

Risdon: Nobody listening to this is gonna know what I'm talking about. But yeah, it's like you said, it's the sort of time-out button to say consent violation. Because . . . there's sexual assault, right. And then, that's a different thing than being like, hey, Mia, you know, we've definitely had moments, you and I, where I violated your consent. I remember so specifically us eating at this restaurant, and I touched your plate . . . do you remember this?

Mia: Yes.

Risdon: Because I was a people-pleaser, in this very big-sisterly sort of way. And you were cutting your steak, and it was moving the plate around, and I grabbed the plate and held it for you, and you were like, ma'am!

Mia: Yeah, but I would not call that violating my consent, Risdon.

Risdon: No, but it's . . . but it's an interesting thing that that happened however many years ago, and if I had been more fragile, or if you had. Do you see what I'm saying?

Mia: Oh . . . yeah.

Risdon: Like, I feel attacked because I annoyed or bothered Mia, or Mia's like, Risdon doesn't believe I can take care of myself. . . whatever the fucking stories are, you know, but it requires resiliency and trust to be like, I can fuck up. And I feel like the way that people use consent sometimes as this red flag . . .

Mia: Well, but, I mean, you just did it. You were like, I violated your consent, and I'm like, no, you didn't! You didn't violate my consent. You kind of invaded my space in a way that made me feel a little smothered. Like, that's what happened. Yeah, I was annoyed.

Risdon: Yes, I did something you didn't like.

Mia: Right, but if I were in a place where I had very extreme black-and-white thinking, or I wanted to figure out how to get out of a friendship with you without actually processing or establishing boundaries, or having any kind of difficult conversation, I could have decided that that was a consent violation, or a boundary violation, therefore Risdon is bad, and I don't want her in my life anymore, and that's that. You said something about knowing your no in your body, and your yes in your body, but I also want to really address also knowing what it feels like in your body when you feel ready to take a risk that scares you, or when you feel trusting enough of the person that you're with to do something with them that makes you nervous, or even when you feel enough trust and comfort and maybe love with a person that you're willing to do something that you don't even really like because *they* like it. And you choose to do it in such a way that afterward, if you decide that you never want to do it again, it's not their fault.

Risdon: Yes, this is so big. I have two things to say about this. Number one is, this is what sex work is all about. People are like, oh, it's not consensual because you don't "want" to do it.

Mia: No.

Risdon: But I am willing to do it, even if I'm not experiencing desire for the person I'm doing surrogate partner therapy with, for example. I might not be, they're not my type or whatever, but I'm willing to do it because it comes from a place of generosity, and I feel really good educating and helping somebody launch in this way. It gives me incredible self-esteem, do you know what I mean? Even though it's not sexual desire, it's still a willingness and knowing that the positive experience will be there on the other side. Does that make sense?

Mia: Yes, yes, I have an example of—not sex work, but a really great example that I would love to hear what you think of. So, a while ago, my partner was out of town for a while on a job, I think. I asked him if he liked phone sex at all, and I kind of expected him to say no. I just kind of didn't get that vibe from him, you know? And he was like, "I don't really get much out of it, but I'm really good at it." And I loved that, because I was like, that's willingness. That's not wanting but willing. And that's being so happy to do something for me, if I want it. Without his own genuine desire to do the thing.

Risdon: Yeah. Isn't that, like, entirely what parenting is?

Mia: Right!

Risdon: Nobody wants to blow somebody else's nose.

Mia: Ew. No.

Risdon: But you do, or, like, you change a diaper. Or sit in a fucking carpool lane, but you do it because it gives you a sense of self-esteem, right? I'm helping build this person. Yeah.

Mia: Right, right. We could get into a whole conversation about the question, Does altruism exist? That would be the philosophical route to go down. Like, if you're actually getting anything out of it, is there such a thing as a selfless good deed?

Risdon: I wanted to loop back to something you said about exploration . . . I did this workshop with Midori, who's a BDSM educator. Something that she said a lot, and that I appreciated, was, "If I came into the BDSM scene now, I wouldn't have stayed." And she's probably our biggest gift in that community, I would argue.

Mia: Oh, yeah, I mean, she's also one of the most well-known people in that field.

Risdon: Yeah, and I don't want to speak for her, but something that came up a lot was this idea that we have taken all of the joy of discovery, and stretching, and trying something new, and exploration, and we've stripped it into . . . everything needs to be so safe, and so sterile. And I think you brought that up, this thing of being like, I don't know if I like that, but I want to explore it. I mean, especially, I would argue, in kink and BDSM, and with sex to some degree, too, vanilla sex . . . you need a little bit of a willingness. Otherwise, it's not really fun. And the whole point is for things to be fun!

Mia: Well, I also feel like you so often don't know if you like stuff until you try it. I'm thinking of, you know, I was nervous to have sex the first time. I didn't know what I liked or what I wanted. If anyone asked me, I would have been like, I have no idea. You can't have enthusiastic sex if you don't know what you like, and you can't know what you like until you do some experimentation.

Risdon: Yeah, and again, you need this resiliency of being able to be like, I feel safe enough to say "yellow" or "red," to safeword on you.[1] This is why I tell

---

1 The traffic-light system is a common safeword practice in BDSM and kink where "red" means stop, "yellow" means anything from "slow down" to "I need a moment" or "I'm not sure about that," and "green" means "yes, good, more."

tops all the time, you have to vet your bottoms. Are they comfortable saying no to you? Because that's where we get into a lot of trouble, you know what I mean?

Mia: Right. Absolutely. That's how you build trust, and it's a two-way street.

Risdon: Yeah. Anyway. Consent's over. It was fun, we had fun doing it.

Mia: Yeah, yeah, we can put it to bed. It's been co-opted and misused, and now it's over. I'm kidding.

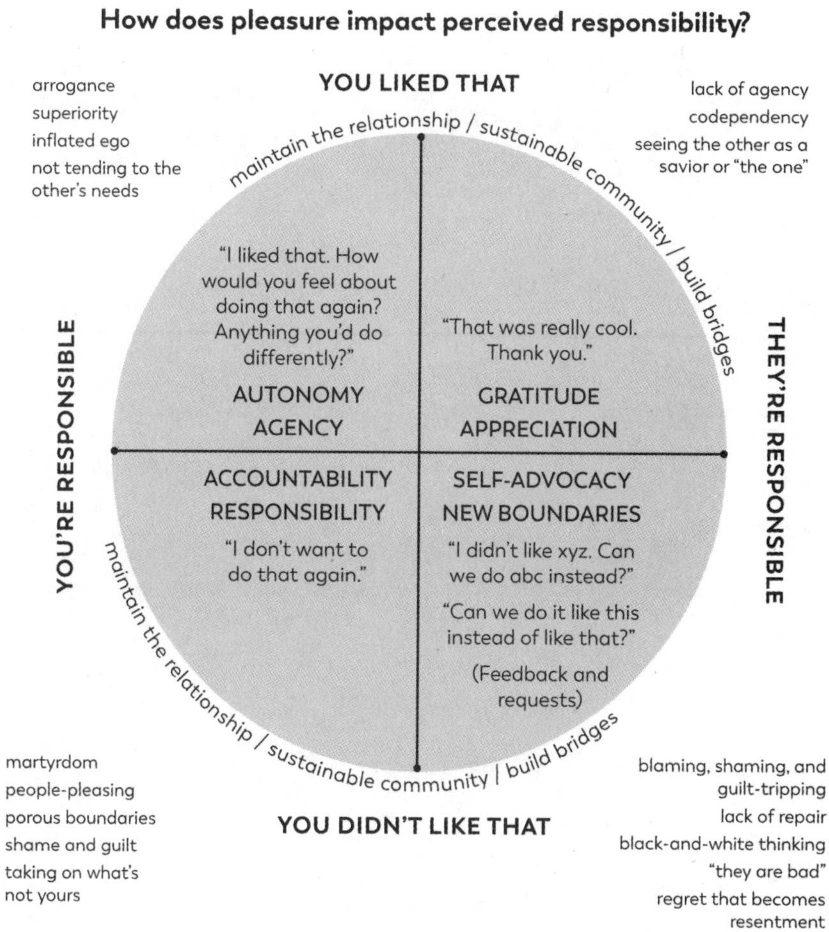

PART VII

CREATIVITY, FINDING YOUR VOICE, AND PUTTING YOURSELF OUT THERE

Consent + Creativity

An Unexpected Link

When I started this work back in 2019, I felt my life rapidly changing. Learning about consent drastically altered my relationship with myself and others and deepened my relationship with my body. This all made sense to me. What did surprise me, though, was how learning consent changed my relationship with my creativity.

As I sat with friends over a potluck dinner this past week, at the home of my dog's puppy's human (my dog had puppies before I adopted her, and I serendipitously found one of the puppies at the dog park last year) we all talked about our relationships to creativity and flow.

"For me, it's been about consent," I said. "Letting my current self to say no to a past self that gave me a to-do list. If I trust that the desire will come and stay open to feeling the creative impulse, then if it's not there, I allow myself to say no."

In order to play, explore, and create, we have to feel safe. Having a personal consent practice has given me a more compassionate relationship with my creativity that has made it easier to find flow because I don't force it. I travel with my sense of safety, knowing that I can feel my desires and needs, ask for them—from myself, from my creative force, from a divine source—and handle whatever answer I get.

That said, I value ritual, which I define as *routine with meaning*. Ritual brings discipline, which is distinct from punishment. For example, I write in my journal every morning. This means that even on days when I don't do any other form of writing, I'm still "a writer." I'm not suggesting that if someone doesn't write every day, they're not a writer; I'm saying that, for me, this practice has helped me maintain that particular sense of my self.

As a creative, there's a constant issue of wanting to want to do something, or wanting to be at the end of a process but not wanting to go through the process. [1] For example, I want to be good at guitar but I don't always want to practice. I want to have the ceramics that I imagine in my mind, but I don't want to get my hands wet and cold.

In consent in our daily life, this could look like wanting to *want* to weed the yard, or wanting the yard to *be weeded*, but not truly wanting to weed the yard. Betty Martin's concept of wanting vs. willingness[2] is apt here: I may be *willing* to weed the yard but not *want* to, and my willingness is enough. I frequently have a list of tasks I simply never want to do (most recently, repairing a mug I shattered and cleaning out the litter box), but from time to time I'll ask myself, "Does that sound horrible right now?" If the answer is no, I'll do it. I know a true desire will never arise, so I check in with some aspect of my willingness. In sex, this might show up as wanting to want to go down on my partner, knowing I'd enjoy it and I'd enjoy their enjoyment of it, but being too tired and having to wake up early, and so choosing sleep. It wouldn't have been the wrong answer or a bad choice to choose sex over sleep. Recognizing the difference between my first-order and second-order desires just gives me more information about how I'm feeling and what I need.

As creatives, wanting to *want* to work, create, or practice is a constant conundrum. I want to write this book, but it's more accurate to say I want to *have written* this book. I want to have a book out in the world. I want to be an author, to be known as a writer, and to be respected for my ideas and opinions, and I want to be able to continue writing books. So I have to write *this* book, even in moments when I don't have a first-order desire to sit down and write.

Sometimes, after many years of wanting to want to do something, it makes sense to let the desire go. If it can't be made into a first-order desire, or never occupies that place in your gut, you may have to reckon with letting go of the dream. All through my mom's career as a magazine editor, she thought

---

1 For more on this, see Harry Frankfurt's writing on first- and second-order desires.

2 I highly recommend her book *The Art of Receiving and Giving: The Wheel of Consent* (Luminare Press, 2021).

she'd write a book when she retired. Once she retired, she tried and tried, but the desire never came. She ultimately ended up taking up photography, her first creative love, and has since learned to use all kinds of equipment and how to do portrait photography, abstract photography, and Photoshop. She's now gotten into gallery shows all over the country. She clung to the second-order desire to write a book for quite some time, finally letting it go and freeing up tons of mental and emotional space and time to make work she truly loved.

But it's tricky! Because making art requires skill, patience, practice, and discipline. Confidence is built through saying, "I'm going to write a book," and then doing it. But arguably, confidence and trust with yourself can also be built by saying, "I'm going to let go of this dream" or, "I'm going to allow this dream to change" as you change. A consent practice with yourself is an incredibly helpful tool in navigating these treacherous waters with many different currents as you check in with yourself and update your maps. You can cultivate a relationship with yourself, with your creativity, and with whatever source you channel from based in consent, reciprocity, and autonomy to support you through the often-painstaking work of creation.

I have a responsibility to foster the conditions in which creativity can flow. This requires money.

The more I've gotten fluent with consent in my life, the more I'm able to ask for what I want and what I need, and believe I deserve those things. I've also gotten more adept at living in alignment with my values while being flexible given the circumstances in which I live and create my art.

There are very real socio-economic and structural barriers to accessing money, but that's not what I'm talking about here. I'm talking about the fact that sometimes, I can create my *own* barriers because of unresolved guilt and shame about having, receiving, and asking for money.

As an artist, no one is going to create the conditions in which my creativity can thrive for me. I have to do this. It's an uphill battle as it is, with the structures set up so that the already-wealthy continue to get wealthier. What I can do is get out of my own way and get on my own team. I can find people who support me, encourage me, and lift me up when they're able, not put me down, guilt-trip me, or become threatened by my success because they're so stuck in their own scarcity mindset.

Money is a strategy, not a value. Within the system as it is currently, we have to have a certain amount of money to live in integrity with our values. In order to fight the current system, we have to live in it, which means we need to have the means to rest, play, and innovate so that we can keep fighting it—and build a new structure as we go.

Attachment healing and letting go

Much to my surprise, as I've healed my attachment wounds and worked toward secure attachment in my relationships, I've seen the healing work show up in my creativity as well.

I took a course on somatic attachment healing in 2022. We were told at one point that having a strong consent and boundaries practice was one of the top three ways to heal attachment wounds. I felt such a deep sense of affirmation, having words to put to the changes I've witnessed in myself and others. For so many of us, our journey into artistic adulthood was paved with criticism, dismissal, rejection, and sometimes even disgust or hatred. We all have core memories that shaped how we view our art and our worth that often only we remember. I didn't get into Madrigals in my middle-school choir and concluded that I couldn't sing, only to learn so many years later to write music and then star in my own musical. We make meaning of these stories and create unnecessary barriers for ourselves.

Working on my attachment has helped me let go of ideas when they're not working, take suggestions with more openness and curiosity, be willing to make garbage on my way to a masterpiece, and trust that if I put a project down, I'll come back to it in due time. I trust my practice and I trust my ability to listen to my body, to whatever I'm channeling, and to the world around me so I can create something only I can make, only in this moment.

Moving from "Is this right?" to "Do I like it?"

In 2019, I asked a friend and coworker if she'd give me guitar lessons. She said, "I've never done that before, and I can't read music." That was exactly what I was looking for.

As a classically trained pianist, I felt stifled by the rules I'd learned. I couldn't improvise, I couldn't write, but boy could I zip through a scale or find you the augmented minor chord in whatever key. Who cares? I wanted to learn to make my own music.

This guitar teacher gave me one of the greatest gifts I've received as an artist: She told me to play something and then asked, "Do you like it?" (The first time, it was four chords from a Taylor Swift song.) Whatever I said, she then told me, "Try it backward." I did, and then the question was, "Which do you like better?" Then she told me, "Now play it major, minor, major, minor." Then, "Minor, major, minor, major." Again, she asked, "Which do you like better?" She helped me cultivate my taste and therefore my voice.

I've long thought that sex is a creative medium, much like any artistic medium. We get to play, create, explore, be curious. We get to try new things, learn new things about ourselves and others, figure out what we like and don't like, and express ourselves authentically. In a sexual encounter, the concern with "doing it right" or doing a "good job" can cloud your ability to listen and gauge what's going on in the moment, as well as separate you from your own desire and pleasure. It's much more advisable to ask yourself, "Do I like this?" and, "How does this make me feel?" Those are better questions to ask someone you're having sex with, too, rather than, "Am I doing this right?" or, "Am I doing a good job?"

The same is true in making art. Art, like consent, isn't math. There's no right answer. There's no formula to follow that will guarantee success. We play, we try new things, we expand our repertoire, and we find what feels good.

Wrestling with my ego

In 2017 I did a ceramics residency in Japan. I was staying in an idyllic town, surrounded by cherry blossoms that bloomed and died in a warm snowstorm-esque flurry of petals everywhere, and all I had to do was make ceramics. But I was more stressed than I've ever been in my life.

I chewed up my lip and the inside of my cheek until it bled. I couldn't stop. I had brought a book on Jewish meditation with me and was journaling and meditating every day, but all I could think about was my ego as an artist. How could I possibly believe that what I had to say and make was worth anyone else's time, and yet, if I didn't, who would? I had to kill my ego so I could believe in myself.

I'm proud to say that now I am my biggest cheerleader, my biggest champion. I am on my own team. I believe what I'm making is important and needs to be put out into the world. I rarely feel my guilt flare, and when it does, I have tools to move through it. I recognize that sure, I could create art in my closet and never share it with anyone, but who would benefit from that? I no longer believe that by sharing my work, I take any space, time, or energy from anyone else; I believe that by sharing my art, I may give permission to others to share theirs.

Here are a few consent practices that can be applied to the creative process:

1. Give yourself five minutes to create, write, or play music, and then teach your body that you can hold that boundary by actually stopping when time is up.
2. Pick up the guitar. Hold it. Feel what it feels like. Open the document and just look at it. Pick up the paintbrush and notice what it feels like in your hand. Do nothing else.
3. Instead of asking yourself, "Is it good?" ask, "Do I like it?"
4. Make dumb shit. Make something for no reason that is totally stupid.

FOMO as a Manifestation of the Pursuit of Perfection

I fell pretty hard for my good friend's girlfriend last year when I was in Costa Rica on a makeshift writing retreat. We can call my friend Jess and her girlfriend Alice. With all my dietary restrictions, one of my go-to, failsafe snacks was sliced cured meat, which is called "lomo," meaning tenderloin. I pulled a package out of my backpack on our weekend trip to Monteverde, and Alice told me, "That's such a move. Like, I would not fuck with someone who pulls meat out of their bag like that."

On another occasion I got some lomo at the grocery store. A stranger sitting outside asked me, "What is that?" I said, "It's lomo." Alice and Jess laughed at me. "It's lomo," they mocked. Later, Jess said, "LOMO is like 'lack of missing out.' Like you're always where you're supposed to be." I said, "Let's get matching tattoos."

I was talking to a friend the other day about perfectionism as paralysis, the panic that sets in at every point of decision-making: "Am I making the right choice or the wrong choice?" This is a binary, and we hate binaries over here. For an artist especially, this will inhibit all kinds of exploration and play. But just in daily life, we can end up spending more time making the choice than doing the thing: Which coffee shop is the right choice for me to get work done in? Tuna or egg salad? This shirt or that shirt?—Fear sets in, especially when we don't know if and how we can get out of the results of the choice we've made.

The nitpicking can go on forever. I've learned that part of making art is knowing when to stop. You can always keep going, but you have to choose when to move onto the next thing. This is a skill in and of itself. Making the next piece is the time to incorporate all you've learned from the process of making the last piece.

FOMO—the fear of missing out—I think largely comes from a fear of making the wrong choice, an endless string of questions like, "What if I'd done the other thing?" But what if you're right where you're supposed to be? What if, when you feel a pang of regret, you could inquire within as to why and use the information you find to make a different choice next time?

There's a conversation about fate in here—about free will vs. determinism. I *mostly* believe that we have very little choice. I understand the irony of holding this belief as a consent educator, but I think if you dig into my work and my thinking on justice, you'll find it's pretty consistent with how I teach. I believe we are *mostly* a product of our circumstances, contexts, relationships, the media we're exposed to, and other forces outside our control. In my work in consent, I ask a lot of questions about why we act the way we do, why we believe what we believe, and what leads us to cause harm. When I studied philosophy in college, these questions were constantly part of the conversation. When I began studying neuroscience and nearly changed my major, I saw the supposed conflict between the two areas of study: Philosophers largely want to believe that humans have free will, whereas neuroscientists largely want to prove that we don't have much choice at all and everything is determined.

I think of the compatibilist view (that both are true) as being like a river: There are certain places where the water can change course, but they're few and far between, and they also have some predetermined circumstances. I've also heard it compared to a tree with different branches, but the choices are not infinite, nor are any of us entirely in control of which we choose. The philosopher Thomas Nagel wrote a piece called "What It's Like to Be a Bat" that posits a compatibilist view, suggesting that no matter how much we can study a brain, we will never know what it's like to be that person or creature, and so, essentially, trying to figure out "which is true" is pointless.[1]

Thinking about choice in this way requires most of us to adjust our view of justice—what justice means and how it can or should be enacted. If we don't have free will, if our lives are largely written for us by our circumstances, our

1 Thomas Nagel, "What It's Like to Be a Bat," *The Philosophical Review* 83, no. 4 (1974): 435–450, https://doi.org/10.2307/2183914.

DNA, our upbringing, our education (or lack thereof), and the systems we're born into, how can we punish each other for choices we are so often forced to make? This line of questioning completely contradicts the tenets on which our so-called justice system is built. It's not easy to move the foundational pieces of a punitive justice worldview to make space for a restorative one and get all the other pieces to Tetris neatly into place, but this is the work I've set out to do.

Now, when it comes to FOMO, a belief in fate can be very soothing. *You are exactly where you're supposed to be.* Of course, when there are factors at play such as depression, illness, disability, restraint, anxiety, paranoia, poverty, and the like, we may need help not only to make decisions but to get out of bed. But in this essay, I'm focusing on making the choices that shape our lives when we find ourselves in the driver's seat, when we have at least some sense of choice, and I do believe that whether or not choice actually exists, the illusion of it is crucial.

When I was seventeen, I applied Early Decision to Sarah Lawrence College, knowing that this meant I was locked in if I got accepted. It was there that I met someone who, many years later, asked me to write a movie about a sex choreographer. In the process, I found out about intimacy coordinators, and I interviewed someone doing that work as part of my research for the script. She then trained me to do the job myself, and my company Consent Wizardry was born a year later.

Recently, I worked on a movie in this very position of intimacy coordinator. I almost didn't go to the wrap party, but I did, and I fell completely in love with someone I met that night. A little over a year later, the printed script of *Just Sex*—the movie I wrote that led me to become an intimacy coordinator—sits in the garage of the home we share together. I don't know how it got there, as I can't remember finding it when I was packing up my apartment. I got chills when I found it presented precisely in front of my car as I parked, almost like it was waiting for me, winking at me. I told my partner, "This script is responsible for us even having this garage, living here, and even meeting in the first place."

I could have had a perfectly lovely evening at home that night, but I chose to go. One way to interpret this story would be that I should say yes more often; I should go to the party, figuratively and literally. "What about all the times I opted to stay on the couch instead? Who might I have met?" And yet, the more

I feel into it, the more I believe that something inside of me, or outside of me, knew that I had to go to *this* party. This comes from a lot of trust and a lot of faith in the magic woven through my life. It's a feeling that I'm protected, that something is looking out for me. It feels like all the intentions I've set changed the beacon that I am and attuned my light to find what I was looking for across a dark ocean, through thick fog. We came together due to a choice I made at seventeen, one that was no doubt informed by countless choices I had made before and countless choices my parents had made before that.

At the end of my time in Costa Rica, Alice tattooed a chain of linked hearts over my shoulder that looks like it's melting into liquid as it drops from my collar bone to my chest. They also gave me a "LOMO" tattoo on my wrist. Jess didn't get one. Back in LA, I felt the shock of not knowing when or if I'd ever see Alice again. I wanted them next to me on my couch. Just their presence. I asked friends, pleading, "What do I do?" and each of them said, "Nothing, Mia. You do nothing." *I guess I have to let it roll off me like water,* I kept saying. Looking in the mirror, the melting chains took on new meaning. *Let it roll off like water.* I looked down at "LOMO" on my wrist: *I am exactly where I'm meant to be.* And so is Alice.

Consent as a Path Toward Knowing Yourself

As I see it, there are three main components to getting what you want:

1. Knowing what you want
2. Believing you deserve it
3. Asking for it

But there are many barriers to each step.

1. Knowing what you want

What do you actually want? This kind of interrogation makes consent possible. It means that I am fully present in the room. Knowing what you want may require you to do some digging into the most honest crevices of your mind. Are your desires truly your own, or are they what you think you're supposed to want?

I think at this point, a lot of people's minds go to romantic comedies and porn. They try to parse out their authentic, inherent desires from those that are learned. But I don't really care where your desires came from, I care what they *are* and what they are *now*. I care about supporting people in getting those desires met safely and consensually, not repressing them or hierarchizing them based on how you got them.

But this also begs an age-old philosophical question: Can the self ever be fully known?

I don't believe so. I think there will always be parts of ourselves we can't know, can't see, and can't access. Some of this is inherited and some made opaque to us by the demands of our society. There are some things we simply cannot face and some that simply remain unknowable due to their incomprehensibility by our human brains. I also think the self is a moving target; we constantly change, impacted by our experiences, our relationships, our ever-changing bodies, time, global events, politics, and new ideas.

We might initially draw the conclusion that consent is therefore impossible. But if we remember the fluidity of consent as an ongoing practice, we can see that consent can hold the unknown. We discuss and agree to risks, and we can surrender to what we can't know. In her book *Sexuality Beyond Consent*, Avgi Saketopoulou argues for what she calls a "negative" model of consent.[1] She suggests that instead of the traditional "affirmative" model where we say, "I'd like to do xyz," "I like this kind of sex," and, "Yes, that's okay," we use a negative model, where we delimit the bounds of what we're agreeing to by clearly stating what we *don't* want to do, and then we agree to the unknown within those bounds. This removes the frameworks of blame and punishment that so often follow any feelings of regret. It opens up space for checking in and giving each other feedback, discussing what came up that might have been surprising, anything you'd like to do differently in the future, and anything you don't want to do again.

As I've said before in this book, I don't really know how anyone can be expected to know what they want before they try things. I don't know anyone who knew what they liked sexually *before* they started having sex. You learn through trying. My partner made a suggestion just last night to me for something to try in bed that had never occurred to me (and would never have occurred to me), but I was very intrigued, tried it, and loved it. Cool—new thing in the repertoire.

2. Believing you deserve it

It might be easy to believe you deserve "a good relationship" or "love" but less easy to believe you deserve some of your more subversive and covert desires. And for some, it might even be difficult to believe you deserve a good

1 Avgi Saketopoulou, *Sexuality Beyond Consent* (New York University Press, 2023).

relationship and love! I often struggle to believe I deserve the kind of care and support I receive from my partner.[2]

But even beyond romantic relationships or sex, you might struggle to believe you deserve to get paid well for your work or art, to have the home life you so deeply crave, to eat that lavish sushi dinner and get the sake or the uni, to have good friends who show up for you, or to be taken care of when you're sick. It might be easier to believe that *other* people deserve those things, and even to give those things to other people, than it is to believe that *you* deserve them.

Confidence itself is a practice. We practice when we look in the mirror and say, "You look great," or, "I love your cheeks." We practice when we notice how good we are at things we take for granted because we've been doing them for so long that they come easily to us, like chopping garlic, making jam, catching something we dropped, rolling a joint, folding a T-shirt. When skills become mindless, we may not notice our aptitude for them. Making them conscious can help build confidence. "Look how good I am at using this kitchen knife." "I really like that thing I just played on the piano." "I'm getting so fast at this crochet stitch!" You can remind yourself of these things while also quieting the voice that comes in to explain why you're not actually so good, knock you down for lacking some other skill, or compare you to others.

We also have to contend with all the social and cultural factors that tell us we don't deserve what we want. The constant messaging we receive from ads, magazines, movies, TV, and music will tell us that there's something wrong with us, but if we spend money on a particular product, we will be more desirable or feel better about ourselves: "Did you know you stink and it makes you unappealing to possible romantic partners? Here's some deodorant with pink packaging so you know it's for women." It's all too easy to compare your body, your hair, your face, your creative output, your income, your partner (or your partnerlessness), or your home to those of other people, including people you

2 I'm taking breaks from writing this to hop off my bed and help him build the shelving unit he designed for our kitchen. I just held up the two sides while he attached them to the base. At one point he stood face to face with me to adjust the sides, looked up at me, smiled, and kissed me. Peak domesticity. To that end, we recently had a friend of mine over. He offered to cook for her for her birthday. She asked for a "Mia meal," so he made steak, potatoes, and broccolini. She asked how it was going, setting up the house and stuff. He said, "I find a lot of joy in domesticity." I think I fell a little more in love.

don't even know! Social media makes this even more constant and subconscious. It's a brutal world we live in, made more brutal when we succumb to the messaging and participate in it ourselves, in our own minds. But without believing we deserve what we want and need, it's nearly impossible to ask for it—and ask for it with confidence.

3. Asking for what you want

Now you have to say it out loud, with words, to other people. I know, I'm sorry. For better or worse, other people can't read our minds. Or maybe they can, to some extent (I like to say, "I may be psychic, but I can't read your mind"), but we can't rely on that, so we have to express ourselves verbally.

One of the beautiful things I've found about having to speak my desires is that the process of finding the words helps me identify the specificity of the desire and helps me stand in my belief that I deserve it. I also have to be honest, by which I mean I can't lie, even via people-pleasing. I can't say I want something because I think *you* want it or I think you *want me* to want it. I have to have done the aforementioned self-excavation.

My partner has taught me to do this during sex. I have to say what I want, and sometimes I have to say it three times. If I just repeat what he's said, he'll often tell me to say it in my own words. Unless I'm willing to lie, I have to be in touch with my desires, moment to moment. I love this method of practicing consent during sex. Hearing myself say what I want is unbelievably hot. Hearing me say what I want or confirming that I want what he wants gives him full permission to do it without hesitation. He gets to do things to me no one else has ever gotten to do because I trust him so much—largely through this process, but also through rupture and repair (see: "We Both Got Too High and Had Sex Anyway"). With him, I've found new things I like that I didn't even know were desires I had or could have.

I also have to be prepared to hear no. Believe it or not, working on the part about believing I deserve what I want makes it much easier to hear no. It's easier to divorce myself from the desire, meaning that *I'm* not being rejected, *my desire* is. And that's okay; that's not about me, and that's actually about the other person's desires or boundaries. Believing I deserve what I want also helps me let go of wanting it with one particular person and allows me to try to find it elsewhere (in a nonmonogamous paradigm, if we're talking about sex).

If you can't ask for what you want, you're going to manipulate people into giving it to you through mind games and deception. You'll couch your requests as offers, trying to convince other people that they want what you want. You'll get resentful when people can't read your mind. You may even just take what you want without asking, checking in, or updating any agreements made previously because you feel owed or because you don't know how else to get it. But the asking is part of the practice. Naming a desire is like casting a spell. It's part of how we become known to ourselves and others, how we grow, and how we connect.

There Is Magic in Desire; Asking for What You Want Is the Spell

When I first started teaching consent, I was really invested in helping people say no. I found "no" to be a magic word, opening up space for other things that you truly love when you reduce the stuff in your life that feels like a drag. But as I've grown in this work, I've gotten more and more passionate about helping people say yes.

I have a history of saying things or writing things that come true. As I mentioned earlier in this book, I became an intimacy coordinator because I was writing a script about one, met one IRL, asked to interview her for my movie, and then was trained by her. It's happened so many times that I have to be very careful what I write or say. Sometimes when I want to write something, I'll ask myself, "Are you okay with this coming true?" Because if not, I shouldn't write it. Now, when I say something that I don't want to come true, I pound my fists together three times and say, "This is not a spell."

In my teens and early twenties, I often shied away from setting concrete goals or having dreams for my future, because I thought that if I never clearly stated what I wanted, I would be able to avoid most disappointment and embarrassment from failure. But at twenty-seven or so, something shifted. I began to name my desires. I don't recall quite what caused the shift, but I remember understanding that I wasn't going to get stuff that I didn't ask for, and I *definitely* wasn't going to get stuff that I didn't even know I wanted, so I needed to figure out what I wanted and be willing to go out on a limb asking for it.

When I began teaching consent in 2019, I experienced a spike in synchronicity in my life. I once left a Zoom meeting with a new friend I had met online through mutuals during the 2020 COVID lockdown, only to get on another Zoom with two people who'd cold-emailed me and find out that they knew my new friend. Soon after that, I ordered a book online called *Decolonizing Non-Violent Communication*, and by the time it arrived in the mail I had met and become friends with the author, Meenadchi. (My interview with Meenadchi is in Part 1 of this book.) I could go on and on.

Others reported the same experience. People who took my classes told me stories of what felt like cosmically divined encounters, asking for something and receiving it within days, whether it was a job opportunity or an email or a date. Someone signed up for a course with me with a very extended payment plan due to financial strain, only to get hired with the highest salary of their life within a couple weeks of starting. My understanding of the magic of consent deepened, and I called my company Consent Wizardry.

But there are certain conditions that have to be met to promote this kind of magic. We have to be able to *want*, which is to say, we have to have our needs met so we can dream, fantasize, desire something more. Struggling to survive doesn't leave much space for wanting anything else. The magic isn't in *need*; the magic is in *desire*.

Hopefully, as you read this, you're able to dream. I hope that at the very least, you're able to set aside some time for intentional daydreaming beyond your current circumstances. There are so many barriers to dreaming, barriers to survival, and barriers to desire—societal, financial, cultural, identity-based, political.

One of my favorite stories of asking for what you want is about Bobbie Esposito. A former student (now friend and colleague), Bobbie came to me because they wanted to work with kids on TV sets as an advocate, helping them navigate consent and boundaries as minors working with adults in a high-pressure industry. They were calling their proposed position a "Youth Coordinator." The only training they could find that could foster their education was intimacy coordination training, which focuses on supporting actors in scenes involving simulated sex and nudity. They wanted to learn and adapt the protocols to working with kids, and yet they were turned away by major training programs who feared industry blowback from a misunderstanding of what Bobbie was trying to do, wrongly associating kids with simulated sex and nudity. I told Bobbie I would train them.

Bobbie joined my Consent Education Training Program and followed it up with intimacy coordination training. They combined what they had learned and tailored it to children, inventing not only their own job but their own field. Bobbie has since invented yet another job for themself: After developing consent and boundaries courses for kids who rock climb, they pitched a job to their rock-climbing gym and got hired with a serious and respectable salary. Bobbie dared to dream beyond what anyone already knew and then created that world, a world we all now live in.

Some of my best ideas come to me in the shower or on a walk. I encourage my students to *cultivate shower thoughts*. This requires them to set aside time to . . . do nothing. To stop working. To step out of their routine, intentionally. But it's not just changing the task or the activity or the scenery: You actually have to actively shift your thoughts. I can go for a walk and end up ideating an infographic, and by the time I'm turning the key back at home, I've pretty much drafted a new Substack essay and accompanying Instagram posts in my head. You have to put metaphorical blinders on your thoughts and let your mind wander. You can prompt yourself by asking, "What do I feel most drawn to right now?" Maybe the answer is writing music, or maybe it's circles, or the color periwinkle. If you catch yourself hating on something in your community or city, you can ask, "What changes would I like to see?" And then, "What role am I drawn to in making that change?"

Let's explore some ways to identify our dreams and make them reality. Before we cast some spells, here are some terms:

Magic: "Any moment of connection, communication, or cooperation between entities . . . be it between two people, you & the sky, a community of trees, a person & their ancestral team, the lungs & the heart." (This was the response of my friend Brooks Herr-Cardillo when I asked them how they define magic.) Synchronicity, serendipity, and a feeling of simultaneous creation and discovery; a feeling of transcendence and experiencing something larger than yourself; being in flow.

Container: The space in which magic is *performed*; the space in which boundaries are established and consent is practiced, beyond which new boundaries need to be established and new agreements need to be made.

Ritual: Routine with meaning; a practice that helps us open and close containers. Ritual can uplift an action or process. It can also prepare your nervous system (e.g., prayer before a meal tells our bodies we're about to eat and need to get into our rest-and-digest, parasympathetic nervous system).

Ready?

1. Tune in. Get comfortable, closing your eyes if you want to, and take a deep breath. I like to do this in the bath.
2. Set the intention / name the desire. *Say it out loud*—this is very important! Don't just throw it away or say it like it's a question; don't shrug it off like it's no big deal. Notice your prosody. Do you *believe* that you want it? Do you believe you deserve it? Say it like you mean it. Try saying it like you already have it.
3. Be specific! Specificity is a creative muscle. It takes focus and precision. It's also how you hear your voice come through. I don't just want love, I want a partner who likes animals, who cooks, who wants to build a life with me, and who takes care of themself. I don't just want to make "more money." I could make one more dollar next year and technically I'd have accomplished my goal. I want to make $150,000, $300,000, $500,000. I can tell you right now . . . as I wrote those numbers down, I believed in their achievability less and less as they increased. My work is to *believe* these goals are not just possible but realistic and even easy to achieve.
4. How do you want to *feel?* This is crucial, because sometimes the specifics change, and that's okay, but you should be able to keep the feeling that you want. For example, the feelings of the things I want in my life include freedom of movement, autonomy, relaxation, security, and abundance. I live in Los Angeles right now, and I'd need to make $300,000 a year to be able to buy a house on my own, save for retirement, have a child as a solo parent, and have some left over to travel, get a better car, and so on. However, if I were to move to Omaha, Nebraska, my cost of living would go down significantly and I would need much less money in order to feel those desired feelings *and* be able to have a lot of those things. So I may ask for $300,000/year, but if I end up moving to Omaha, that amount could change while still giving me the things I want.

5. How will you know when you achieve these things? In order to avoid perpetually moving the goal post, lay out in advance how you'll know when you've reached your goal. This will hold you accountable, so you don't keep kicking the can down the road.
6. Now, listen . . . just listen. Notice your thoughts as they pass. Move your body as you feel the impulse. Let out a sound if your throat opens. We're not pushing ourselves to do anything in particular, but we're listening to what comes and obliging when we receive instructions.

Change and augment this practice as needed, or as you feel called to. Ultimately the magic is in you and around you, so you can find your own process of tapping into it. This is what works for me.

Happy spell-casting! Be careful not to underestimate your power. :)

Something Bigger than Yourself

I think that when people first meet me, they find it very surprising to learn that I believe in god. They see me as very rational, as a believer in science and reason, and they see a belief in god as contradictory to those principles. But those who know me well know that I am fascinated by what we can't know and can't prove, and they know me to be someone who doesn't really believe in binaries, someone who perpetually lives in the gray.

I don't think that science and religion are mutually exclusive, nor science and spirituality, nor science and god. But even if they were, I actually think that believing in god is one of the most rational choices a person can make—and I do believe it is a choice.

In 2019, when I was at my sickest, I was getting ready to die. I thought that if my body didn't simply give out, I'd have to choose an exit strategy—not because I wanted to die, but because I wanted to live, and the life I was living wasn't it. I did a lot—*a lot*—of research on how people healed from autoimmune and gut-related illness, as well as what's called "radical remission," when people with terminal cancer diagnoses suddenly and often inexplicably improve and even fully recover from illness. I watched a documentary that I would now be hard pressed to find (I can't even remember what it was called), but it looked at hundreds of people who experienced healing against all odds and what they had in common. The most common life changes and choices included several things I was already doing (changing your diet, herbal treatments, movement/exercise, a mindfulness practice, an active social life), but one I hadn't yet considered: Believing in something larger than yourself. You can call it god, the universe, or whatever you want, but the results were clear that the belief itself had healing qualities. I remember being shocked by statistics (my own research shows the same) showing that people who believe in god live longer, on average, and heal faster from wounds and surgeries. There's a correlation between a belief in god and a stronger immune system and better mental health. At the time, I was so desperate I thought, "Sure, why not?" I would have tried anything, and I just about did. This was one more prescription of sorts.

Ritual, spirituality, and a belief in something larger than you are good for you. I'd heard the same about yoga, about an anti-inflammatory diet, about meditation (what is meditation if not prayer?), and so many other things I had been willing to try without hesitation. How was this any different? When I say I think believing in god is one of the most rational things a person can do, what I mean is that if you look to science for how to be healthier, happier, and live longer, believing in god is a proven way to achieve those goals.

But I knew I couldn't fake it for it to work. I had to really let myself go there. Surrender. So here's where I landed:

1. I don't think something that doesn't exist can affect change.
2. Believing in god changes me.
3. Therefore god exists.

To put it another way, the belief in god and god are one and the same. That's faith. The rest is unknown, and that's where I choose to surrender.

Okay, what the heck does this have to do with consent? One more bit of background before I tie it all together: When I was twenty, I took a theater-acting class with a woman named Sondra Lee. Theater acting is very different from TV or film acting. You pore over a text until it becomes totally embodied, not just learning the words of the script and where to cross stage-left when, but letting it seep into your body and flow through you. Sondra used to say, "You have to do the homework until you can forget the homework." You listen deeply to your scene partner/s, you react honestly, and you don't plan ahead. You have to be incredibly present. This is why I don't think actors make good liars, contrary to popular belief.

At the time, acting was the closest thing I'd found to a spiritual practice. The mindfulness of acting brought me closer to myself. The practice helped me achieve transcendence, flow, and an out-of-body experience of tapping into something beyond myself. I surrendered control to the moment, to the space between me and my scene partner, to the text, to the playwright who might be dead, or at least was rarely in the room. I was able to tap into a deep kernel of humanity within myself, something that tied me to every other person, alive or dead or not yet born.

Then I found consent. When I began learning about consent beyond "no means no," in a way that incorporated trauma, boundaries, the body, risk, and my relationship with myself, I once again found myself with something akin to a spiritual practice. I had to listen to myself and others, react honestly, and be incredibly, deeply present. I had to continually make updates based on any and all new information that came my way (including nonverbal information) from myself and others, rather than just continuing with my goal or plan.

This kind of listening—full-body listening—is how I seek guidance from and commune with something bigger than myself.

My bat mitzvah was October 12, 2002. At the time I'm writing this, we're just about back to where we were then in the annual cycle of Torah reading (in which different portions are read each week of the year), which means we're reading the same portion that I had to learn to read twenty-three years ago: Noah's ark. I wrote my drash (interpretation or speech) on climate change and George W. Bush's treacherous environmental policies.

Upon revisiting the portion in fall of 2024, I focused on a quote that I hadn't really paid much mind to all those years ago: "Noah walked with god." Many interpreters have written that Noah may have needed god's help to walk, but "If we're considering the interpretation of that phrase to mean that Noah needed god's help, don't we also need to consider the interpretation that god needed Noah's help? Just logically speaking," I asked.

The rabbi facilitating, Aaron Leven, who I'm lucky enough to be friends with, seemed surprised. He said, "Write that drash."

I never wrote it (maybe I am now), but that interpretation of the passage has changed my prayers ever since. Every Shabbat service, we're given time for a silent prayer. One of the many things I love about Judaism is the way we're encouraged to build our own theology and have our own, unique relationship with god, whatever god is to us. For a few years now, in my prayers I've expressed gratitude for my clarity of purpose in life. Since October 7, 2023, I've prayed for the families of the dead in Gaza, that they may find healing. I've also thought about the increasing number of lost souls, automatons, or zombies doing the bidding of the money-hungry, murderous narcissists who currently run some of the most powerful countries in the world, and I've asked god to help them find their souls again. But since that day in Torah study, thinking about Noah helping god, I've also asked how I can help god. "What do you need? How can I best be of service?" In consent terms, I've gone from making requests to making offers.

If this is a leap for you to think that perhaps there's something you could offer something like god, I'd like to challenge you on your humility. You might think, "God doesn't need my help. God is omnipotent and all-powerful; how could god need help from little old me?" Even if you're not a believer, perhaps you think that *if there were* a god, god wouldn't need the help of humans.

But this is where I often find myself suspicious of humility. I'm all for being honest and realistic about one's capabilities, but when humility stops us from thinking we could have anything to offer the world or those around us, we hoard our gifts. When humility leads us to deny the power and influence we have, we are almost guaranteed to waste it at best and abuse it at worst. You can remain confident without losing your humility by knowing what you can and can't offer and being clear about the difference.

A friend of mine recently called me crying because she's having sudden and serious health issues. She's having to change how she eats, how she relates to her body, and how she relates to her partner, her friends, and her larger community. She asked me how I do it, how I moved through the grief.

First, I told her, don't rush it. Grieve. Mourn. You are different—different from other people and different from who you were before. Your life is not what it was. Don't rush your feelings about that. You have to change how you perceive yourself. Your identity shifts: You are disabled.

Second, know that how you feel right now—scared, anxious, stressed, sad—is not how you will feel forever. You will build new habits that will become second nature, like checking the nutrition labels on foods. You will get better at asking for what you need. You will find the foods that work for you, the restaurants where you feel safe to eat, and the recipes you like to cook. (Upon hanging up, I created a Substack account called "No Burden Recipes" for low-impact, anti-inflammatory meals.)

But the third thing I said, which I think feels most significant, is that you will learn to listen to your body in deeper and more intimate ways, which will ultimately bring you closer to god. When you practice consent with yourself, when you practice full-body listening *with yourself*, you deepen your relationship with god. I knew who I was talking to when I said this, and I wouldn't have said it to just anyone. This friend is a practicing Muslim, and we talk about god from time to time.

It's curious to me how many people believe in finding their purpose or their soulmate, or feel that their partner and they were "meant to meet," but say they don't believe in anything bigger. They'll say they believe in science, as though science and faith were mutually exclusive. And then there's those who feel that any mention of god feels like pressure to have the same beliefs as the person speaking. (Maybe you're feeling this right now.) On TikTok, I posted a video that said this and only this: "Here's my take on god. I find that believing in something larger than me brings meaning to my life, so I . . . choose to believe in something larger than me. That's it." The comments ranged from, "That's fine, but the problem is when people push their beliefs on other people," to accusing me of being delusional or dumb for believing in something, which I see as . . . atheists pushing their beliefs on me and everyone else.

Consent is showing up in a few places here, huh? I'm talking about the full-body listening that I mentioned earlier. I've talked about the link between consent and creativity, and I believe that when we achieve a flow state we tap into something larger than ourselves. I'm talking about finding purpose and meaning, and I do believe that when we practice consent in this deeper, embodied way beyond contracts, beyond permission, beyond yes and no, we often begin to pick up on things we didn't use to notice, which can feel spiritual, like a channeling. I'm talking about consent bringing you closer to your body. And I'm talking about consent regarding forcing beliefs on others. I've mentioned *choosing* to believe. Yes, a choice. And isn't consent ultimately about choice?

I'm finding more and more that musicians and trans people seem to believe in something larger than themselves more frequently than other people in my life do. Perhaps it's because we listen differently. Perhaps it's because we find flow as we remove the friction from the outside world and simultaneously uncover and create our selves. But I've also noticed that so many people around me do believe in something larger than themselves, even if they don't want to call it god. If at one point we thought science would replace religion, I hope we can move toward a compatibilist view that allows us all to find meaning in our lives and allow each other to believe whatever we each *choose* to believe.

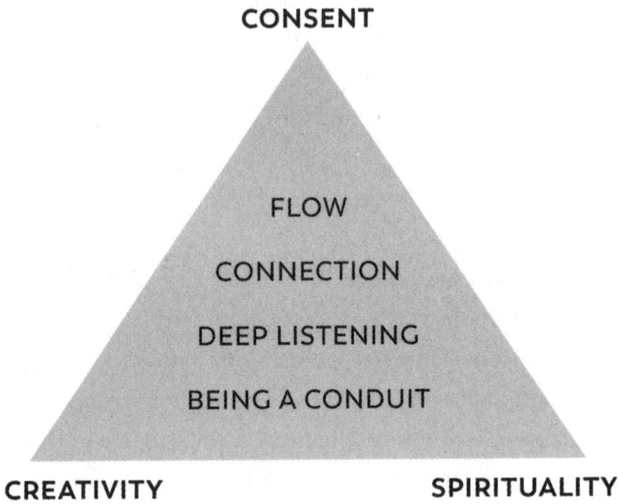

Interview with jo Valdés and bahar baharloo

BDSM, Kink, and Creative Sexual Expression

jo Valdés is always doing the most, to say the least. They're a queer, nonbinary, Afrolatinx writer; a sexpert, intimacy coordinator, cultural worker, foodie, barista, and sometimes DJ. They have an absolute obsession with kink, BDSM, and leather. They've recently been published in Condé Nast's *Them* and *Our Time Press*. Right now, they are working on a pilot TV show about the queer underground in New York City as well as a nerdy book about kink and neuroplasticity. jo is currently based in Flatbush, Brooklyn. They were born and bred in the Boogie Down Bronx so they rep the Yankees really hard even though they don't know shit about baseball.

bahar baharloo is an Iranian, queer, trans, nonbinary intimacy coordinator and bike mechanic based in New York City. Their background in theater and acting often explored themes of gender and sexuality, paving the way to their role as a sex educator and consultant. They are passionate about biking, karaoke, and tinned fish. You can find them on Instagram @baharloo.intimacy

Mia: jo, you were saying that you want a work dom/me?

jo: I want a work dom. Yes.

Mia: To do what?

jo: To make me meet my deadlines. I think that it's helpful to be bossed around by someone that is not me, in a lot of areas of life.

Mia: I love this, particularly because I feel like so many people are inclined to hate their bosses; it's almost built into workplace culture. But now that you're working for yourself, you're like, "Oh man . . . there was something about that." [*Both laughing*]

jo: Yes. For my own business, if I had a boss that was hired to boss me around, I'd just work for that person. I would be like, "Oh my god, yes, make me work on my calendar today, I'll do anything for you." [*All laughing*] That's how I really feel about it.

Mia: I get it, I relate.

bahar: I feel, for some reason—and maybe it's the top in me being like, "Don't tell me what to do"—but I can't have that. I have a little app that tells me when my plants need to be watered, and I'm like, "I know, shut up!"

Mia: I gave myself a reminder on my phone a few months ago for when I was gonna be PMSing, just like, "You might be PMSing right now, in case you're having a rough few days," and when the reminder went off, I was like, "I know, bitch! Don't tell me how I'm supposed to feel!" *I* set the reminder! [*All laughing*]

bahar: Super condescending of you to remind me. Thank you.

Mia: Exactly!

jo: Yeah, I think that it's funny, because in every area of my life, typically, as soon as I have a boss, as soon as I sign my onboarding paperwork, we're fighting. I don't like you. Even if I like you, I don't want to like you. Adversarial headbutting—it's been this way my whole life. I'm completely resistant to authority. Every scenario. Except for in kink, usually, where I'm just like, I will bottom out for . . . it just is a thing that feels so much more natural to me. And I think that because there's so much intimacy with working for yourself and working at home, even in part, that that amount of self-reflection also breeds space for me to think about it that way. Just, like, god, if there were a way that I could be bottoming out for myself in a way that would feel effective, I don't know.

Mia: Well, you're making me think . . . I have a theory as to why those are different. I'll tell you my theory, and then I want to hear why you think they're different. I'm thinking that, in a dom/sub dynamic, the sub has a lot of control over what happens. Whereas, in a boss-employee dynamic, the employee really doesn't. So it feels entirely different.

bahar: Yeah . . . we're boiling domming down to just being an authority. It's not necessarily just authority. It's so much more; there's a back and forth. . . . It's not necessarily about being paid to be there. It's a whole slew of other things that you are exchanging in a dom/sub relationship versus, "You're my boss."

Mia: Right, and ultimately, jo, in the dynamic that you're talking about, that person is in service to you and your goals.

jo: Y'all are making really good points here. Exactly. Yeah, I think that link is so much more than authority, and I think that I do also think about labor. Maybe it's also because of my work background and having had a lot of different kinds of jobs. I often feel very empowered at work in a lot of ways, because I'm like, you rely upon me to keep your business running. And also that could be just because of the way that kink is kind of woven into my marrow, and it makes me think about power across the board. It's almost the opposite when I'm by myself, you know what I mean? Does that make sense?

bahar: Sort of? It's the opposite when you're by yourself, how so?

jo: I don't know. I think I need to sit with that a little bit.

bahar: If you're saying to a boss, "You need me. If I'm not here, no work gets done, and you don't have a job," but in terms of yourself—are we talking about the *need* aspect?

jo: I think I was more thinking about the labor aspect of what is being offered. When you're in a work situation, and you're working for a boss, I feel like you're offering your labor, you're offering this thing that your boss often can't fulfill on their own, or without you in any capacity.

I have to let the bones on that thought cook a little bit more. I haven't really thought about that before, until having this conversation. Why does it feel so different to be laboring for yourself and in service to yourself, when the power dynamic is, in fact, subverted? It's like, oh, if I do this thing for myself, then I will be able to be prosperous. Or maybe it's some kind of internalized resentment toward the boss man. Or whatever.

bahar: Well, I have a perspective on that, because I used to be a boss, I used to be the manager of a place, and what I perceived my job to be was to take care of my employees and have their interests in mind so that we all could have a happy and productive workplace. But there was such a culture of mistrust, and whether it was within the culture of the place I was working or it's just part of this infrastructure of our society that the boss is bad—regardless of what I did, I often would just get misunderstood, and my actions were misconstrued as harm all the time. I mean, I was the boss of these people, but I had a bigger boss, and I was essentially a messenger of this bigger boss who was never around and didn't really know what the needs of my employees were, you know, so . . .

Mia: And didn't you also go from being one of those employees to getting promoted? Yeah, I mean, I think that dynamic is also really complicated.

One thing that you're all making me think of is, I have a friend who's a rabbi, and at one point, we were talking about the subby nature of religion, and how getting these directives of, "Here's how to be good, and here are the rules, and the structure, and just follow the things that I tell you to do, or that this book tells you to do," can be really freeing, and really gratifying, because it's so clear, and you know exactly what you're supposed to do. It kind of blew his mind, and he brings it up a lot. I really loved thinking about it that way. jo, you were talking about how kink is woven into the marrow of your bones and makes you think about power in so many different ways. Thinking about religion in this way kind of allowed me to look at power within the context of religion in a way that I had never really thought about before. I'm curious what you guys think of that.

bahar: I have a lot of thoughts. I think that, also, I never grew up with any religion. I'm not a religious person, and I never was very spiritual either, but the closest thing that it makes me think of is learning something new. Even learning a skill physically, and getting this internal feeling of, "I'm good." This feeling like, "Wow, look at how my brain just did that." It's like a flow-state feeling. If we're talking about creativity in kink, it is a flow state, and I think that I have heard other people who are religious or have deep spirituality liken it to just being like, "I don't understand why, but I'm not necessarily thinking about my next moves." I just know what's set before me, my tasks. Whether spiritually or literally, it's like I'm cleaning my room. And I just go about it in this way that makes it feel effortless. And that, I think, is very, very much a part of that, the kink dynamic of, "We've set a structure, we've made the Bible together, and now we are good." Now it's just good, you know?

Mia: Yeah, yeah. The word coming to mind as you're talking is "surrender."

jo: Yeah, if we made a Venn diagram of work, play, and religion, that's exactly what came to my mind, too. And I also appreciate that you put change or learning on par with god, or religiosity, or spirituality, because there's also a part of me that is thinking about this Octavia Butler idea that god is change. That's the only constant thing that can be relied upon. And learning is kind of just a practice of change. And that kind of feels heartening in some ways. There are some things, even outside of the realm of religion, that you can kind of rely upon within the self, but also, whenever you're learning something, you're always tapped into some kind of force. You know? Even if it's not a higher power, let's say, even if it was horizontal. You're still kind of in a matrix with everything else that has been learned, or you're within a lineage of learning or thought. So I think that thinking about learning as a way of tapping into some kind of life force is pretty cool. Thinking about flow state and thinking about yoga, for instance—I've had yoga as an on-and-off but pretty intensive practice in my life. I know that Mia, you go to yoga all the time. I can't remember, bahar, if you're into . . .

bahar: Yeah. I go, like, three times a week.

jo: Yeah, so I feel like when I'm really deep in a practice, and beyond the point of the fumbling of, "Okay, this is really hard," and all I'm thinking about is my body and how frustrated I am with trying to get the poses, and then the nice teachers telling me not to think about that, and then I think about . . . you know, being guided toward this point of being so strong and so regimented with it that you can surrender, and you don't have to think about thoughts anymore, and you can actually connect with breath.

bahar: And thus, you allow for the change to continue, because when you start to do yoga, you suck, you know? You're not strong, you don't have stamina, you don't understand what the teacher's saying, they're saying the Sanskrit name for the pose, and you're like, what the fuck did you just say?

Mia: Especially with hot yoga. I know you do hot yoga. When I did hot yoga for the first time, I was like, someone has to be murdered for this. [*All laughing*] Yeah, I was like, this is so fucked up.

bahar: Yeah, this is cruel. This is cruel [*laughing*].

jo: I'm sweating . . . I'm stressed and I'm sweating. And I'm sweating more because I'm stressed.

Mia: And I'm mad, I'm so angry.

bahar: Yeah. But then later down the line, you're like, "Oh yeah, I'll go into the such-and-such pose, da-da-da-da," and you know exactly what that pose is. It's weird. I never sat and read a book about it.

Mia: Right, it becomes kind of second nature. I love how you guys are talking about this so much, because the way that I lay out consent at the very beginning of this book is that it's like a language or some kind of physical practice; it can become embodied. At first, you know, if you're learning a dance, or you're learning an instrument, or you're learning a language, you're sort of like, "Oh, I have to do this, and then I have to do this," or, you know, "What is chair pose? Where do I put my feet?" And then eventually, it just moves with you, or it flows out of you. And I think when so many people learn about consent, they feel at first like it's just gonna be robotic forever. And once you find that flow with it, it can feel like a very spiritual experience.

jo: I absolutely agree with that.

bahar: I think also, if I'm thinking about consent, I'm thinking about kink. So much of the mainstream perspective on kink, or the perspective people have when they begin their kink practice—and it's a practice, right? Like any creative practice [it takes practice] . . . sometimes you are interested enough in something and start to do it, but it feels clunky, it feels wrong. And you will make mistakes. All the time. It doesn't necessarily mean you're not kinky enough, or you're not creative enough, or you're bad at something. You're just starting, and sometimes the superimposing works, and sometimes it doesn't, and part of that flow state, I think, is to listen and parse out what's working and what's not, you know?

jo: So, one of the projects I'm working on right now is a book on kink and neuroplasticity. There's very little scientific research on kink and its somatic effect on the body, so I'm reverse-engineering experiments to research that. I'm looking at things that are hard but that you do anyway because the outcome is so great—that's probably the most succinct way that I've figured out how to say that. But I'm looking at Alcoholics Anonymous, or recovery models, and yoga and meditation. The first two I have a lot of experience with and thoughts about. Meditation is a little bit harder to access for me.

But I think that one of the things that feels consistent there is that, with kink, you show up and you're like, I'm searching for some vague, amorphous experience that I understand in my body or [have been told] culturally is going to be good. For some reason, I have a desire toward it. Same with yoga. You're like, hmm, people talk about it. I need to work out, sounds like it's gonna be good. But you know, culturally, people tell you that yoga is really, really hard. Popping those headstands, getting the regimen of it, the routine of it—it's arduous on the body. But it takes you to some kind of transcendental level, and you're curious about it coming into it, but oftentimes you're not necessarily even quite sure what you're gonna get out of it. You know that you're gonna get *something* out of it, but you don't have a reference point for it; it's similar to an orgasm. When you're pre-orgasmic—people are like, oh yeah, you'll know it. You'll feel it, you'll know it. And you're kind of working awkwardly and diligently toward this vague feeling, and for some people, it's very uncomfortable.

When thinking about yoga or recovery, for instance, it's like, I know that my life is shit right now, and I need to get to the other side of it, where it's somehow vaguely amorphously better.

So I'm gonna take this rigorous set of steps, which usually involves being in a lineage of thought with other people who have taken these same rigorous steps and are now on the other side of it, and it's better. I think with kink, it's a harder sell, because it often is also in a constellation with all of the deepest and darkest and most depraved behaviors of humanity. So you're kind of coming directly in contact with both a lot of elation and also the worst things that people do and are capable of, and all of your demons. And also, I think that sex in general, across a lot of cultures, has a bad rap.

Mia: Well, and a lot of shame sometimes, you get very confronted with that.

jo: Yeah, and also, in some spaces, you know, especially with gay sex, queer sex, it's like, "You're a sodomite, you're not allowed to have this." And I'm also kind of tethering this back to the conversation about religion. I'm a former Catholic schoolgirl, and also, my parents practiced Santeria. So there was a split my whole life between my home-based religion and the one at school, and a lot of my shame, slut, kink stuff comes from the Catholic thing, which is not very uncommon. But anyway, I think that the common thread between all of these big systems is there is this idea on the other side that things will be better, and that you'll find some sense of comfort, peace, relief, transcendence, community, on the other side . . .

Mia: Release.

jo: Release.

Mia: Yeah.

jo: . . . on the other side of these rigorous steps that are laid out either by bodies bigger than you or the people who have done it before, or even just driven by this kind of awkward self-motivation toward rigor and ardor. I think that that's kind of just generally why people pursue a lot of things. I think people are often trying to change, and kink puts you in direct confrontation with how fucking awkward it can look to want to want something, and to want change, and to want that catharsis—instead of it being like, okay, I did my yoga class move, that was great. So much of yoga culture is about being more private and to yourself, and kind of having this private experience, as opposed to facing the gross parts of wanting.

bahar: Thoughts on all the things you were just saying . . . let me just word vomit a little . . . so about the grossness of wanting, or the shame of sex. It's like that living-in-vulnerability thing that is a big part of learning, or scratching the surface of what you're curious about. I think with sex, especially with kink and stuff, like . . . okay, I get AA and yoga, both of those are implying a sort of trajectory of betterment, or improvement . . . whereas I think kink and sex are their own special category of not necessarily improvement, but just curiosity, and discovery, and . . .

Mia: Play.

bahar: Play. Yeah. A thousand percent, because in my classes, I would talk a lot about what you think is hot versus what you *actually* think is hot. Sometimes the things that our environment feeds us—we're inspired by things around us all the time. But you have to be very good at listening to what is actually working and what you're doing just because you thought that it was the hot thing to do. And I think arousal happens when we are both feeling safe and secure and going into uncharted territory at the same time. Because I think you cannot spark any sort of curiosity or excitement if you know exactly what's going to happen next. There has to be a little bit of the unknown, but you also have to feel confident going forth and doing it. So I think that's where we're literally on the edge of things. So it's not necessarily "before and after," but it's kind of just playing, yeah.

jo: I agree with a lot of that. I'm almost kinky by orientation, which is something that I've been thinking about a lot recently. I don't always necessarily think about kink in the same category as sex, especially because we all know that sometimes you can have kink experiences that have nothing to do with traditional sex or genitalia at all, or arousal in that particular kind of way that most people think about sex. And also, I think that it can have a lot to do with sex. I think it can be sex in and of itself, too.

With that being said, there is one layer of kink that feels almost like that initial phase—exploratory, curious, or even in waves, with different partners, or over time, discovering. But there is also a part of it I've been kind of sitting with a lot recently as I try to improve certain skills, like needle bottoming, or learning how to rope top. There is a part of it that is kind of connected to just the rote learning and mechanics, and it is motivated by eroticism, but it is also motivated by that human desire to learn new skills. And there are certain heights of creativity and I guess, therefore, curiosity that you can't reach until a certain baseline of learning improvement has happened. For instance, if you're like, okay, I'm trying to get to a point where I can suspend people so I can have these new experiences—one of my friends is a newer rigger, but he has learned crazy fast. He's gotten so good so fast. And hearing him talk about his experiences now doing suspension versus doing floor work is so different. It's like, you've kind of labored for these new heights of experience in a way. So I think there is a part of it that's just kind of fun and playful and explorative, and then also the Virgo in me is like . . . there is also some kind of . . .

Mia: It's homework.

bahar: Homework, yeah.

Mia: I mean, you're talking about honing your craft, which is practice, ultimately. And, as an artist, sometimes making your art feels like homework, but to think about it as honing your craft so that you're ready when that flow state strikes—that's what it's all for. You're not always in the flow state, you're not always transcending, or channeling, or you know, like, "Wow, I am profoundly changed by this experience."

bahar: You can't belt the hymn if you don't know the words or the notes. Right.

Mia: Right.

bahar: Aww.

jo: I love when the segue is organic. Exactly, yeah.

Mia: I love drawing attention to the segue.

jo: In terms of thinking about this larger idea of how kink influences my creativity, or my art, or who I am, I do think a lot about that rigor and that erotically motivated or sensually motivated desire to just do better. It also is a space of confronting deep fear, because as I've talked to both of you about extensively, I get really bad stage fright, which is actually the motivation for starting to write this book . . . I'm gonna get personal, is that okay?

Mia: Absolutely.

jo: So I had started, after a certain point, doing more public kink scenes, just more public impact-bottoming scenes—nothing too crazy, but it felt like a very big risk for me as somebody who was kind of averse to doing anything in public. I feel like I labored a lot in different kinds of therapy modalities and different kinds of conversations to get to a point where I was like, I'm comfortable doing this. And then I think it had some reverse-engineering effect, because historically, I haven't been able to get myself to do karaoke. I had a few youthful karaoke experiences that were very bad—another conversation for another time—and I just skipped out on it for a long time. But I love pop music, I love musicals, and I love having a good time with people. So I went to karaoke with bahar the other day, and they were like, "Are you gonna sing?" And I'm like, "Absolutely."

Mia: You did? Oh my god, you know bahar and I love karaoke. Every time I'm in New York, I'm like, "Where's the karaoke night?"

bahar: I remember going to your birthday once, jo . . . it was a karaoke at that Korean restaurant.

jo: Yes, that was one of the moments where I was like, "Oh, this is a strange thing that I'm doing, because I don't like this, but it's my birthday, and I'm making myself do it." And there was also the intimacy of having our own room. But even before, historically, even if I'm by myself, or with one other person that I trust deeply—or fuck, even my best friend—as soon as I'm holding a microphone, it's like a frog is in my throat. So, after this set of experiences where I'd started to do public kink scenes more, now I'm able to hold the microphone. I'll sit it out a lot of the time still, but I am able to do it.

bahar: I really, really want to talk more about this, because my friend is always like, "I'm so scared and shy, but I want to do it so badly," and she was telling me I should teach a class about how to do karaoke, and I was like, "I don't know how to, because how do I break through . . ." Anyway, I don't want to distract from your train of thought.

jo: Maybe you just whack everybody, and then they do it. I think maybe that's the map . . . just whack everybody [*all laughing*], because basically what

I realized was, doing a handful of public impact-bottoming scenes kind of unwound something that was seemingly unrelated. It's like almost when you are getting a massage, and you work out a knot in one part of your back, and then the rest of your back feels a release or something. It's like, the karaoke thing happening over here in this part of my brain felt like it was related to this over here, and then I'm like, well, that's the neuroplasticity.

Mia: Neuroplasticity! Yes! Right, and I'm thinking of the trauma therapy treatment EMDR, where you heal one memory or trauma, or you desensitize it so it's not as triggering, but then many, many other things also get lumped into that, because it's not an isolated event, it's part of a whole neural network. So it makes so much sense to me that as you're opening up in this one particular area, of course you're seeing that happen in other realms of your life. That tracks for me so much. When people sign up for my classes on people-pleasing, or boundaries and consent, it's because they're having an issue with their roommate, or their ex, or with their mother . . . but so often the feedback that I hear after the class is that they've started painting again after years of not painting, or they've suddenly decided that they wanted to finally take guitar lessons, or whatever it is. People do experience this kind of creative boom. So it makes a lot of sense to me that as you open up and also experience new sensations of maybe not fully safety, but something more like comfort in an arena where you used to feel nervous . . . you know, getting on stage can feel so dangerous. It makes total sense to me that you're suddenly willing to fall on your face, willing to be embarrassed, willing to put yourself out there, willing to try new things—and it doesn't matter if you're choking on the words, or your voice is stuck in your throat, you're just sort of like, "I'm just gonna do it."

jo: Again, I don't think a lot of people are doing this with kink on purpose, but I do notice a kink glow-up that sort of happens when people start to situate themselves in their power, whether they're tops or bottoms or switches. There is this part of the whole manufacturing of an identity, whether that is the worst, most villainous parts of yourself, or the subbiest, most humiliated parts of yourself, that makes everything else seem so much more chill. So I do think that there is a part of me that after this handful of experiences of public bottoming, there is some part of me that's like, okay, if that's the worst of it, and I could survive that—it manufactured a stretch zone around karaoke where I'm less worried about what kind of fool I'm going to appear as on stage. Because I was like, this is too scary; I will not do this. Danger! Bad things will happen, you know? There is a part of it that created a buffer zone in a completely unrelated arena, and now, karaoke is still not my favorite thing in the world, but I guess that's because I need to do more public bottoming scenes. *[All laughing]*

bahar: I think you just do. Yeah.

Mia: Yeah, it's the medicine.

jo: Yeah.

bahar: Have you met your deadlines? Have you drunk some water? How many public bottoming scenes have you done this week?

Mia: Water break. [*All drink water, laughing*]

bahar: I think the anti-authoritarian in me is like, "Don't tell me to drink water," and I'm famously not a water drinker.

Mia: Me too, I know, we're two Cancers who hate water.

Okay, bahar, I'm wondering what you have learned about yourself that has perhaps surprised you through kink and BDSM exploration and play.

bahar: It's funny, for me, I think that it is not surprising that the things that I found arousing—like, oh, this is part of my sexual library, this is my sexual vocabulary—were so rooted in things that are roleplay [*all laugh*]. Roleplay and playfulness, silliness . . . I think that it's too on the nose, and I was like, well, if I'm actually feeling horny or slutty, or whatever, I won't really be that silly, will I? Turns out, yes, 1,000 percent, I'll be the silliest. I'm not a deadly serious top person. I think the most surprising thing, I guess, was that it was a little too on the nose. [*All laugh*] At least in the beginning, for me.

Mia: Well, I think it's easy to dismiss the stuff that you've acclimated to in yourself, but I think that there's something in there that could be really surprising to a lot of people. Silliness isn't often thought of as sexy. To discover that there's this really silly part of you that comes out in this role, I think that's really cool.

bahar: Especially in a power exchange. I think I did not expect it. When you think of power exchange, you think it's so serious. You have this first perception of it being like, someone is telling you what to do, and blah blah blah. For me, that's more bullying territory [*laughs*]. There always has to be a thread of humor for me. I guess that's surprising. Because when I watch other people do scenes that are not silly, I'm still very into them. I think that they're really hot, and I love them, but on *my* body, it doesn't work on my body, per se.

jo: Yeah, that does feel super relatable, because I similarly kind of bought into the narrative that in order to be hot, in order to be a good top or a dom, you had to be very stoic and bitchy. And again, I also love that shit too, but I feel like I'm such a troll and a clown when I'm topping, and it is one of the things that reminds me that I can bring my whole self to a scene, and I ultimately should be trying to bring as many parts of myself as I feel comfortable bringing to a scene. Even if it's not an intentional tool, humor breaks the ice even with myself, and even breaks that shyness that I have a tendency toward. It's like, well, what if I just had fun? It opens up space for play, which I think is really cool.

But I think one of the things that I'm perhaps most surprised at is how much I can take. I think it's helped me discover not just more of an internal sense of power, but more just generally, it opens up a sense of expanse for what I'm open to tolerating, and it also gives me permission in other areas of my life to *not* tolerate things. Like bahar was talking about earlier, you need to have a sense of curiosity about what you actually are into versus what you think you're into—which is a lot harder if you're not having partnered play, or if you're feeling really rigid about what you should like and what you should do, or if you're acquiescing to what other people want of you, or if it's work, or whatever. I think that it's easier to be like, "This is how this all *should* go."

There is something about leaning into dynamics that feels really exciting, and I'm really into psychological edge play and head games. And it's so hard to walk out of those environments and then not see everything for what it is, if that makes sense. It's like, "Oh, this person is trying to make me feel small; not sure why that's happening," you know? Like, "Oh, this person doesn't know it, perhaps, but they're bullying me, or replicating dynamics that don't feel great." So I think it's helped me grow a little bit of a thicker skin. I think that we live in a culture that gaslights folks that have been through a lot of crazy stuff, occupy marginalized identities, or just generally disagree with the status quo. There are certain things that are always gonna feel a little bit funny, but you don't necessarily know *why* until you start playing with power. And then you realize that, actually, most of the time, people know exactly what they're doing.

Mia: They may not *know* that they know. That's something that I've tried to talk about sometimes, and I frequently get pushback from people, who are like, "No, you can't be manipulative or malicious or lie without intent." And I'm like, right, but I think you can do things intentionally without *knowing* that you're doing them intentionally. Dogs do that, and they're not thinking consciously that they're trying to manipulate you. Babies, toddlers learn to fib and trick and stuff before . . . they're not actively thinking, "Oh, I can really get away with something." It's not conscious. I totally agree with you, jo, and I think that often the most dangerous liars, and most successful liars, are the ones who don't know that they're lying to themselves. Because then they don't know that they're lying to you.

jo: Oh, yeah.

Mia: I was in a relationship for about six years where I was sort of relied upon to be the top, sexually, and I kind of learned to do it, and I enjoyed it. I guess I was also sort of relied on to be more dominant, but . . . I don't know, it's blurry, overlapping space. I would be in the bottom position, but I was never the sub in the dynamic. Then when I started working for myself—to bring it all the way back to the beginning, jo—I really started to crave a work dom, but more along the lines of someone being like, "You have to *stop* working now." Like, a tech dom. And I had one, briefly, someone who told me that I wasn't allowed to be on my phone. They would take my phone away. They would tell me, "You can't check your phone for an hour. I want you to write yourself a letter about all the things you're really good at." And I really felt like I was making so many decisions at work. I was having decision fatigue, and I started thinking that it would be really nice to have someone else just take that responsibility away from me in a lot of other areas of my life.

But it wasn't until recently that I discovered that I do really enjoy being a sub, sexually. And one of the things that has surprised me so much about that is that the trust that I experience in that dynamic has made my body capable of doing things that, until recently, I didn't think I was capable of doing. Ways that my body opens up, or ways I can tolerate things, or, like one of you said, ways that you can take more than you thought, whether it's impact, or pain, or pushing, or being restrained. So, yeah, that's something that has really, really surprised me, because I've recently had several experiences where I'm like, "Whoa, I did not know that I could do that." It's really cool.

bahar: Yeah, I mean, it's part of the adrenaline, too, I feel like. One of my favorite things to do, whether it's kinky or sexually, or both, is wrestling. I love wrestling, whether it's mini little tiny fights or full-body wrestling. I don't care if you're three times my size, I'm gonna go for it. And that's because, first—we're bringing back the idea of vulnerability—I'm curious, I'm playing with you, and second, I'm discovering my threshold. Like, I'm gonna give this my all in a way that I wouldn't give anywhere else in my life. And I'm telling this person, before we wrestle, "Please don't touch these places, and we'll tap out if something starts to hurt, but don't hold back." Then you kind of learn . . . sometimes wrestling is three seconds. I'm like, oh, you fucked me up, I have to go. [Playing with] threshold is really fun when suddenly I'm pinning someone down, and I'm like, *woooo* [*laughs*].

Mia: Yeah, it's exciting. I took a fetish-wrestling class in New York last year from my friend Lola Jean. She's a pro fetish wrestler.

bahar: jo, weren't you there? We were at one of those parties where I think I started to wrestle.

jo: Yeah, you wrestled with my ex. It was really fun.

bahar: Yeah, I definitely wrestled your ex. I just remembered that. [*Laughing*]

jo: It was actually a really good match. You both definitely put up a really good fight, and . . .

bahar: Yeah, I think they put me down very quickly.

jo: It wasn't as quick as you think [*laughs*]. Yeah, it was a fun fight. I love watching wrestling. I love WWE wrestling.

bahar: Oh, nice. The horniest stuff I've ever seen in my life.

jo: Oh my god, I know. It's filthy, and I think that it's crazy that people think that it's not gay. It's one of the most overtly . . . everybody's in a Speedo, like, 90 percent of people are in Speedos.

bahar: And they're performing. They're literally performing.

Mia: Oh, yeah! It's a show!

bahar: Oh, it's so gay. Yeah, they're in drag.

jo: Right, and people will be sitting on each other's faces.

Mia: Yeah. Swinging each other around with the other person's crotch in their face.

jo: Right! Or throwing someone to the top of the ropes, and then they'll just kind of bottom out, wobbling there, and you're shoving their head in your crotch . . . it's insane. It's disgusting. And it's so fun. It's one of the most fun things I watch. Especially recently, because I've discovered that the women's wrestling league has gotten so much better. It used to be very much like, this is the opening act, you know? And now it's like *Bring It On*, where the cheerleaders are the main event. The costumes are better, the storylines are better—but anyway, I digress. I think that wrestling is hot, and I would go with you to this class.

Mia: Okay, well, let me find out when she's doing it again. She also does Kinky Karaoke.

bahar: What does that mean?

Mia: Okay, I'll tell this story, and then we'll have to wrap up. So I went to this fetish wrestling class, and then I went to Kinky Karaoke. People come with an act, and they've practiced their song, and sometimes they do a BDSM scene that they've rehearsed, or they do a burlesque striptease. And I did not know that, you guys, because I didn't do my homework. And I went and decided with the other fetish wrestling instructor—there's two of them—I asked her if she would be willing to wrestle me while I sing "Casual" by Chappell Roan. And the reason why I love this story is because I love this example of consent where I'm agreeing to a certain amount of risk. Here's what happened. I was like, "Okay, as my act, would you wrestle me?" We had, like, two minutes. She said, "Yes, what's off-limits and what's okay?" And I was like, "I don't remember any of the terminology, you're the instructor; anything that we covered in that class is fine with me, and I trust your judgment." So part of what I was agreeing to was the unknown, and I also was agreeing not to be angry with her, even if something happened that I didn't like, or that hurt me, or that I regretted. Like, I was saying, "I am putting my trust in you, and it's not that you're not going to be capable of doing anything wrong, but that I am taking responsibility for agreeing to a bunch of stuff that I can't possibly know ahead of time." And then we did it, and it was so much fun.

bahar: Were you able to sing?

Mia: Kind of. I'll send you the video.

bahar: I have to see this.

Mia: Yeah, it was really hard. Plus, I'm just laughing the whole time.

bahar: Yeah, that's the best.

Mia: And I think I was upside down at one point, and couldn't get the microphone, and I couldn't see the words, you know?

bahar: That's amazing.

Mia: But I really think it's so important to look at consent as agreeing to a way to take risks, and leap into the unknown in a supported way—with care, but without expecting or demanding 100 percent guaranteed safety.

bahar: Yeah, yeah, you're not asking to be coddled.

Mia: Right.

jo: Even if you *are* asking to be coddled, I think that's cool, if that's what you want and need. But I think that I kind of learned this through working in venues, trying to create safer spaces. You can harm people the second you agree that the space that they are entering is risk-free, or that it's a safe space—as opposed to being a space that's safer, or is risk-aware, or is engaged in harm reduction. Once you're guaranteeing safety, you're kind of putting forth this idea that you exist in utopia. I'm sussed out as soon as I hear this.

Mia: How? How is that possible? It's not possible.

jo: If a hurricane hits, this is no longer a safe space, it's a crisis. So, yeah, I'm sussed out by the idea that because you're consenting to something, everything that transpires is gonna be great for you. And that if it's not, it's still somehow on the person that you're engaging with, even if you agreed to it. As opposed to the understanding that everybody's coming into this as risk-aware adults, and maybe we're working toward a point where we're like, "Okay, if shit hits the fan, or after the fact, this is how we'll care for each other, or this is how I'll follow up with you to make sure it's okay, and you get back to stasis." Or, "This is not my responsibility, but I'm encouraging you to take care of yourself afterward."

I feel heartened even by this conversation, because a lot of people are just trying to seek safety, for lack of a better term. People are often just trying to feel assured that everything is gonna be okay, and I think that that's poetic, but it's also not possible. So, I think that sometimes the idea of surrendering and knowing that things are actually not gonna be okay, things are gonna be really painful, and things are gonna be uncomfortable and messy, or might not go how you want them to—that feels actually more like living in the world for me than anything else.

Mia: I feel more inclined to trust you if you're anticipating that, expecting that, prepared for that, equipped for repair and check-ins. I immediately distrust someone who's trying to guarantee safety. I'm like, that's not realistic.

bahar: It's not like this impenetrable force field of perfection. It's weird. No.

jo: As one last straggler thought about the tether between consent and negotiation, a lot of the time, people think that negotiation in kink has to be so flat. And so un-hot. But there is a part of me that's like, yeah, if you're doing the negotiation thing right, it should be one of the hottest parts.

Mia: Absolutely. It's also sometimes the most creative part, because you have to get specific. And sometimes, one of the most exciting sexual experiences that I have consistently, still, as an adult—because I'm not doing a ton of stuff that I haven't done before—but one of the things that always feels new is if my partner says, "Do you want to do this thing?" And it's just something I've never thought of. It's not like a new sex act, it's just like, "What if we put lube there?" And I'm like, oh, I've never thought of that. Sure, let's try that. And even still, and we've been together for a year and a half, I frequently get asked, "What do you want to do tonight?" while we're in bed, talking about the sex that we want to have. And I feel like that's a part of sex that people often either don't ever have or only have when they're first getting to know each other. But it's so fun to make a plan, even if you deviate—that's so hot.

jo: I think it's also fun to shine a light on desire, no matter what. Like, having to be really explicit. It's like dirty talk. If you're like, okay, I have to lay out a menu of all the things that I want you to do to me. And then you get to reiterate to me what you're going to do to me, or what you want to do to me—that's so fun.

Acknowledgments

I'd like to thank my editor Gillian for taking a chance on me and for his patience. After losing my first deal, I was hesitant to try again. Gillian was so supportive and ready to go to bat for me, and he was so understanding when I hit road blocks. Thank you, Gillian. And a huge thank you to Erin Wiegand for copyediting. I really felt like she understood the message of this book. Her suggested edits often rephrased my writing in ways that sometimes felt even truer to what I was trying to convey.

I want to thank my parents, who've sculpted my writing over many years. Big thank you to my mom, who edited my fifth-grade essays at the dinner table, often while I whined and complained about the notes. And to my dad, who always has so much faith in me and tells me I can do anything I want to *because* I want to.

To Andis, I love you. You've been such a gift in my life these past couple of years, and it was truly a joy to edit your interview while you snored next to me in our bed. This book unintentionally offered such a sweet history of the first two years of our relationship, and I look forward to many more. Thank you for being such a wonderful muse.

To all my friends who let me interview them: Thank you all! Meenadchi, Janice, Risdon, jo, bahar—you're all so talented and brilliant. And Kai Cheng, I'm so excited to see what we cook up in the year to come.

Special thanks to Hannah Said, Charlie James, Dean Spade, and Sophia Cleary. You all keep me going and keep me thinking. And Romaric, you've been such a wonderful source of support from afar, even though we've never met in person. Thank you for reading my writing and continuing to be a champion of my work, even from prison. I hope you are able to read the next book in hardcover.

Index

A

Abstinence Lite, 8, 60
acting, mindfulness of, 234–235
Adults, 187
alcohol, 10
Alcoholics Anonymous (AA), 245, 247
Amazon, 193
Ansari, Aziz, 186, 189
Aristophanes, 13
armchair philosophy, 9
attachment healing, 214
attraction, 157–161
authenticity, 30–32, 141
autonomy
 consent and, 44–45
 giving up, 44–45, 142
 polyamory and, 130–131

B

baharloo, bahar, 239–258
BDSM, 89, 206, 239–241, 251–255. *See also* kink
binary thinking, 45, 78–79, 122, 126–127, 185
blame
 consent and, 35–37
 impulse for, 17
 of others vs. self, 17
body
 listening to, 11–13, 22, 24, 79, 143
 separation of mind and, 13, 79
boundaries
 changing, 112
 crossing, 17
 expressing gratitude for communication of, 71–75
 misuse of term, 68
 as mutual effort, 115
 setting, 16
Burke, Tarana, 49
Bush, George W., 235
Butler, Octavia, 243

C

cancel culture
 alternatives to, 190–194
 definition of, 195–196
 effects of, 65, 186–187, 189–190, 196–197, 199–200

cancel culture (*continued*)
hypervigilance and, 181–182
infighting and, 177–180, 192–193
nonparticipation in, 65, 168, 190
policing by, 177–178
repentance and, 173–175, 199–202
Cartesian dualism, 79
Casper, Sarah, 43
children, 43–44, 228–229
code-switching, 32
coming out, 149–151
commitment, 83–86
compersion, 131
comphet, 157
confidence
building, 213
as a practice, 223
connection, prioritizing, 181, 190, 192
consent
as an art, 41, 60
confidence and, 51–52
as connective tool, 56
control and, 2, 38, 40–41
creativity and, 211–216, 238
definition of, 1, 3–4, 54
discomfort and, 18, 36
as dynamic process, 54–55
enthusiastic, 44, 60, 121, 125–126
freedom and, 100–101
FRIES acronym for, 121
as harm-reduction strategy, 38–39
iceberg metaphor for, 3
making hot, 139–140
mind-altering substances and, 10, 111–115
mistakes in, 113
misunderstandings of, 1–3, 35–49, 53–68
as mystery, 58–59
negative model of, 222
overusing concept of, 19–20
as path to knowing yourself, 221–225
perfectionism and, 2, 39, 62
permission vs., 3–4, 40–41
practicing, without sounding like a robot, 108–109
pressure and, 18–19
punishment and, 2, 35–37, 202
resiliency and, 203
retroactively withdrawing, 185–186, 203
rules vs., 1, 38
self-, 11–13
as shared responsibility, 18–19, 43–50, 115, 185
spectrum of, 53
spirituality and, 235, 237, 238, 244
trust and, 18–19
unknown and, 222
violations of, 19–20, 25–26, 202–205
weaponization of, 37–38, 159, 203
willingness and, 57–58, 60–62, 205–206

consent education
for children vs. adults, 43–44
as continuing process, 91
healing and, 178
patterns in early stages of, 15–20
Consent Wizardry, 219, 228
container, definition of, 229
control
cancel culture and, 191
consent and, 2, 38, 40–41
people-pleasing and, 63–64, 89–90
creativity, 8, 211–216, 238, 243, 245, 248, 250, 258
Cuddle Sanctuary, 15, 71
curiosity, importance of, 125

D

Decolonizing Non-Violent Communication, 21, 228
Descartes, René, 79
desires
deserving, 222–224
first- and second-order, 212
knowing, 221–222
letting go, 212–213
magic in, 227–231
naming, 224–225, 227–231
sculpting, 158–161
determinism vs. free will, 218–219
dirty talk, 139–140, 258
disability justice community, 191
discomfort
avoiding, 18, 20
danger vs., 20
fear and, 37
domain, definition of, 40
drugs, 10, 111–115

E

ego, 215–216
Eilish, Billie, 149
EMDR (Eye Movement Desensitization and Reprocessing), 36, 250
enthusiastic consent, 44, 60, 121, 125–126
Esposito, Bobbie, 228–229

F

fandom wars, 66–67
fear
discomfort and, 37
of missing out (FOMO), 15, 84, 217–220
feedback
as gift, 74
lack of, 119
receiving, 71–75
flow, finding, 211, 237
Foell, Jens, 126–127
FOMO (fear of missing out)
commitment and, 84

FOMO (*continued*)
no-happy phase and, 15
perfectionism and, 217–220
Frankfurt, Harry, 212
Franzblau, Jean, 15, 71
free will vs. determinism, 218–219
Friends, 167
friendships, ending, 16–17
full-body listening, 22–23, 83, 235, 237

G

gatekeeping, 149–151, 154
gender
binary, 45, 150
identity, 157, 161–163
sexuality vs., 155
god
belief in, 233–238
as change, 243
helping, 235–236
grammar, policing, 166–168
Griffith, Janice, 87–101
guardrails, language of, 25

H

help, asking for, 117
Herr-Cardillo, Brooks, 229
High Maintenance, 137
how-to articles, reading, 77–81
humility, 236
hypervigilance, 181–182

I

inner critic, 92–93
intimacy coordinators, 219, 227, 228–229

J

jealousy, 131–135
Just Sex, 219

K

Kant, Immanuel, 9
karaoke, 249, 255–256
kink
creativity and, 243, 245, 248–249
identity and, 250–251
learning skills and, 247–248
misconceptions about, 98–99, 246
negotiation and, 257–258
neuroplasticity and, 245, 250
practicing, 245
safety and, 206–207
sex and, 247
willingness and, 206
Kink.com, 99
knowledge
a priori vs. *a posteriori,* 9–10
self-, 75, 87–88

L

Lauer, Matt, 26, 185, 189, 196
Lee, Sondra, 83, 234
Leven, Aaron, 235
listening
  to the body, 11–13, 22, 24, 79, 143
  full-body, 22–23, 83, 235, 237
LOMO (lack of missing out), 217, 220
Louis C. K., 189, 196

M

magic
  definition of, 229
  in desires, 227–231
  of saying "no," 227
Martin, Betty, 40, 56, 108, 123, 212
masking, 32
Maslow, Abraham, 94
Meenadchi, 21–32, 228
memory
  changing nature of, 112–113
  trauma and, 178
men
  consent and, 44–46, 48, 185
  #Me Too movement and, 186–187
  misandry, 49, 183–184
  as potential perpetrators, 44–46, 48
  universalist myth of cis, hetero, white, 78
#Me Too movement, 26, 49, 183–187
Midori, 206
mind and body, as separate entities, 13, 79
misandry, 49, 183–184
mistakes, making, 113
money, 213–214
monogamy, 130–133, 136–137

N

Nagel, Thomas, 218
neuroplasticity, 245, 250
"no," hearing, 224–225
"no," saying
  to everything, 15–16
  magic of, 227
  people-pleasing and, 118–120
  struggling with, 124
  trust and, 18–19, 117–120
Noah, 235, 236
nonbinary people
  consent and, 45
  #Me Too movement and, 183
  pronouns and, 166–168, 180–181
  sexual assault statistics and, 64
Non-Violent Communication, 21–25

O

Ono, Yoko, 127
opinions, forming, 80–81
orgasms, faking, 140–141

P

people-pleasing
  control and, 63–64, 89–90
  definition of, 118
  identity and, 118
  lying and, 118–119
  mindset of, 62
  relationally caring vs., 66, 95, 126
  trust and, 118–120
perfectionism, 2, 39, 62, 84, 191, 217–220
permission vs. consent, 3–4, 40–41
Planned Parenthood, 121
pleasure
  giving others, 153–156
  other considerations besides, 125–126
  perceived responsibility and, 207
polyamory, 129–139
Poor Things, 84
porn, 97–99, 160
power, abuse of, 51–52
prejudices, disguising, 159
pressure, 18–19
projection, 72
pronouns, 165–168, 180–181, 190
prosody, 1, 108, 230
Proust, Marcel, 166
Pro Villain. *See* Woodman, Tim

Q

queer-baiting, 149–150
queerness
  becoming vs. born this way, 163
  coming out, 149–151
  encouraging others, 149, 151
  gatekeeping, 149–151, 154

R

rape
  labeling an experience as, 125–126
  sexual assault vs., 46
reality, lack of shared, 179–180
rejection, 112–113
relationships
  as collaborations, 16, 18
  deserving good, 222–223
  ending, 16–17, 41
  monogamous, 130–133, 136–137
  polyamorous, 129–139
  risk and, 24
repentance, 173–175
resiliency, 203
responsibility
  personal, 49–50, 185–187
  pleasure and, 207
restorative practices, 198–199
rituals
  benefits of, 211–212, 229–230, 234

definition of, 211, 229
repentance, 173–175
Roberts, Risdon, 178, 195–207
A Room of One's Own, 165, 168–169
Rosenberg, Marshall, 21

S

safe space, 191, 257
safewords, 206
Said, Hannah, 117, 119
Saketopoulou, Avgi, 23–24, 222
Sarah Lawrence College, 219
The School of Consent, 56
Schwenteck, Matthias, 40
self-consent, 11–13
self-knowledge
conscious vs. unconscious, 87–88
consent as path to, 221–225
importance of, 75
unattainability of full, 221–222
sex
a posteriori knowledge of, 9–10
creativity and, 8, 215, 243, 245, 248, 258
lack of experience with, 153–156
moral panic around, 7–8
risks of, 7, 24
shame and, 246–247
stretching yourself and, 18, 206
talking about, 7–9, 139–142
unenthusiastic and consensual, 121–124
sexual assault
defining, 61
labeling an experience as, 113, 125–126, 184
rape vs., 46
statistics on, 64
sexuality
changing, 157–163
gender vs., 155
Sexuality Beyond Consent, 23, 222
sex work, 54, 60, 89, 122, 127, 185, 205
Shakespeare, William, 165, 166, 167
shame, 246–247
shower thoughts, cultivating, 229
social media. *See also* cancel culture
comments on, 72–73
effects of, 224
fandom wars on, 66–67
Solomon, Andis, 129–145
speech, effects of, 64
stealthing, 46
Stone, Emma, 84
Styles, Harry, 149
surrender, 234, 243, 244
Swift, Taylor, 215
swinger culture, 137
synchronicity, 228

T

"thank you for telling me," saying, 71–75
therapy, 36

"they," as singular pronoun, 166–168
Thom, Kai Cheng, 53–68, 90
time constraints, 19
trad-wifery, 123
traffic-light system, 206
transformative justice, 53, 198–199
trans people
    #Me Too movement and, 183
    pronouns and, 166–168
    sexual assault statistics and, 64
transphobia, overcoming, 127–128
trauma
    healing, 182, 191–192
    hypervigilance and, 181–182
    memory and, 178
    projection and, 72
    unresolved, 178
    use of term, 199
Trump, Donald, 127
trust
    saying "no" and, 18–19, 117–120
    with yourself, 213

V

Valdés, jo, 239–258
victim
    blaming, 36
    identifying as, 192
violence, 199

W

wanting vs. willingness, 123, 212
Weinstein, Harvey, 26, 185, 186, 189, 196
The Wheel of Consent, 56, 108
willingness, 57–58, 60–62, 123, 205–206, 212
women
    consent and, 44–46, 48, 185
    giving up autonomy, 44–45
    #Me Too movement and, 26, 49, 183–187
    objectification of, 150
    as writers, 165
Woodman, Tim (Pro Villain), 96–98
Woolf, Virginia, 165–169
wrestling, 254–256

Y

"yes," saying, 227
yoga, 234, 243–247

About the Author

Mia Schachter is a writer, multimedia artist and musician, educator, and intimacy coordinator for TV, film, and theater living in their hometown of Los Angeles with their partner, Andis, and three pets, Lucy, Button, and Tennessee. Mia has a Substack full of their writing at consentwizardry.substack.com. They've put out two EPs (*To-Do List Dreams* and *Costumes*) and a full-length musical soundtrack (*Squirm: A True Story*) under the name Max Silver. Their autobiographical musical, *Squirm: A True Story*, about their torrid love affair with their tapeworm, has been performed all over Los Angeles.

Mia graduated from Columbia University with a BA in Philosophy and special focuses in gender studies, neuroscience, and visual art. They teach classes in person and online. Go to consentwizardry.com to read more and sign up. Mia still does ceramics and crochets squishy, cozy hats, which you can find on their website as well.

About North Atlantic Books

North Atlantic Books (NAB) is an independent, nonprofit publisher committed to a bold exploration of the relationships between mind, body, spirit, and nature. Founded in 1974, NAB aims to nurture a holistic view of the arts, sciences, humanities, and healing. To make a donation or to learn more about our books, authors, events, and newsletter, please visit www.northatlanticbooks.com.